ADVANCE PRAISE FOR MANIFEST LIKE A MASTER...

As a father, a Marine, and the CEO of a multi-million-dollar real estate business, I've encountered a lot of voices offering advice on how to "live better" or "create success," but Dale Halaway's *Manifest Like a Master* stands in a league of its own. This book grabbed me from the beginning and didn't let go. Now I normally don't even read a book straight through, but this one pulled me in. Chapter 3 especially hit home, diving into the Law of Vibration and the relationship between our conscious and unconscious selves. Dale doesn't sugarcoat things. He gives it to you straight, and that directness resonated deeply with me as both a Marine and a father. Sometimes we need the truth, not fluff, and that's exactly what this book delivers.

    I'm endorsing this book because it challenged me, expanded my thinking, and made me a better version of myself in multiple roles of my life. If you're serious about manifesting a life on purpose, this book is a must-read.

—**Billy Alt**, *Realtor, Marine Veteran and Father*

This book is a true gem... it's a remarkable read, a remarkable project, and a remarkable mission. As both a colleague and student of Dale Halaway's for over 37 years, I can speak firsthand to his depth of wisdom, the sincerity of his heart, and his unwavering dedication to spiritual awakening and personal transformation. Dale has long been a living example of embodied truth... fully committed to learning it, living it, and generously sharing it. I can honestly say he lives what he teaches.

    In this third book of his transformational trilogy, Dale offers a treasure trove of higher principles, universal laws, and soul-stirring insights. Through intuitive teachings, enriching stories, and powerful, reflective exercises, he invites us deeper into the journey of self-discovery and into communion with the divine essence of our soul. As we absorb the vibrational frequency woven through these pages, *Manifest Like a Master* inspires us to become the greatest version of ourselves.

    I hold Dale in the highest regard and will proudly share his work with those I love.

—**David Corbin**, *four-time Wall Street Journal bestselling author, and mentor to mentors*

Dale has a rare gift for translating the Universal Laws into practical guidance for everyday life. With clarity and neutrality, he walks you through these timeless principles, helping you recognize and resolve personal challenges... even those you weren't fully aware of. His thoughtful exercises are designed to deepen your self-understanding and bring forward the unique essence of who you are.

This book is enlightening on many levels. Dale helps you clearly see the role that family, friends, and other influences play in your life. Both those that uplift you and those that may hold you back. Knowing the difference is key.

Whether you're just starting your journey or reinventing your life... this book is a sacred tool for personal, professional and spiritual transformation.

—**Carolyn Jacobs**, *Talk Show Host and Entrepreneur*

Book three of Dale Halaway's Transformation Trilogy is a guide for creating a richer, healthier, more fulfilling life. It provides more than just inspiration; it offers structure, clarity, and direction.

His teachings blend deep spiritual wisdom with grounded, practical insight. They've helped answer many questions I've carried with me for years. Questions about purpose, existence, and the role of creativity in our lives. As someone who has always felt called to create, the book's message about becoming a co-creator of your reality deeply resonated with me.

This book isn't just about manifesting a super successful career, or a prosperous life. It's about becoming the person you were meant to be, from the inside out. If you're serious about your art and your life, start here. *Manifest Like a Master* will not only serve you now, but along your life's journey in the years to come. It's definitely a keeper.

—**Kelly Vohnn**, *Nashville Entertainer of the Year, and Canadian Country Artist of the Year*

Dale Halaway has been transforming lives for decades and mine was one of them. From the moment I met him, I saw his rare ability to inspire, teach, and lead others into lasting personal transformation. His newest book, *Manifest Like a Master*, distills that same transformational power into a practical guide for unlocking your potential and creating a life you truly love.

ADVANCE PRAISE FOR MANIFEST LIKE A MASTER...

I've known Dale for nearly 30 years, and our paths have crossed and reconnected at just the right times, moments I now see as divinely orchestrated. Over the years, I've witnessed his extraordinary growth... spiritually, personally, professionally, and as a mentor. His relentless commitment to being the best version of himself... for others, for the planet, and for his own Soul's evolution—is what makes this book so powerful.

As the CEO of a health and wellness company for 18 years and an entrepreneur for over four decades, I deeply appreciate the practical and spiritual evolutionary wisdom Dale shares. This book is now a must-read on my list—for friends, family, employees, and colleagues alike.

—**Rick Bergen**, *CEO, Business Man, Innovator and Alchemist*

Throughout my career working with major clients at one of the largest commercial insurance companies, I've relied heavily on instinct, focus, and intention—tools I believed aligned with the principles of manifesting. But it wasn't until I read Dale Halaway's *Manifesting Like a Master* that I truly grasped the depth and transformative power of authentic manifestation.

This book goes beyond surface-level concepts. It deepened my understanding of the underlying energies and practical applications of manifesting in every area of life—personally and professionally. Dale's wisdom clarified what I had sensed intuitively for years and gave it structure, language, and a greater sense of purpose.

—**Michele Costa**, *Senior Account Manager, Commercial Lines, and Athlete*

Manifest Like a Master is more than a book. It's a transformational guide from someone who's been walking the talk for decades. I first met Dale Halaway nearly 50 years ago, and even then, his ability to inspire change and empower others was undeniable.

I saw firsthand how Dale helped people rise, myself included. Under his mentorship, I went from part-time sales to becoming the top performer, all while working full-time as a senior police officer. What made him different was not just his knowledge, but his presence. He has a gift for awakening potential in others—and helping them act on it.

Despite struggling with a speech impediment in those early years, Dale's presence was magnetic. His ability to create energy, unity, and high performance within a team was unlike anything I'd seen. He built people up, and built successful organizations in the process.

Now, decades later, his third book delivers the same transformational power I witnessed firsthand. Dale's teachings have always been rooted in Universal Laws and masterfully blended with real-life experience. This book is a stand out, as it distills decades of wisdom into practical tools that can help anyone break through their limitations and start living their purpose. If you've ever struggled to realize your dreams, this book holds the keys to manifesting the life you're meant to live.

—**Harvey Crich**, Retired Police Officer of 26 years, Business Man & Entrepreneur

As a young professional in my mid-20s working in business development at a growing bank in Austin, I've been fortunate to start seeing real momentum in my career. At the same time, I'm deeply committed to community involvement through organizations like the Chamber of Commerce, Center for Child Protection, the Real Estate Council of Austin, and the Texas Advocacy Project.

Reading *Manifest Like a Master* at this stage was a powerful experience. Dale Halaway speaks directly to the inner journey that often gets overlooked when you're focused on results, deadlines, and external success. This is the kind of inner alignment that allows you to build success with the soul.

—**Mackenzie Comer**, Athlete, Business Development Officer, and Real Estate Council Member of Austin, TX

THIS BOOK IS A GAME-CHANGER. To become your most powerful self, you must align with your dreams, your purpose, and your goals... and *Manifest Like a Master* shows you how.

For over two decades, I've had the privilege of working with Dale Halaway... personally, in supporting the alignment of his nervous system for optimal health, and professionally, as we walked a shared path of helping others become who they were destined to be. I've always known Dale as a leader who walks his talk. He's always led by example, with what it is he teaches.

ADVANCE PRAISE FOR MANIFEST LIKE A MASTER...

His vision for humanity has always been expansive, and his passion is contagious. In this groundbreaking book, Dale delivers transformational teachings that resonate deeply with the laws of life, love, and healing. He meets readers where they are, helps them recognize their potential, and then empowers them with tools to take aligned action.

Manifest Like a Master, along with the first two books in the Transformation Trilogy, should be a staple on every bookshelf. They certainly are on mine and will be shared with my family, friends, and patients.

—**James Matthew Paige**, *D.C.*

Dale Halaway offers each of us a profound opportunity to reshape the manifestation patterns that have quietly governed our lives. Manifesting is not a mystery. It's a natural ability we all possess. Yet the beliefs we hold are the key drivers of what actually materializes in our daily experience.

In Chapter 5 of *Manifest Like a Master*, Dale takes us on a powerful inner journey--one that explores the connection between personal freedom and belief systems. His insights struck a deep chord within me, answering long-held questions about why we so often manifest outcomes we don't consciously desire.

If you're ready to move beyond survival and start shaping your future with clarity and purpose, *Manifest Like a Master* was written for you. It's an inspiring, life-changing guide to manifesting your best life.

—**Stephen Jacobs**, *Producer, Entrepreneur and Business Man*

Engaging in Dale's book *Manifest Like a Master* ultimately placed me in an inner space of empowerment and clarity. By under-over- and inner- standing the importance of aligning my mind to Universal laws, it was quite a journey.

I have experienced Dale as an individual who operates on a genius level of intuitive wisdom along with many years of personal growth and commitment to helping others travel the inner realms of self-discovery. He's like a well-seasoned scout who knows the inner wilderness, which allows him to blaze new trails and pathways like a wildfire burning through the inner weeds of confused programming in a person's mind.

This book has taught me that it is truly okay to love my life, acknowledge my self worth and cherish these things as part of the gift life gives to us all. Accepting these things as truth I can now see is essential to my peace. Before reading this book I didn't realize I was in a mentality of constant struggle, but no more thanks to Dale's in depth teachings. My eyes are opened and I see the gift in each present moment, therefore leaving no room for anything but a constant evolving into the experience of true happiness.

This book shows you how to shift perspectives allowing the alignment to what you truly want! Voilà: You Manifest Like a Master.

—**Mortonette Stephens**, *Ph.D.*

Why do we read books? The answer to this question is as varied as the topics of the subject portrayed on the cover. This book, *Manifest Like a Master*, is a masterpiece created by Dale Halaway, a Teacher of Teachers, a Coach of Coaches, a Leader of Leaders, to enable every person on this great planet to realize one's full potential.

As I read through the manuscript, I was in awe of the information condensed in this book. And the question that permeated my brain as I read and digested the information was "I wish I had this information when I was starting my adult life, or for that matter, even at an earlier age." I am 85 now, and certainly have learned a plethora of information to have a fulfilling life, but what if I had this masterfully created condensed information way back when? I think you know the answer, and if you don't, the book will give you the answer.

This book would make a great textbook for a class on this subject. It is a book you can continue to refer to. The good news is I am still learning and the dynamic information in the book is still applicable to my life's desires and dreams. That never stops. It is a book of the ages which means the book has lasting importance, not just a moment of popularity.

—**Ed Costa**, *Athlete, Professor, and Entrepreneur*

The Transformation Trilogy™

The Transformation Trilogy™ consists of three books with a common theme—transforming yourself into the person you were always meant to be.

The first theme in the trilogy is *transformational change*. What is change? How do we embrace it (instead of resisting it) ·when it comes knocking on our door? How can we let go of that which is no longer working in our lives? If something isn't working, why isn't it easier for us to let go?

The second theme is *achieving our greater destiny*. What is destiny? And, more importantly, can we affect our destiny? If so, are we affecting it in a positive way or a negative way? Where and how does choice or free will come into play? And, does karma have anything to do with our destiny?

The third theme is *manifesting dreams and realizing goals that are in alignment with the soul-self*. Can we consciously create our own reality? If so, why would we manifest something that's negative and painful in our lives, rather than creating something wonderful and positive?

By applying the innovative principles and unique processes that are shared in this trilogy, you can become the person you were born to be!

Learn more about the Transformation Trilogy
www.DaleHalaway.com

MANIFEST
like a
MASTER

Create The Life of Your Dreams in
Harmony with Universal Laws

DALE HALAWAY

All rights reserved.

Copyright © 2025 Dale Halaway

No part of this book may be reproduced or transmitted in any form or any means, electronic or mechanical, including photocopying, recording, or by any information storage or retrieval system, without permission in writing from the Publisher

Any unauthorized use, sharing, reproduction or distribution of these materials by any means, electronic, mechanical or otherwise is strictly prohibited. No portion of these materials may be reproduced in any manner whatsoever, without the express written consent of the publisher.

DEDICATION

I was lucky to be richly blessed with more than just a few phenomenal people at an early age in this life. That said, I want to bring extra recognition to three amazing gentlemen: Bob Proctor, Jim Rohn, and Brian Tracy. Each of these influential men, in their own unique way, contributed to me and my life beyond measure.

They are a few of my heroes that almost immediately, after we first met, I knew I wanted to become like, or to embody some greater aspect of theirs that they were in complete expression of.

It is who they became along their own unique journeys in their lives that inspired me most. They moved me to manifest better things in my own professional entrepreneurial world and to rise up in doing better in my own life as well.

There is no amount of money I could give them, as they all built very successful businesses and became wealthy. The best I can do to repay all that they did for me is to continue to serve others in the way that I was served by the Divine through these remarkable and incredible Divine Beings.

So, it's with the deepest love, respect, and gratitude I dedicate book number three of the Transformation Trilogy, *Manifest Like a Master*, to my dearest mentors...

Bob, Jim & Brian

—from Dale

*Until one is committed
there is hesitancy the chance to draw back,
always ineffectiveness.
Concerning all acts of initiative (and creation),
there is one elementary truth,
the ignorance of which kills countless ideas
and splendid plans:
that the moment one definitely commits oneself,
then Providence moves too.*

*All sorts of things occur to help one
that would never otherwise have occurred
A whole stream of events issues from decision
raising in one's favor all manner
of unforeseen incidents, meetings
and material assistance,
which no man could have dreamt
would have come his way.*

*Whatever you can do, or dream, you can begin it.
Boldness has genius, power, and magic in it.*

—William Hutchinson Murray

Contents

THE TRANSFORMATION TRILOGY™..........................vii
DEDICATION.. xi
FOREWORD 1
A MESSAGE FROM THE AUTHOR........................... 7

INTRODUCTION 11
   A New Approach 11
   Stop Struggling.. 12
   No Quick Fixes 13

CHAPTER 1: GETTING STARTED........................... 15
   The Current State of Humanity.......................... 17
   Manifesting Is a Natural Ability 20
   Reflection Question for Parents with Adult Children 25
   Additional Questions to Ponder… 26
      Question #1... 28
      Question #2... 28
      Question #3... 29
      Question #4... 29
      Question #5... 29
   Exercise: Remaining Conscious........................... 30

CHAPTER 2: THE LAWS OF MANIFESTING................ 34
   Law #1: The Law of Energy................................ 37
   Law #2: The Law of Attraction 38
   Law #3: The Law of Vibration............................. 46

Law #4: The Law of Consciousness........................ 52
Law #5: The Law of Belief 55
Law #6: The Law of Correspondence...................... 58
Law #7: The Law of Patterns 61
Law #8: The Law of Seeking................................ 62
Law #9: The Law of Gestation 62
Law #10: The Law of Environment......................... 64
Law #11: The Law of Process............................... 66
Law #12: The Law of Growth 71
Law #13: The Law of Perpetual Transmutation of Energy 78
Making These Laws Work Together 79

CHAPTER 3: MANIFESTING FROM THE CONSCIOUS/ UNCONSCIOUS SELF 80
The Continuum Experience 82
Continuous Creation 89
Conscious and Unconscious Manifestation 94
Our Life Force Weakens When Manifesting from the Unconscious 98
Finding the Right Mentor 100
The Music Inside 101
Earning It to Keep It 102
Why Manifest What We Don't Want? 104
Two Common Denominators 105
   #1 – Past Programming............................... 105
   #2 – Lacking Understanding of the True Self............. 108
Manifesting What We Want 111
Exercise #1: 113
Exercise #2: 113
Exercise #3: 116
A Final Question to Ponder.............................. 120

CHAPTER 4: THE THREE SELVES 121
#1 – The Past Self....................................... 121
#2 – The Present Self................................... 126

Ego Pushback 130
Managing Resistance 134
#3 – The Future Self 137
Reflection Question 140

CHAPTER 5: BELIEFS 145
Belief Systems 147
Exercise: Other's Beliefs 150
How Belief Systems are Developed 151
Unlimited Beliefs and the Law of Correspondence 156
The Two Places Our Beliefs Come From 158
Social Media and Children's Beliefs 160
Generational Beliefs 162
Exercise: Uncovering Our Beliefs 167
    Exercise Question #1 168
    Exercise Question #2 169
    Exercise Question #3 169
    Exercise Question #4 170
    Exercise Question #5 173
Freedom Beliefs and Prison Beliefs 178

CHAPTER 6: THE CREATIVE STATE 182
Area 1: Wanting Your Life 182
Area 2: Gratitude for Your Life 188
Area 3: Loving Your Life 189
Area 4: Feeling Good Naturally 192
Maintaining the 4 Areas: Your Baseline for Manifesting on a Conscious Level 197

CHAPTER 7: THE INNER MANIFESTING POWERS 201
Power 1: The Power of Imagination 202
Power 2: The Power of Goals 207
The Greater Reason for Goals 214
The Deeper Purpose of Goals 218
Goal-Setting Exercise 224

Select 3 Goals from Your List of 10 228
Your 3 Most Important Goals 229
A Final Question to Ponder… 229
Power 3: The Power of Thought 230
Power 4: The Power of Feeling 239
Power 5: The Power of Aligned Action 249
Aligned Action Step 253
Power 6: The Power of the Spoken Word 254
Power 7: The Power of Discipline 259
Disciplined Action Step 264

CHAPTER 8: PRINCIPLES OF MANIFESTATION 266
The Principle of Suggestion 266
The Principle of Association 269
An Exercise Around the Person You Spend the Most Time With 272
The Principle of Gain 277
A Simple Exercise for Building Inner Confidence 280
The Principle of Detachment 281
The Principle of Active Visualization 284
Exercise: 6 Steps of Active Visualization 288

CHAPTER 9: THE THREE PILLARS FOR MANIFESTING 291
Pillar 1: Conceive 292
Pillar 2: Believe 294
Pillar 3: Receive 298
State of Being 303
State of Doing 304

CHAPTER 10: BECOME WHAT YOU DESIRE 308
The Principle of Becoming 309
The Principle of Acting As If 321
The Principle of Aliveness 325
Exercise… 331
The Law of Perpetual Transmutation of Energy 332

CONTENTS

CHAPTER 11: CHANGING YOUR REALITY 337
    The Power of Responsibility. 339
    4 Steps for EmbracingOur Inner Power of Responsibility. 347
    The Power of Control 357
    Questions for Further Reflection 359
    Using This Power Correctly. 360
    The Power of Control and the Law of Consciousness. 367
    The Power of Intention. 372
    Living Intentionally. 380

CHAPTER 12: YOU CAN MANIFEST ANYTHING 390
    The 5 Guidelines 392
    5 Steps to Mastery 397
    The Power of Faith 399
    An Exercise for Working with Fear 405
    The Power of Commitment. 427
    Live Long and Prosper 433

ACKNOWLEDGMENTS 436
NEXT STEPS 438

Foreword

By: Jesse Krieger

As I sit down to write these words, it marks the completion of a project nearly 10 years in the making. As fate had it, in 2016 I had a call with a wisdom teacher and evolutionary leader who was inspired to write books. I recall as though it were yesterday, stepping away from a friend's birthday party in Santa Monica to take the call, because from the moment I heard Dale Halaway's voice, he sounded familiar, like someone I've known for eons, just resonating on every level. The conversation was about not just one book that he had in mind, but a trilogy on how to transform one's life from the inside out; how to embody one's soul, take responsibility for clearing their karma and learn to Manifest Like a Master.

At the time I was in my thirties, running a fast-growing publishing company that focused on entrepreneurship topics as well as spirituality and self-development. Following that first call, Dale and I met in person and talked for hours about his vision. I admired how he carries himself, upbeat, positive and with a knowing smile that invites you to open up, to speak the words on your heart, without your mind getting in the way. So, while our relationship began as an author and publisher, it evolved to me becoming his student and attending many of his seminars over a span of years. One of the things I love about publishing books is that I get to live through my own experience of the content as it evolves, takes shape and is released into the world for others to have their experience with it. That curiosity and open-minded approach led me deeper into Dale's vast body of knowledge and wisdom that he has accumulated across 40+ years as a teacher...and that is just in this lifetime. If you've read *Being Called to Change* and *Transform Your Destiny*, then you know how our life lessons evolve, play out and resolve over a course of lifetimes.

Well, Dale has been at this for lot longer than 40 years, and in fact he has shared that he has conscious memory of him and I in the times of Atlantis, and even before where we shared a similar dynamic of him as a teacher and guide, and myself as an earnest initiate in service to the Divine, living in accordance with Universal Law. A time that his books in this Transformation Trilogy will help to bring about again, when enough have embodied the wisdom teachings herein.

Dale Halaway is unique in that his commitment is unwavering. His commitment to his own growth as a master strategist and success coach, as well his commitment to his students and his readers, which now includes the one and only You! As I opened myself up more and became more honest and authentic with myself, my life began to change at a rapid clip. In the process of publishing *Being Called to Change* I invited Dale to be a partner in the publishing company. We aligned on a vision of helping our authors unlock their next level of growth and setting a new standard for book publishing, one where the author is honored and supported (which is sadly not the industry norm).

We got into a rhythm of doing a quarterly call available to all the authors I was publishing and Dale would share a teaching and inspire those present. On one of those calls he talked about falling in love with your book, and from that place of love sharing it far and wide. That talk resonated with an author who worked with inmates in maximum security prisons to help them overcome addictions and learn new skills so they can build a life after incarceration. I was inspired as well and helped that author place books in hundreds of prison libraries across America. The stories some of those inmates shared that someone cared enough to try and help them are truly heartwarming. I share this story as it is indicative of Dale Halaway's speciality - bringing light and love to dark places and integrating parts of us that have lived in the shadows too long.

Dale and I worked over 4 years on the second book in the trilogy *Transform Your Destiny*, which is all about embracing the life you are meant to live in partnership with The Divine. As the book came closer to completion, my personal experience from immersing myself in the 500+ pages of material over and over again was a full transformation of my own. My former publishing business had skyrocketed during 2020, having our best year ever when much of the world was shut down. But then into 2021 the aftershocks were rippling through supply chains and our finances took a turn for the worse. I worked myself sick doing everything I could think of to turn things around and save the company. My body was breaking down under the stress of the situation, and Dale was there for me every step of the way. All the way to and through the collapse of the publishing company weeks before the release date of *Transform Your Destiny*.

But fate and destiny have an amusing way of dancing with us through the difficult times. Even though the company collapsed, the book was already printed, distributed, in retailers and available on its release date. The book made its debut to great acclaim and the testimonies of those who read it are nothing short of remarkable. As I sorted through the winding down of a business I put everything I had into, I made sure to be as present and responsible as possible every step of the way. I read *Transform Your Destiny* four times back-to-back through this process and sought to embrace the lessons that were there for me to learn, to resolve the karmic patterns that drove my actions and to set the stage for my own personal New Beginning.

In this process of death and rebirth, I emerged a new, better, more humble and gracious version of myself. No longer in a rush to do a million things and hope some of them work. No longer willing to ignore my inner knowing and rush into relationships that weren't a match from the start. I let it all go, transmuted aspects of my lower nature in transformational fire, and waited patiently for the winds to raise me up like a phoenix from the ashes. I told Dale Halaway that I would like to be his personal publisher and recommitting to seeing the Transformation Trilogy through to completion.

That was nearly 3 years ago now. By honoring each step of my process I am now blessed to say that by the time you read these words I'll be married to the love of my life. I am thriving in a new career and still love books as much as ever. It is hard to do justice to the true and lasting change that I have personally experienced by immersing myself in Dale Halaway's teachings and using the results in my life as a reflection for where I'm at in now time.

Now in *Manifest Like a Master* you will learn the most exciting aspect of growth and transformation - how to create the life of your dreams in alignment with Universal Laws! This book is a veritable goldmine of transformational magic. Dale begins with a deep dive into the many Universal Laws that are integral to manifestation, and connects them in a way that is totally unique. This sets the stage of learning about the continuum of conscious creation and how to become aware when you're *unconsciously* manifesting something you don't want in your life, so you can change it.

FOREWORD

From there you'll learn about The Three Selves and how your past, present and future selves play into manifesting more of what you truly want in your world. Dale will guide you through your inner manifesting powers of imagination, goal setting and taking aligned action. You will learn essential principles for manifestation as well, such as the principle of becoming and the principle of aliveness. Ultimately you will learn how to change your reality through the conscious application of these timeless principles so you truly can Manifest Like a Master.

May you manifest all you truly desire,

Jesse Krieger
Publisher of *The Transformation Trilogy*

A MESSAGE FROM THE AUTHOR

Conscious Manifestation is, in my view, one of the most important topics currently on the planet for us to be learning and ultimately mastering. It's also one of the most exciting topics, as it opens us up to much greater possibilities in both our personal worlds as well as the collective world that we are all a part of. In order to rise up to a better, richer, kinder world and successfully sustain our residence there, we need to be masters of our own selves. Thus, the title of this book, *Manifest Like a Master*.

A few years back when the seed for this book originally began to grow within my consciousness, my intention was to write a series of books on the topic of manifestation. Since that time, I was inspired to have my first book on manifesting be the most in-depth book of the Transformation Trilogy. I wanted to give you, the reader, the most comprehensive body of teachings, along with exercises, examples, and stories. To do this, however, would mean a much longer book (which I did clear with my amazing publisher, Jesse Krieger, in advance of writing this book)—at least two books in one. My intention was to not only write a book but for it to be a textbook for life that the reader could return back to for further discovery, application, and learning.

For some of you, this book will help you remember what it is you already knew. For others, you will learn or discover some new ideas, which, when applied, will help move the needle forward in your personal and/or professional worlds. And for a select group, it will help you refine and expand on what is you've already been working on.

It's also possible that for many readers there'll be parts of this book that will challenge you. This book could challenge your approach to life that you've had for years, or something, as in one of your beliefs, that's no longer serving you. Or, for that matter, it could challenge anything that is in the way of you creating the life of your greatest dreams, which is to be let go of. As I often say to my students and private coaching clients, what challenges us has already been designed to change us at soul level.

The subject of manifestation first grabbed my attention when I was a young man in my early twenties, and I experienced the type of success in my life that neither I nor anybody else at the time could understand. Around the age of 26 I remember being invited onto a television show to talk about the success that had manifested in my life. I had a lot of trepidation going into that interview. I didn't know what the talk show host was going to ask. But the more stressful part of it all was that I was concerned I wouldn't be able to give them a good answer to whatever their questions were. In short, I was scared. The interviewer eventually got to the question, "What do you credit your success to?" To which I answered, "Hard work." He asked me the same question again, and again I answered the same. To which he replied, "Really? That's all you're going to give us today?" I repeated my answer yet again. He grew frustrated, as he thought I was holding out on him and his viewers.

What he didn't know that day is that I really didn't have another answer to his question. He closed out the show, and I left feeling disappointed in the way I showed up that day. That experience would haunt me in the best of ways in the months and years ahead. So, I eventually went on a secret mission to learn, to uncover, to discover what it was I knew I was missing. And from that moment to this, I've never stopped. I promised myself that I would mature to the place within where I could go onto an interview in the future and speak openly, spontaneously, and masterfully on the topic of success and manifestation. I would eventually go on to speak and teach on this topic by giving public seminars, customized training programs to businesses and organizations alike, private intensives to select clientele, and now sharing my accumulated knowledge here in book number three of our Transformation Trilogy.

To this, I would also like to acknowledge my many students throughout the decades of teaching and coaching on this incredible topic, for you all, in your own unique way, helped move me along in my discovering, learning, and ultimately becoming a master student myself on this most important topic. From my students to my personal coaching clients, to my company and business clients, to my family, friends and mentors—I send you my deepest appreciation and gratitude.

From the depths of my being to yours, a heart-felt mahalo…

My love and Aloha,
Dale

INTRODUCTION

When somebody comes along who has really been struggling for a long time, and they learn the lessons contained in this book, and then work through them for a sustained period, odds are they will find a way to punch through those struggles. The opposite of struggle is manifesting what you want on a conscious level. And that is what this book is all about. When you can manifest on a conscious level, with precision, it will change your life in the best and brightest of ways.

How do I know this? I've been doing this for a long time—teaching people from all walks of life, from all nationalities, and all ages—from teens to people in their seventies and eighties. For decades, I've traveled the globe, helping others effectively work through whatever it was they needed to work through. But ultimately, I was there to help them learn to manifest whatever it was they truly wanted.

A New Approach

For the most part, just working hard and trying to make something happen doesn't work. And if you do that long enough, you will burn out and you might even crash and burn. You might end up in a hospital bed because you burnt through all your energy during that phase of your life's journey. You could find yourself with no or very little energy for weeks or months to come after that. Now, you can keep on living that way, and if that's your approach to go about manifesting and achieving your goals (and you really believe that's what you need to keep on doing), then have at it. Go for it. Hey, you're not gonna get any pushback from me—far from it. But given that you've picked up this book, it is my promise to you that I'm going to do everything I know how to do to get you to see this in a newer, refreshed way—in a way that is ultimately more aligned with who it is you really are to become in this life.

When you're finished with this book, you can turn me off. You can never come back to this book again should you choose to do so. I wouldn't take it personally because you're entitled to do that, and I'm not here to force you into this way of thinking. Rather, I'm here to remind you of what's possible for you. I'm here to help open a doorway so that perhaps you can see a higher possibility for your own personal, professional, and spiritual life again. Perhaps you can see the greater truths that are at play. And then, it's up to you. It's up to you what you're ultimately going to do with this.

Stop Struggling

Learning how to *Manifest Like a Master* not only enables us to live our dream lives and attain our goals, but we also learn how to stop manifesting what it is we *don't want*. If somebody is struggling with a health issue, and they've been struggling with it for, say, five years, that sends off an alert signal to me that they aren't quite doing the right things yet. Now, they may be trying, and they may be doing plenty of things to try to fix the issue, but they haven't accessed the *right* thing for their particular issue. How do I know? Because that's a long period of time to struggle. Some people who come to me have been struggling with a certain issue for 10 years—even 15 years, sometimes more. Imagine that... you might find yourself asking, "Now how did that happen?"

In this book, *Manifest Like a Master*, we're going to take a deep dive into this question and others, because it's really important to get a deeper understanding of the struggles we experience in our world and what we're supposed to learn from them. The only way we are going to get out of the struggle is by going into it. We've got to learn from that struggle. We've got to uncover all of the little golden nuggets that struggle has to offer us.

No Quick Fixes

I'm not going to give you a quick fix in this book. As far as I know, there is no fast way to do this—and I've been around some pretty powerful healers. There is no, "I'm going to read this book, and 24 hours later, I'm going to be completely healed of this thing that I've been struggling with for the last five years of my life."

In the event that somebody does come into your world and is able to wave their magic wand, and all of a sudden you are healed—but you haven't actually learned anything—it's probably not going to last. If you haven't learned whatever it was you were supposed to learn from that experience, then the issue could repeat itself all over again. I've seen this play out a number of times with individuals over my decades of teaching and helping people to heal, change, or get better at manifesting on a conscious level.

So, if you're ready to stop struggling, if you're ready to start creating the life of your dreams... settle in and prepare to take the stairs—one step at a time. In other words, it is generally not the best strategy to take the elevator approach and attempt a bypass.

CHAPTER 1
GETTING STARTED

As we go through our experience together here, you're going to discover some of the most powerful teachings around how to get better at manifesting on a conscious level. My guess is that some of these teachings will be new to you. Some of them might be familiar but you just don't know how to practice them, integrate them, and realize them.

> Throughout the book highlighted in shaded boxes for you to easily refer back to, are many exercises, action items and questions that will be posed to you. To get the most out of the teachings contained here, it is suggested that you take the time to answer the questions in a designated notebook or journal each time a question appears. Some of these questions will have a certain level of meaning for you. And with others, the meaning will be even greater.

Every now and again you'll come across one of the questions found in these pages that will have you thinking about, being with, that question for several days. These are the questions that I suggest you spend the most time with. In doing so, take whatever that question is that's really speaking to you, open up your journal to a clean page, and write that question down on the top of that page. Then let yourself simply be with that question for the rest of the day or for several days and see what comes up for you. Whatever that is, be sure to write that down as well.

These questions are designed to open you up to a higher and greater possibility. They are designed to engage you into that of your own sacred inner process. The more time you put into your answers, the more you will get out of this manifesting journey you are embarking on.

If you find yourself becoming distracted or zoning out, put the book down and take a break. Let what you have read sink in and then return at a later time when you can be more present. You are going to want to be as conscious as possible for this experience. This is too important to skim over. If you are conscious throughout this process, it's going to result in a victory—which is what we're all looking for when it comes to manifesting.

So, before we begin, I want you to take a moment and slow everything down inside. To do that, I'd like you to start off by closing your eyes... Then, just take a couple of deep, slow breaths... and now go ahead and take three or four deeper breaths.

And as you do that, with your eyes closed, what I'd like for you to do is put your hands up on the center of your chest... and just gently hold that part of your body. Now simply go into silence for 60 seconds. This is an opportunity to slow everything down on the inside.

Now take three more deep and slow breaths, giving yourself permission to completely and totally relax into your physical temple—your body... just let yourself relax.

You've come a long way on your journey to this point in time. And wherever it is you're headed, you're going to get there. So for now, could you just let yourself cherish this moment of complete relaxation?

And whenever you're ready, gently stretch out your arms and let your hands drop down towards the floor and simply let them dangle. Move them around a little bit—just a little bit of gentle movement. You might even move your shoulders in a circular motion from front to back.

Now that you're a little more relaxed and present... let's get to Manifesting Like a Master.

The Current State of Humanity

The goal for this book is to help you *Manifest Like a Master*—to be able to create the life of your dreams. And yes, that is not only possible, but it is what we were intended to do from the very beginning of our Soul's journey.

Did you know that only 3 percent of the world's population has actually created the life of their dreams on Planet Earth? Think about that for a moment. That means 97 percent of humanity has not yet created the life of their dreams. This is something that one of my first mentors and teachers—the late, great Bob Proctor—would often say.

Boy, that sheds a lot of light on what's going on currently on the planet right now, as well as what has been amping up for many decades—the upheaval, the unrest, the dysfunction, the division, the separation, and on and on and on.

Well, of course, if I've gone through almost an entire lifetime, and I'm now in my seventies, and I still haven't created the life of my dreams, I'm probably not going to be a happy person. Let's call a spade a spade here. In fact, there's a chance I could become the complete opposite of happy and literally be one of the most miserable, stressed-out human beings on the face of the Earth. And where's the fun in that?

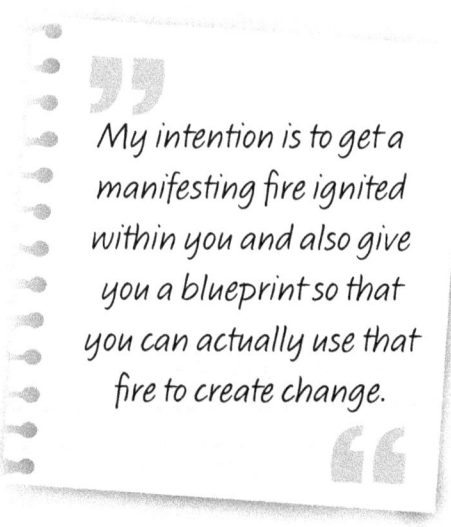

My intention is to get a manifesting fire ignited within you and also give you a blueprint so that you can actually use that fire to create change.

So how do I go about creating the life of my dreams? It's all going to come down to my ability to manifest on a conscious level.

In this book I'm going break this down in multiple ways for you, from multiple angles—to the point where you might even become a little frustrated with me LOL. But that's okay. Because my intention is to get a manifesting fire ignited within you and also give you a blueprint so that you can actually use that fire to create change.

You're reading this book because you want to get better at manifesting—because you recognize (and good for you for being able to recognize this!) that you need a little help with this manifesting thing.

This is big stuff, and it makes sense that you might need a little help—that you might not be very good at manifesting at this point in time, because 97 percent of the world's population isn't! Or another way of looking at this is 97 percent of the world hasn't yet created the life of their dreams.

You're already on your way to being part of the other 3 percent because you've made the choice to pick up this book! You've made the choice to invest in yourself and a better outcome for your future.

Now, is this the be all end all? Of course not. How could it be? For you, this might be the accelerator point, but it could even be the very beginning, and that's OK. It completely depends on where you are currently at in your journey.

The next choice after choosing to pick up this book then becomes: What might you do with this information? How long will you stay on a conscious manifesting path come the end of this book? Will you stop there, or will you continue on? Just as we learned about in book two of this Transformation Trilogy: *Transform Your Destiny*, you get to choose how you show up here—whether you are all in or just dipping your toe in the pool. Clearly, I can't force this upon you or make choices for you. What is next for you—this gets to be your choice.

Manifesting Is a Natural Ability

Now I'm going to share something with you that I discovered as a result of teaching these concepts for decades. Every single one of us was born into this life with a natural ability to manifest.

In this regard, we are born equal. One of the most profound discoveries I made about humanity, as a result of my experiences over the years, is that the natural ability you were born with to actually manifest on a conscious level has gotten blocked (at least with most of us).

The 97 percent of the people on this planet who never create the life of their dreams have this ability just as much as the 3 percent of people who do create the life of their dreams. The ability simply got blocked, and now they're experiencing an energetic separation to this natural ability.

Obviously, they've got the results to back that up as well. Here they are, going through their life... They're now 70 years of age and they still haven't figured this thing out. Then they wonder why they're so angry. They wonder why they're so bitter. They wonder why they can't forgive somebody who wronged them. Well, that would be a tough go because they've spent 70 years struggling through this life and still not manifesting their goals. They're still not manifesting their dreams... and this sucks for them.

I can't tell you how many people have said to me that they feel like their life has become a hell. That's right. A hell.

The question eventually arises: "Why wasn't I taught this?" Then they take it a little further into their schooling. They spent all those years in high school, all those years in college, all those years in university, getting one degree after another, and yet they still don't know how to consciously manifest. Some of my students end up connecting this pain and anger they later feel towards their Mom and/or Dad.

In my early twenties, I taught a seminar that was focused on getting better at manifesting, specifically, on achieving your goals. There was a student at this seminar who was about 27 years old, and at this point, they'd gone through three of my seminars over a period of about six to eight months.

> *Every single one of us was born into this life with a natural ability to maniifest.*

Something I was teaching sparked a feeling in them, and they became really angry. Now, you're probably wondering, *Why would they become so angry?*

Well, they had been in the classroom with me three times now, and they were learning about manifestation and how deep, expansive, and remarkable this subject is, and suddenly, we were at the end of the third seminar, and a revelation came upon them.

So, I began helping them get in touch with their anger and where their anger was coming from and who it was directed towards. And, if you're wondering, it wasn't towards me... rather, it was toward their parents.

I have seen this over and over again in young adults over the years. Anger seems to come up from inside, out of nowhere, when learning about manifestation. This anger has been accumulating over a period of time.

Why? Because Mom and/or Dad never taught them how to manifest. In fact, in some families manifestation was never a conversation topic—whether around the dinner table or just in regular day-to-day activities. I ask you, the reader, as you reflect back on your past... Can you think of a time when your parent sat you down and focused the conversation on how to get good at consciously manifesting? Probably not.

Now, in all fairness to Mom and Dad, they were also children once and they had a mom and dad too. And guess what? Odds are they also likely found themselves with suppressed anger inside that dated back from their childhood years when their parents didn't teach them how to consciously manifest either.

As I began to help my students clear their anger, I'd ask them how it feels to be at this place in time. Most would say they felt like they were in a wheelchair—energetically crippled, or that they felt they missed out on something that would have been very important for them to learn.

I want you to think about this... If you are 30 years of age and you are still not able to consciously manifest that which you really have a genuine desire for, how happy are you going to become over the next 10 years of your life? Exactly. You're not. You're going in the opposite direction, baby. That's what happens when you don't learn how to do this.

Here's something you might want to ponder... I've worked with doctors throughout my career in the holistic field, and this is one of their biggest frustrations. They're super skilled as doctors, but they often struggle with manifesting. They're part of that 97 percent.

This is a big problem on Planet Earth. And it's been going on for thousands of years. This is not something that just crept up.

And just because this is the status quo, that doesn't mean it can't have a catastrophic result. I know people who have literally committed suicide. They've taken their own life. This is serious stuff. Do you know of anybody who's taken their life? If you do, ask yourself this question: Prior to taking their life, how were they doing when it came to manifesting on a conscious level?

You'll see it right away. Even though they had that ability inside, they separated themselves from it. And then they went on for months or even years, not accomplishing their dreams, not manifesting or realizing their goals. Then they became down, depressed, angry, bitter, and resentful. Next thing you know, the thoughts are running rampant in their mind. One of the easiest and fastest ways out of all the pain and suffering is suicide.

Now, nobody's ever done a study on this to my knowledge, but I have no doubt if somebody were to do one, they would uncover what it is I've uncovered in the many different situations that I've been privy to throughout the years. And that is when somebody is not good at manifesting on a conscious level, they become angrier, more depressed, and they might even have a lot of hatred inside of them.

What happens when you're living that way? All of the fun and joy that you really are supposed to be having in your world gets squeezed out.

Recently, somebody from my past had a massive heart attack and died. They weren't very happy, clearly; they weren't fulfilled; and they definitely were not creating the life of their dreams. They were doing everything but that. Yet, nobody talks about things like this. And it's because most of us aren't even thinking this way.

Einstein said, "We cannot solve problems with the same thinking we used when we created them." In other words, in order to solve any problem, you've got to rise above the problem, and you've got to think at a level that's higher or greater than the way of thinking that you were using when the problem was originally created.

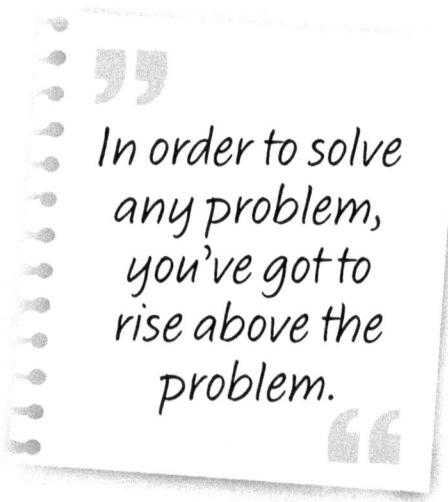

In order to solve any problem, you've got to rise above the problem.

The same applies with this situation, or problem which is our ability to manifest on a conscious level. If you have difficulty manifesting on a conscious level, then you need to address this problem with higher-level thinking.

Many of us have invested tens of thousands of dollars into higher education. I know countless people who have a degree, two degrees, three degrees, who, at some point, end up serving tables because they cannot manifest a successful career with their degree—even though they have the credentials. This has been widely studied in the recent past and is becoming somewhat of a widespread issue. Why can't these people manifest a career? They have all of the practical tools, but they haven't tapped into this natural manifesting ability, and it has been holding them back.

Reflection Question for Parents with Adult Children

This is the first question of many that will be asked throughout this book. Take a moment now to get your notebook that you have devoted to the exercises and questions contained here. Be sure to date your entries so you can track your progress and changes as time goes by.

Get your pen ready and keep it handy to write your answers for later reflection, beginning with this question:

If you have adult children, meaning they're in their twenties or older, I invite you to think about them and answer this...

On a scale of one to 10, 10 being really good, 1 being not so good, how would you rate your adult children when it comes to them being able to consciously manifest the life of their dreams in current time? (Be honest with yourself.)

Now why would I present such a question? Because it's a way to look at our results as parents regarding how good a job we did of teaching our kids how to manifest on a conscious level. If we did well, then we've set them up for the rest of their lives in the biggest and brightest of ways.

If, on the other hand, we have not done very well, then our adult children could be downright stuck in their anger, self-pity, or their own misery.

So how well are they doing? Look for the result. The results don't lie.

Again, if you are a parent, there was a time when you were a kid, and you had parents too. And your parents were either teaching you how to do this or they were teaching you how to suppress and bury this natural ability you were born with. Were they aware that's what they were doing? Of course not. Not at all. They were unconscious. This is a really important piece to remember here, as this will help minimize the tendency to beat ourselves up for possibly messing up with our kids.

As you will learn throughout this book, all manifestation has got to come from somewhere. And that somewhere will always be within us when it comes to our own personal world.

Additional Questions to Ponder…

As we get into the mindset of manifesting, here are a few more questions that will give you a clear idea of your starting point when it comes to the overall blueprint we're developing. You will then be able to refer back to these as you progress on your manifesting journey.

> With your notepad and pen in hand, I encourage you to answer these questions with total honesty. In fact, it is important that you become brutally honest with yourself throughout this process. Now if you're not willing to do this just yet, it does not make you a bad person, of

course. But if that's the case, then more than likely, you're going to stay within the 97 percent of people who have not yet created their dream life.

Why is that? Well, think about it. Of that 97 percent group, how honest do you think they are with themselves? Not just with their partner, not just with their kids, not just with their parents. How honest are they with themselves?

> *When you're in the presence of someone who really knows how to Manifest Like a Master, you're in the presence of somebody who knows how to manifest on a conscious level with precision.*

This "honest with yourself" theme is something you're going to get a lot of reminders from me on throughout this book, because you'd be amazed at how many people are dishonest when it comes to themselves. Remember you've got that ego in there—which might have a lot of your power right now—and the ego does not like honesty. Let's call a spade a spade. Honesty is a very powerful dynamic that can do all kinds of beautiful things for you. And that threatens your ego—especially if it's still untamed and hasn't been trained properly. Keep that in mind, as you are possibly being tempted to bend your truth a little here.

Take a moment to get out your notebook and pen and answer the following questions. Remember to be honest.

As you think about manifesting—I'd like for you to think about yourself and your natural ability to manifest—when answering the following questions...

Question #1

At this exact moment in time, how good would you say you are at manifesting what you would really like to have manifest in your world on a conscious level? On a scale of 1 to 10, 10 being you're really, really good and 1 being you have no clue how to consciously manifest what you would really like to have. Once again, be honest. Whatever your number, there's no right or wrong answer here.

Question #2

Reflect back on your past timeline and where you were one year ago. Pinpoint a specific moment during that time that you can visualize. Think of one specific time—not multiple events.

What were you up to? Who were you with? What were you doing? What was happening?

Why is this so important? Because what you wrote is now anchored to a point in time, approximately a year ago in your past. And this is crucial for the next question...

Question #3

Now that you are anchored to a specific point in your timeline, one year ago, consider where you were at then when it came to how well you could manifest at a conscious level. Again, be honest. On a scale of 1 to 10, 10 being that you manifested everything you wanted, 1 being you were not that good at manifesting at all, or somewhere in between. Whatever your number, write that down.

Question #4

Take a look at your responses to Questions 1 and 3. Contrasting your responses to both these questions, did you get better, or did you get worse at manifesting from a year ago to today?

Once again, be honest. What actually happened? What's been happening with you in relation to manifesting on a conscious level over the last 12 months?

The cool thing that we can all count on, whether we believe in this or not, is that the results that manifest in your world, day to day, week to week, month to month, year to year, never, ever lie.

Question #5

One more question... How conscious would you say you are, in current time, of the manifestation process in your personal world? On a scale of 1 to 10, with ten meaning you're really conscious and one meaning you're not very conscious at all.

Now, if you say you're a 10, what that means is you understand all of the mechanics, dynamics, and energetics that drive the manifestation process. And more specifically, if you really are at a 10, that would mean you're not just manifesting consciously, but you're manifesting consciously with precision. Also, remember that (at least up until now) only around 3 percent of the world knows how to manifest with conscious awareness and has mastered it. That means that everyone else is either still trying to figure this out or doesn't even know it is possible.

When you're in the presence of someone who really knows how to *Manifest Like a Master*, you're in the presence of somebody who knows how to manifest on a conscious level with precision.

EXERCISE: Remaining Conscious

Here's a simple exercise that is designed for you to begin to have some kind of a conscious experience with manifesting.

> Before you write anything down, think of something that you would like to manifest. Now, in this case, I want you to purposely go for something that is easy and within your reach. In other words, if you've never manifested thirty thousand dollars before, then it's probably not going to be in your best interest to write down a million dollars. That's your ego trying to trick you. We've learned much about the ego in the first two books in the Transformation Trilogy, which you can refer back to as needed

What we're looking for here is for you to have some kind of an experience in remaining conscious around something you've chosen to manifest up until the point where it actually manifests for you on a physical level.

> To do this, go ahead and write down something that you would like to have manifest within the next _____ days. (Choose the number of days that seems realistic and is within your current reach. The key here—what we're after—is remaining conscious throughout this process. So be sure you don't pick a time frame that is too long.)

An example of this might be to manifest a smaller sum of money. Have you ever come across a $100 bill unexpectedly before? Like an actual $100 bill, just out of the blue? If you haven't, maybe that's what you go for. Or maybe you say, "I'm going to manifest three $100 bills in the next 30 days."

> So, whether it's a $20 bill, a $100 bill, or the perfect parking spot, get clear on what you want. And now go manifest it. You could very well pleasantly surprise yourself—because remember, you've got the natural ability inside of you. This exercise is meant to help you unlock it.

This is the premise that we're all operating from; that inside of each of us is a natural ability that we were born with. What we want to do is recall that ability—we want to get it fully activated. And then we want to learn how to correctly utilize that ability.

No matter your situation in life, regardless of whatever handicaps or limitations you may have, you can overcome them. This ability is still inside of you. It's just waiting to be awoken. It's waiting to be utilized correctly by you. You've got it. You've had it all along.

So now, connect with what you're going to manifest. And remember to make it something that's simple, easy, and within your reach. Maybe it's three $100 bills, or maybe it's a $1,000 check. For those of you who are in business and serving others, maybe it's a new paying client. If you are new in business, don't attempt to manifest 10 new paying clients. Just keep it to one (at least for now) and see how it works out. If you want a bonus or possibly a raise at work in your career, remain mindful to keep it within your reach. Or, if you're in sales, maybe you've been struggling for a while and you haven't closed a new account, so you set your goal to manifest one new account, or maybe you have an account that you want to go more vertical with. Perhaps you want to manifest a new dress, a new suit, or maybe a new piece of furniture for your house. All of these are great starting points.

So now that you are thinking about what it is you want to manifest, let's put a time frame on it. For this exercise, we aren't going to go beyond the 30-day mark. We want to keep the time compressed so we can stay consciously aware of the process. So, with the parking spot example, "I want to manifest the perfect parking spot at work three times within the next seven days." This could be a great starting point.

So, write the number of days, whether it's seven days, like the example above, or any time frame up to 30 days.

Whatever your intended manifestation is… double check, is it realistic? Is it within your reach? Keep it simple, realistic, and tangible. This is important for your psyche, for your Soul. If you let your ego get in there, it's going to try to trick you into either choosing something unrealistic, or it will try to trick you into not believing in your ability to manifest this, and you aren't going to have good results.

We want the victory to create a foundation for believing we can do this. On a psychological level, you are going to love the benefits you will derive from really taking this to heart and doing it properly.

CHAPTER 2

THE LAWS OF MANIFESTING

Universal Laws are not like the manmade laws that our police officers enforce. These are spiritual laws, and they are laws that you cannot bend, change, or work around. Universal Laws are those that work 100 percent of the time, just like the law of gravity or the law of electricity.

When I was a young man, I studied Universal Law, and then I became a teacher of it. I taught thousands of people what the Universal Laws are, and then, more specifically, I taught them how to integrate these laws into their day-to-day world personally and/or professionally.

I had people from all around the world coming to my classes during that time—I was in my mid-twenties at that point—and I became quite skilled at it. Therefore, my name got around the campfire throughout western Canada, which is where I was living at the time. So much so that a producer of a television station, Jim, and his wife came to one of my seminars on Universal Law.

It was a weekend class, and we had maybe 400 or so people in the room. During that weekend, at the first break of day number one, they were in line to talk to me. Jim said, "I just want to see if you would be interested in doing a television show on the Universal Laws."

Initially, my response was, "No, Jim, I'm not interested."

He was surprised by my response, but he asked me to just consider it and told me how much he and his wife were enjoying my seminar and how they couldn't wait for the rest of it. He asked, "At the end of the seminar, could we just talk because I've got the director of the station on standby, and he wants to meet with you first thing Monday morning?"

> *Universal Laws are spiritual laws that you cannot bend, change or work around.*

I said I would consider it, and we would see how it goes.

So, Monday morning came, and I went to the station to meet the director. That following Friday afternoon, I was in the studio recording my first handful of TV episodes. That show, called *Reach for the Stars*, went on to become the number one show on that station within about a six-month period of time.

On average, we'd get hundreds of letters each week, with a few of those weeks receiving as many as 1,500 letters. Back in those days, there was no internet, so people had to hand write a letter if they wanted to ask me a question or express appreciation. I had that show for another couple of years before I ultimately made my journey to the U.S. It was a huge success.

After that show ended, I continued integrating the concept of Universal Law into my teachings. These are laws that govern not only the universe, but our own personal universes as well.

Back in my twenties, it became obvious to me that the majority of people I came into contact with didn't know the term Universal Law, let alone what the Universal Laws were, how they worked, how to integrate them, how to align their lives with them, and so forth.

If you've read my two previous books in the Transformation Trilogy, or if you've attended any of my classes or seminars, you'll know that I integrate these Universal Laws into all of my teachings. On this specific topic of Manifesting Like a Master, there are a handful of laws that are essential to this process. So, I'm going to now introduce these specific laws and explain how they operate.

In this chapter, I'll provide you with an overview of each of the Universal Laws that relate to manifesting, and you will then be able to deepen your understanding of them as you work through this book.

LAW #1: The Law of Energy

The first related law is known as the Law of Energy. It states that everything is energy, that everything around us contains energy. The shirt you're wearing right now is energy. The body that you're currently residing in, right now, is made up of energy. The walls in your home are made up of energy.

Everything is energy. Everything. No matter what it is. Now, this is really important because inside of each of us we have thoughts and feelings. Every one of those thoughts, every one of those feelings, is energy. We also have behavioral patterns, and we have languaging patterns, all of which are made up of energy.

When you understand this law, you can put it into action and actually transform energy. You can transmute energy. If I can, so can you. You may have already had experiences that have shown you that you can do this.

Now, when somebody is struggling to manifest on a conscious level, then they probably don't have a deeper understanding of this. If I'm going to get better at manifesting on a conscious level, I've also got to get better at bringing this law—the Law of Energy—into the way I'm living my life. What this ultimately means is that in order to transform my life, I'm going to be transforming the energy that makes up my field of consciousness, my brain, my heart, and my physical vessel—as well as the many different aspects that make up my physical life such as my health, my career, my relationships, my finances, etc. I'm transforming the energy molecules of all these areas to their higher octave

LAW #2: The Law of Attraction

Now, another law that we're going to hone in on is the Law of Attraction. Everybody has heard of the Law of Attraction, but what's so fascinating is how few actually understand this law. Even if they've watched the wonderful movie *The Secret*, they still don't fully comprehend it.

One of my mentors, as mentioned earlier, Bob Proctor, was the major star in that movie before he passed. When he was speaking to an audience prior to his passing, he said that what they put out in that movie wasn't the whole truth. He went on to say that he almost wished they could have redone it. Why? Because people only got half of the story. Three hundred million-plus people came across that movie, yet they're still a part of that 97 percent of the world's population who are not creating the life of their dreams.

The Law of Attraction says energy must seek its own. Like energy attracts like energy, period. This means that if I've got a pocket of negative energy inside of me, that negative energy must attract more of its like to itself. Just like if I have positive energy that's real and sustainable inside of me, that, too, must attract.

This is one of the big misunderstandings that has plagued humanity for thousands of years. Energy can only do one thing and one thing only, which is to seek more of its own. And that's why these people who think it's all about just thinking positive only have half the equation. Yes, it is about that, but it's not *just* about that because if you have a lot of negative energy inside of you, if you have a lot of pain, a lot of hurt, a lot of unresolved karma, or a lot of anger inside of you, that is considered negative energy, and that negative energy must attract more of its like to itself.

Whether we believe in this or not, this energy could care less. That's one of the beauties of Universal Law. It's completely impersonal. It's non-emotional. If we choose to violate this law (consciously or unconsciously), simply out of ignorance, then we will bring more pain upon ourselves. We will bring more unconscious, unnecessary suffering upon ourselves. Even if we try to blame it on our parents, or our kids, or the economy, and so on, the reality is that it's coming from inside of us.

> The Law of Attraction says like energy must seek it's own—whether positive or negative, it will attract more of its kind to itself.

And if you're in violation of this law or any other law, there will be a negative consequence. It might not happen right away. It might be weeks from now. It might be months from now. Heck, it might even be a couple years from now.

I had a student who came to my four-day-long Magic of Attraction class years ago. Her life wasn't going very well at the time. More specifically, she had a severe physical issue that was spinning out of control in her world. She was going to a psychiatrist, and she was on all kinds of meds to help her manage this issue.

She had been diagnosed with a severe panic disorder. In fact, she had a couple panic attacks in my class. She was having panic attacks daily. The only way she could survive through this was by going to a psychiatrist. Without help, she would have died. It was just a question of time. She had been suffering with this for some time, and it was building. It was growing like a bad weed in a garden.

At the beginning of class, she announced this issue to me. I saw almost immediately the opportunity that was present for her, should she choose to step into it, as a way to begin to change this. So I asked her, "Whenever you have a panic attack, would you be willing to bring it to my attention and give me an opportunity to work through the energy of the panic attack with you?"

Although she was foreign to this kind of thing at the time, something inside her told her to say yes, and she did. When this type of situation arises, I will only ask this question if I know that opportunity is present for them to be ready to step into this. And I knew the opportunity was present, given by the permission of her Higher Self.

She has since remarked that the Magic of Attraction course was a game changer for her. It changed everything and ultimately led to the healing of her panic disorder, to the point where eventually her psychiatrist said that over time, they were going to reduce the medication. They reduced it gradually, and eventually, there was no more medication.

She healed herself of it naturally, organically. It took a while, no doubt about it. But her starting point was literally in that first class, the Magic of Attraction.

Well, why was that? Because during that class, I was teaching the Law of Attraction—the full version, not the abridged version taught on *The Secret*. For example, one of the teachings in the Law of Attraction is called the point of attraction. Whatever it is you attract in your world, in order for that to be attracted, you've got to develop a point of attraction. And that point goes into your magnetic field. Oh yes, you have a magnetic field. Once that point has been developed, it then becomes an energetic point of attraction.

It's similar to acupuncture—the energy points on the meridian lines. When I look at somebody's magnetic field, I can see these points—just like a highly trained acupuncturist can see these energy points. It's not necessarily something you can see with your physical eye, yet, if an acupuncturist comes along and touches these points, and you are stuck, or that energy is backed up, you're going to feel something right away. It's the same thing in your magnetic field. You have points of attraction in your magnetic field. When any one point of attraction gets strong enough, it starts to consume the magnetic field.

Once it begins to consume the magnetic field, now you're only days or weeks away from manifesting whatever it is that is going to manifest—or attracting whatever it is you're going to attract. This could be your next relationship with one of the most dysfunctional people on Planet Earth. The attraction could be a choice that you're about to make that's going to cost you $23,000. It could be that you're about to go somewhere, and something is bound to happen. You're going to get really stressed and anxious, then something will result—you might fall and break your knee. The outcomes are endless. And I've seen this play out in countless ways.

Because here's the deal. If that point becomes strong enough, it must, by law, attract its like. Of course, anybody who ends up attracting something bad—like an abusive relationship, financial loss, a broken bone, etcetera—is completely unconscious. If they were conscious, they would be disarming that point of attraction, rather than continuing to power it up. And then, more importantly, if they really were aware of this and knew how to truly operate within this law, the first thing they would be doing is developing new, positive points of attraction and/or strengthening the positive points of attraction they already had.

So, if you already know about the Law of Attraction, from *The Secret* or from another book or course, and you have tried to implement it already but are unsure if you are implementing it correctly, a good way to gauge this is to simply look at your results. We will come back to this point often in this book: Whatever the results that have manifested in your life, they never lie. If you really are developing better, higher vibe points of attraction, if that really is your truth, then at some point, as they get stronger, they're going to consume your magnetic field.

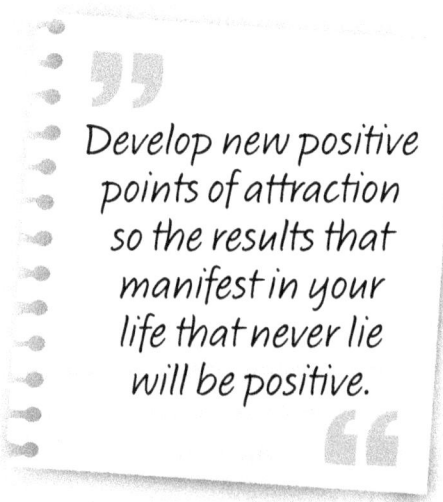

Develop new positive points of attraction so the results that manifest in your life that never lie will be positive.

And once they do, you will be pleasantly surprised with how quickly whatever it is that you're in the process of creating or manifesting… just manifests. Maybe you're manifesting a positive relationship. In this case, you'll realize, *I didn't do anything. I was just guided to go here. I went there, and there he/she was.*

Think about it. If and/or when you attracted a dysfunctional relationship in your past, you didn't "do" anything. One day, you just turned right, and there he or she was. Then, 18 months later, you're wondering, *How the heck did we get here?*

That was your point of attraction. Your point of attraction is either of a higher-vibing nature, or it's of a lower-vibing nature. It's one or the other.

If it's a lower-vibing nature, what's one of the ways you'll spot it? You'll notice you feel bad. You'll notice that while in this state you'll feel a lot of negative, heavy or dense emotion. Usually, it's a repetitive emotion, and/or a lot of negative cyclical thoughts over and over again. That feeling is driving the feeding of your point of attraction, and it's going to attract something negative—like a magnet.

Now on the other hand, if you want something of a higher nature, then it's also going to be found in your feelings and in your thoughts.

This would be a good time for us to reflect on a few questions that are related to this law.

> So remember to be honest with yourself as you answer the following...

What do you typically feel most of the time? What do you find yourself thinking about when you're in conversation with someone close to you? What do you think about most when you're by yourself? What do you find yourself imagining most of the time—and is it mostly positive or mostly negative?

All of these things come into play to serve in the creation of a higher-vibe point of attraction, as well as a lower vibe point of attraction.

And just like with a lower-vibe point, as that higher-vibe point of attraction gets stronger, there's a time when it just starts to spread throughout one's magnetic field.

One of the things you'll notice, if you're really skilled with your dreams, is that they will start to reflect the very thing you're about to manifest, whether it's a higher-vibe or lower-vibe point of attraction. Your dream space is clearly reflecting back what is coming. When it's a lower-vibe point of attraction, it can be really scary. And it can even show up as a nightmare.

However, it is more common for a person who is manifesting from a lower-vibe place to be unconscious. These are the people who are always numbing themselves out with the next bag of potato chips, a whole plate of fried food, copious amounts of alcohol and/or drugs, a bunch of sex, compulsive shopping, or a whole lot of negative thinking. Those people who have numbed themselves like this often aren't in touch with the content of their dream space.

Their dreams might be warning them of what's coming in terms of a manifestation, and there's a good chance they don't even know how to interpret those dreams properly. For example, they might see what seems like monster, such as a real distorted animal or looming figure, in their dreams and thus they can easily become frightened. And if they misinterpreted the languaging of that dream, they will react with their emotions and feelings, which only serves to further power up that dream and what it's portraying.

Yet all of this can be rerouted. All of it. We can stop that negative vortex. If I can do it, you can do it. Anybody can do it. But, if you're ultimately going to pull this off, you'll need to get a handle on the Law of Attraction.

The point of attraction is a key aspect of this law. It is a very powerful concept that most people don't know about. Most people don't want to hear about this concept either. And maybe that's why it never made it into the movie. Dealing with your shadow—going into the underbelly of consciousness—isn't necessarily good for business. And if you're going to disarm these lower-vibration points of attraction, that's what it's going to take. It's not pretty work.

> *If you're really skilled at working with your dreams, they will start to reflect the very thing you're about to manifest.*

If you're one of those people who wants everything to be comfortable—who likes everything to be pretty—you're never going to get there. Which means these lower points are going to get stronger... until, like a bad weed in the garden, they consume that garden (or in this case consume your own magnetic field).

This is where you get to choose. This is where you get to be conscious. This is where you get to become more aware of what's really going on. This is where you get to understand the Law of Attraction more deeply and ultimately learn how to utilize it like a master.

LAW #3: The Law of Vibration

The Law of Vibration states that everything moves. Everything. Your thoughts, your feelings—everything's got to move. Nothing rests. Nothing remains idle in the Universe. Think of the seasons here on Earth—change is constant.

Those of us who have deep-seated control issues are attempting to block this process. We are attempting to block an emotion or thought running through us instead of just letting it do what it's supposed to do.

If I don't want to feel what's inside of me, I'm simply not going to allow myself to feel whatever that is. Even if I'm not consciously aware that's what I'm doing. In other words, I'm going to literally park that emotion—which is nothing more than energy in motion. But this is where that emotion can become stuck. This is a violation of Universal Law. And if I violate it, and choose consciously or unconsciously not to correct it, this is where the process of a consequential effect begins to manifest in my life.

The Law of Vibration is the primary law to the Law of Attraction, meaning the Law of Vibration influences it. Our energetic frequency, in motion, determines our vibrational state—which determines what we attract.

Now, if all you're doing is thinking positive thoughts, this is not going to help you get there. Because it's only one piece to this larger equation. You see, attempting to use positive thoughts to override your negative emotions simply won't work. In doing this, you're just pulling the wool over your own eyes.

People who only think positive thoughts can still end up getting sick and lose money. Why? Because when we're only focused on our thoughts and there are these negative emotions running rampant inside of us, ultimately those negative emotions are going to win. They're going to take center stage. They will pull us down because they also carry a frequency. They will pull us down to their level of frequency, and we'll then be in that lower vibrational state—despite our thoughts. If we're in this place, this then becomes the vibrational state in which we are creating from.

So, in other words, if we are upset and in a bitchy, grumpy mood and we choose to stay there for hours, we are literally going to attract more of the bitchy, grumpy mood. Somehow, some way, someone or something is going show up in our own personal universe. Maybe someone shows up, and they're bitchy or grumpy too. Maybe they're downright mean. Maybe they're going to make us feel guilty or give us a hard time. Our low-vibrational emotions will continue to perpetuate, despite whatever thoughts we are attempting to cover these emotions up with. And then, something else will happen. It might be our computer. All of a sudden, our computer might go off, and for the life of us, we can't get the computer back on. So, then we will try harder and harder to get it to turn on, but the cycle will continue until our emotional state has been addressed.

You see, when you're in a low-vibrational state, it becomes your creative state—whether you like this or not, whether you believe in this or not, whether you're conscious or unconscious to this, and whether or not you're trying to think positively. You're manifesting 24/7, and you're creating from whatever vibrational state you're in.

On the other hand, I could train myself to *feel* good. In this case, if I have a negative feeling come up—if I were to become activated and feel really afraid, or insecure, or depressed—I could sit with it for a couple hours, rather than a few days. We don't want to ignore the feelings that come up or deny them, but it's not a wise choice to sit in them for an extended period of time. We don't want to wallow in it. We want to process and consciously work with and through the feeling. When people who are close to me come to me with a negative emotion, I most often tell them, "If you go beyond two or three hours, that's completely your choice—because there's no reason on earth you have to sit in this for longer."

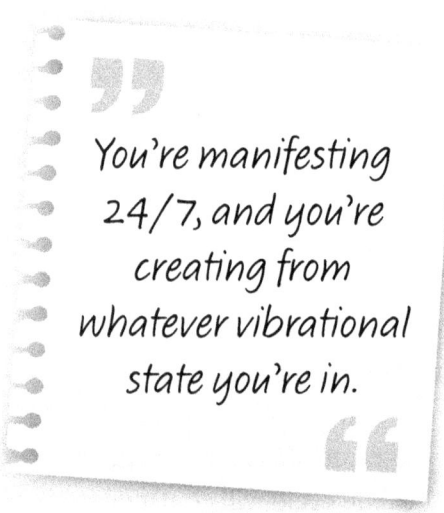

You're manifesting 24/7, and you're creating from whatever vibrational state you're in.

Once we've processed the negative material, we can work our way back into a higher vibrational state. How cool is that? How productive is that? When it comes to getting better at manifesting consciously, you'll want to get this down.

But most people are completely uninformed about this or are unconscious to it, so they get activated. And then what do they do? They might choose to stay in it for the next week—maybe they vent about it, or they engage in self-pity, or they try to think positive without addressing the emotion. Now this isn't their fault. They just simply have no idea what they're doing to themselves. And if they did, there's no way they would continue doing it this way. When we do this, we're sucked down to the lowest vibrational state, and it's from here that we potentially manifest something we don't want. This is a lower energy pattern that if not checked regularly and transformed can repeat over and over again.

Another point to consider is our need to be positional. This "need" is one that runs against the Law of Vibration and can really impact our ability to manifest whatever it is we want to have manifest in our world. Now when I say "need," I am referring to a needy energy, which is an extension of our ego.

Perhaps you can think of someone who is really stubborn. In other words, they're just hell bent on doing something their way—and there is no other way. Nobody's going to advise them. They aren't going to take any suggestions. They already know exactly what they're going to do. They've got their heels dug in. That's it. That's the bottom line. Whether it's a good choice or a bad one, it doesn't matter. They're just plain stubborn.

Our Soul is always prompting some kind of a change. Maybe it has been continuing to prompt the exact same change for the past five years. When a person becomes positional and ignores these nudges, they can no longer receive anything. Their Higher Self can't get through. Their guides can't get through. The Universe can't get through. They might have an angel in their world, disguised as a teacher, a coach, a mentor, or some kind of guide. They can't get through either.

When somebody digs their heels in, it locks things down. There can be physical consequences to this as well. In this person's body, their circulation could start to jam up; their natural flow could be restricted. And yes, it can actually be quite alarming. As they dig their heels in even more, they can become whiter than a ghost—because this is a serious "hanging onto" energy that can have their life force grow weaker while they're literally locking everything down inside themselves. And, of course, as these sensations are going on in their body, they are no longer even aware of the Law of Vibration and how it truly works.

For example, someone could have a real strong need to be positional. And upon getting really triggered by something someone else says or does, they take a position against that other person—which strengthens in intensity the longer they hold onto it. This could stretch out over weeks or even months of holding tightly to that activated energy. Obviously, again, in all fairness to them, they have no idea what they're doing to themselves or to their life, but nonetheless, they could get sucked back down to that lower vibrational state, which means they run the risk of potentially hurting themselves, of sabotaging something they really value in their world, and whereby possibly manifesting something in their life they never really wanted to have manifest in the first place.

I've seen it happen over and over again throughout the years... it's unnecessary suffering. As mentioned in book number one of the Transformation Trilogy, *Being Called to Change*, there are two types of pain that every person experiences on the course of their journey. One of them is completely optional. The other one is not.

Most people go after the one that's completely optional, and that's the pain that they live in. This is the sabotage of all sabotages. This puts their life force at risk. This completely negates the thing they want to manifest, right from the very beginning of the process. When people do this, they never get to stage two in the manifestation process. They get stuck at that first stage once they get activated because their need to be positional takes center stage—and they get stuck in that low-vibrational energy for days or possibly even weeks. Heck, this can be nasty stuff. And it has nasty, negative consequences. So, if we're going to learn how to *Manifest Like a Master*, it is critically important to get this down.

There's so much at stake when we decide to be positional—and it's all unnecessary. There's no law that says it has to be this way. It all comes down to personal choice, and now that you understand this, you can choose differently; by starting first with reminding yourself that holding onto your own activated energy for two or three hours of time is enough, and by then reaching out to your teacher, mentor, or guide and asking for help. Remember that once we get really good at processing this stuff, it can often be dealt with in a matter of minutes.

> *If we want to get good at manifesting on a conscious level with precision, we'll need to be in that higher vibrational state on a more regular basis.*

If we get this down—if we learn how to process these negative emotions quickly—what does that mean? It means we're back in that higher vibrational state. This is where we want to be. If we want to get good at manifesting on a conscious level with precision, we'll need to be in that higher vibrational state on a more regular basis and eventually 24/7—that's where we're ultimately going. We've got to turn this into a lifestyle, and it takes time to do this. And more than likely we're going to need help and support to get to this level, and it's going to take some work. But it can be done.

Now the other type of pain I mentioned earlier in this section, which is not optional, would be the pain that comes with our karmic lessons. This is a type of lesson you came into this life with—implying that if you're going to learn the lesson, you're going to have to go through the lesson by experiencing it. I might add that learning lessons at this level is uncomfortable—and they most certainly can be even painful. For when we learn the lesson really well, we will also have grown as a person—as a man, as a woman, as a Soul. Another way of saying the same thing would be this is growing pains. Remember when you were a kid, and your body was growing? There were actual pains that came along with your body getting bigger. These two examples would be the pain that we all get to experience that is not optional, for it has already been chosen for us prior to coming into this life.

Another way of looking at the Law of Vibration is that we are to be increasing our vibration or raising our frequency. When we are truly growing as a person, this is also what we are doing—we are raising our frequency. And as we raise our vibrational frequency, we naturally attract a better, richer, more radiant quality of life.

LAW #4: The Law of Consciousness

Now let's go on to the next law—the Law of Consciousness—which we could say is another primary law that fuels the Law of Attraction.

This is another part of the missing piece out of the movie *The Secret*. And it happens to be a huge missing piece. Now, the Law of Consciousness is really unique because it says that consciousness is the cause and substance of the entire world.

If you've read my second book in the Transformation Trilogy, *Transform Your Destiny*, you might recognize this law from when you learned about the Law of Cause and Effect and the Law of Karmic Return. While those two laws drive the Law of Consciousness, the Law of Consciousness is at the root of everything. Everything. The Universe, at its root, at its essence, is consciousness. Your beingness, at its root, at its essence, is consciousness.

Consciousness is the cause as well as the substance of the entire world—and not just your world but the world as a whole, the collective world.

This law also says that consciousness carries a vibrational frequency. Now, despite what you've learned about in the past, there are many frequencies of consciousness. Never be fooled into thinking that you've accessed "the" frequency of consciousness. That would be your ego tricking you, big time.

When you understand consciousness and when you begin to understand the many frequencies of consciousness, it starts to open something up inside of you. You could say that you might even get cracked open in a way you've never been cracked open before. If you don't understand what I mean by that, I'm talking about your upper energy centers being cracked open to a higher, greater truth. (This is something I teach in a one-day online class that I do on a rather regular basis for the general public called the Energetics of Relationships, which dives into the Upper Energy Centers. It can be found on dalehalaway.com.)

Now the frequency at which consciousness is vibrating determines its natural effect. So once again, if we go back to *Transform Your Destiny*, under the Law of Cause and Effect, our world is made up of effect. With every effect, there must be a direct cause. And more than likely, it is not what you think.

In order to get to the cause, you're going to have to do some work, baby. You're gonna have to do some peeling away to get to the cause. But here's the deal. Whatever the frequency of that level of consciousness is, it'll vibrate at a certain speed. This then will determine its natural effect in your body, your brain, and in any external part of your life—such as your finances, your relationships, and your health... you get the idea.

A deeper understanding of this law alone and the method by which it operates will allow you to create the life of your dreams.

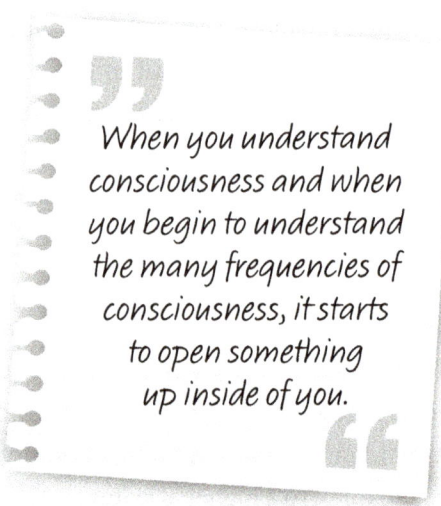

When you understand consciousness and when you begin to understand the many frequencies of consciousness, it starts to open something up inside of you.

Now, of the 97 percent of people who have not been creating the lives of their dreams, do you believe that they even know of the existence of this law, let alone how to actually operate it in their life?

Probably not, as that would likely only apply to the 3 percent. These are the people who are manifesting the life of their dreams, or their heart's deepest, greatest desires. The results never lie. These are the people who are working *with* the Laws of the Universe.

LAW #5: The Law of Belief

Now, another law we're going to take a pretty deep dive into is the Law of Belief. The short summation of this law says that whatever we believe with feeling and conviction becomes our reality.

As wonderful as it sounds, the Law of Belief is actually a tough one because if you're going to get this law working for you, if you're going to bring your life into alignment with this law, you're going need to roll up your sleeves. You're going to need to do some serious transformational work.

When you have a deeper understanding of this law and how it actually operates, and more specifically, how you could be operating your life in alignment with this law, that's when the magic really gets released... the transformational magic, the spiritual magic, the manifestation magic.

Why? The bottom line is this: At the root of everything that you manifest, there will be something that you believe to be true about yourself.

When I first came to know this law, it resonated with me right from moment number one. It was almost like I felt I'd gone to heaven. I found myself wondering, *How could I have possibly forgotten about this?*

I started to dive into it, study it, work with it, and bring it into my day-to-day world—including into my dream space. I'm a real avid dreamer, and I get tremendous information and insight from my dream space about the people I work with and the content for my seminars, courses, and books—as well as my personal life.

When I first started diving deep into this law, my dreams became so colorful. Of course, this was my Higher Self downloading even more teachings around this law.

The Law of Belief says that it's our strongest emotionalized beliefs that manifest in our day-to-day world. When any belief inside of you—positive or negative, destructive or constructive—becomes emotionalized, it has a super strong effect on your psyche. It has a strong effect on the way you're going to live your life and the choices you're going to make. It has a strong effect on the behavioral patterns that you engage in. In fact, beliefs that have been emotionalized literally determine the type of success that you're going to experience, the type of love you will have in your life, the level of wealth or financial wellbeing you aspire to, and ultimately, the level of happiness you will experience.

Your strongest beliefs, whether you believe in this or not, are at the root of whatever you're now experiencing. If you are struggling for love in your life, it's because you have at least one strong emotionalized belief that is not in support of you having true love.

As a young man, I was physically ill a lot. In fact, from my first two years in this life through to the age of 33, I had a few near-death experiences. I came close to dying when I was just a toddler, and then, at the age of 33, I was being told by two doctors that there wasn't much more that they could do for me because there was something going on in my body that they didn't yet understand. They could see that I was ill and didn't see me getting out of this anytime soon. Basically, they suggested that I get my affairs in order because at that point in time, they didn't see me living more than 18 months longer, at most.

Well, what was I going to do? The medical professionals said there was nothing more they could do. Where does a person go from there at 33 years of age? I knew then that I had come to a fork in the road and that one of two things was going to happen to me. One was that I would die early in this life. Option two was to find a new way. Years ago, one of my earlier students would often say to me, *Dale, you are the trailblazer of trailblazers.* Back then, I wasn't really sure what he meant. Now I am.

When I was told I was going to die within 18 months, I did not know where to go, and I didn't know what to do… and yet, over a short span of time, I healed myself of all of those physical ailments—without any medication or surgery.

> *Your strongest beliefs are at the root of whatever you're now experiencing.*

Now, I'm not saying you should never put medications in your body. That gets to be your choice. I'm not saying you should never have surgery. That also gets to be your choice. Obviously, if you break your arm, you're probably going to need medical attention. And I'm not making that wrong here.

But please understand that for me, that was no longer my journey. And this was partly because I came to a fork in the road. I was either going to die or I was going to uncover something that was going to help me heal myself naturally and organically.

Eventually, I got to some of my own emotionalized beliefs that turned out to be at the core of my illness. How about that?

Now, no one helped me with this because, quite frankly, at least back in those days, I didn't have access to anybody who could help me. And those that I went to didn't seem to know what the heck was going on.

And yet, somehow, some way, I uncovered these truths. Yes, it was uncomfortable. Yes, it was unpleasant. And yes, it was downright painful. There were times where it was excruciatingly painful, especially since I was no longer taking prescription drugs for these conditions.

That's when I really discovered for the first time in this life that our beliefs determine the type of success we will have in this world—or lack thereof. They will determine the type of happiness we will have—or lack thereof. They will determine the type of health we have—or lack thereof. They will determine the type of love we have—or lack thereof.

Whether our beliefs are rooted in fear or love, they will produce a corresponding reality. If your beliefs are rooted in fear, they will create a limitation—a blockage. Whereas if your beliefs are rooted in love, they will produce a freedom—an expansion.

LAW #6: The Law of Correspondence

The Law of Correspondence is secondary to the Law of Belief. The Law of Correspondence says as within, so without. This means that if I have something going on in my external reality, there is a deep-seated root for this inside of me. I may not even be aware of it.

But if inside I have a strong, emotionalized, fear-based belief, which must, by law, produce a corresponding reality in the external world—if that's what's going on inside of me—then it must, by law, show itself and even play itself out.

Your body, in this context, is part of the external world, not the internal world. You are not your body. You are a Soul living in a body. You *have* a body.

An emotionalized belief can exist whether you are aware of it or not. For instance, if you have an emotionalized belief from ten years ago, you may have very little awareness around it, let alone how you created it. And yet it got created.

A fear-based belief will show itself in a specific limitation. New Year's Eve will come, and you'll make your New Year's resolutions... and by February 26, you will have forgotten it. It's like New Year's Eve didn't even happen, just like in previous years. Why do all of those resolutions go out the window, so to speak? Because you have a blockage. You're dealing with a limitation. It's a restriction.

For example, if a person is dealing with a blockage like this, wanting the same thing year after year, you will never hear them say, "I'm working through my blockage, which is _____ (you fill in the blank)..." In all fairness, this person likely isn't aware of their blockage; they haven't connected with it. That blockage is nothing more than a limited, emotionalized belief, rooted in fear, which hasn't been addressed.

Another example of this is when we have a belief inside that says, "I'm not good enough." And I'm now in a relationship with someone that does or says something that makes me feel "not good enough" or makes me feel that there is something wrong with me, when, in fact, there might not be anything wrong with me at all. It might be this belief that is driving the way I think, driving the way I see myself, and influencing me on what I'm about to do next—as in possibly shut myself down from my partner or my friend. Or go on the defense and possibly make him or her wrong. Which now can potentially sabotage the love I could be experiencing in this relationship.

So we can now see how these things play out, when this hasn't been cleared or transformed. It's just going to keep producing its corresponding reality. It must because it's governed by law.

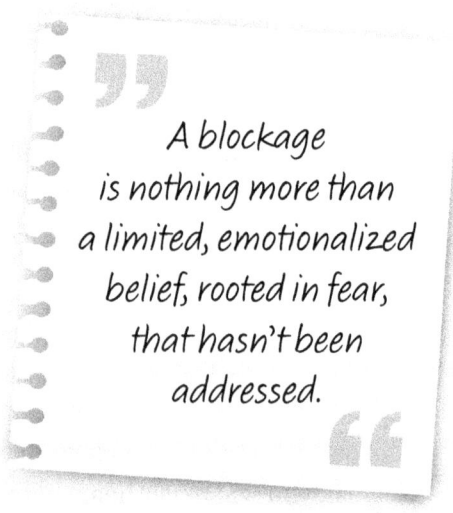

A blockage is nothing more than a limited, emotionalized belief, rooted in fear, that hasn't been addressed.

Now, when you look at an emotionalized belief rooted in love, you're going to experience this differently. That corresponding reality is going to show up differently for you. An example of this healthier expression might be where we now have a belief that has become emotionalized within us that says "I am worthy of love, I am love." The way we spot this in our external world is we notice just how loving we are. And how those around us, especially those most dear to us, somehow, in some way, find a way to love us back.

This is where we might even feel that high current of love so ever-present in our day-to-day life. And it then feels like it is flowing through our veins… we love our job, we love our kids, we love our husband or wife, we love God or the Universe, and we especially love ourselves.

LAW #7: The Law of Patterns

The Law of Patterns, similar to the Law of Belief, says that we live by our patterns. And when I say we, I am talking about every living creature on this planet, not just humans. This includes the animal kingdom, the plant kingdom, and the mineral kingdom.

Dr. Joe Dispenza is a wonderful researcher—which is one of the things I really respect about him. And one of the conclusions that he drew by sifting through scientific studies is that 95 percent of what happens in your personal world is because of programming. By the way, spiritualists have known this for eons, whereas science is now catching up.

Patterning is programming. A belief system is programming.

Now, here's the other thing I discovered long, long ago. No one can hide from this law. Ultimately, no one can avoid this or bypass it.

I guarantee you that someone will always try. However, they'll attempt to go for the bypass because they just don't want to do the work, for whatever reason. Maybe they're afraid of it. Or maybe they think they shouldn't have to do it because they're entitled to something. Or maybe they think they've already done it (the work, that is). Maybe they believe they shouldn't have to earn their way. The list of possible reasons goes on and on.

But here's the truth… and this applies to everyone: If we're going to punch through, if we're going to become very, very good at manifesting on a conscious level, those sleeves need to be rolled up really high.

Maybe not right away. Maybe we roll them up an inch at a time. And then another inch and another. No matter how long it takes, our patterning, and more specifically, our negative patterning, needs to be consciously addressed and ultimately dismantled.

LAW #8: The Law of Seeking

Now the Law of Seeking is probably one of the most misunderstood laws from when Jesus walked the face of this earth. He said, "Seek, and you will find." What did he mean by that?

Seek it, and you'll find it. Now, notice how simple and profound this is. Did he say to seek something positive, and you shall find it? No. He said seek—meaning you get to decide what you're going to seek.

If you're seeking to find the negative in me, or seeking to find what I just did wrong, you don't have to go very far. In fact, I might even help you. Because if you are the one who's using this law in this way, where you're seeking to make somebody wrong or to find something wrong in somebody... guaranteed you're gonna find it, baby.

But if you're seeking the positive, that is also what you are going to find. This is a Universal Law. It's absolute. And it's up to you to decide how you are going to make it work for you.

LAW #9: The Law of Gestation

The Law of Gestation... Again...oh my gosh. Talk about a misunderstood law. This law, when it comes to manifesting, says there is a natural gestation period for all acts of creation. The period of time it takes is unique to whatever is in process of manifesting.

How long would you say it would take if you were to plant a potato seed in your garden for it to sprout and produce potatoes? First of all, is there a gestation period? Or do you believe that you just plant the seed, and then, next morning, you have potatoes to harvest?

Obviously, there's a gestation period. So, the potato takes X number of days or weeks to ultimately sprout. It has a specific gestation period. If you have been to or possibly lived in Hawaii, let's apply this to the taro, another root vegetable. How long does it take for the taro root to go through its period of gestation?

> *The Law of Gestation applies to the period of time it takes that is unique to whatever is in process of manifesting.*

Let's just say it takes much longer than your regular potato. Much, much longer. The point is this... Everything that manifests on this planet here in this dimensional reality has a period of gestation. And every single thing has a different timeline for that period of gestation—including two different types of root vegetables.

When you were conceived, how many days, how many weeks, how many months went by? Probably about nine months. It would have been impossible for you to emerge after only 30 days from your mother's womb because of this Law of Gestation.

Now, if you're one of those people who likes to hurry and rush and push your way through life, that doesn't make you a bad person. However, it might make you a frustrated person because you're not going to be very good at manifesting on a conscious level if you are trying to rush the gestation period of whatever it is you are intending to manifest.

Rather you're going to end up doing the opposite and get really good at manifesting on an *unconscious* level. And you're probably going to end up in some major doodoo that gets manifested, partly because you are not respecting this law—and that could be because you haven't had an awareness of the law until reading this book.

LAW #10: The Law of Environment

And lastly, another major law that I've structured these teachings on manifestation around, is the Law of Environment. Now, this law governs our humanity. It governs what happens in people's personal worlds. To sum it up, this law says we are nothing more than a product of our environment—the environment that we spend the most amount of time in is what we become. Period.

Let's say that a person is brought up on welfare. Maybe they spent 18 years of their life on welfare. What do you suppose happens in their twenties? What do you suppose happens by the time they turn 23?

Exactly. Most of the individuals will end up on welfare too. It was their norm, and it becomes their norm again. This law says you and I literally become a product of our environment.

You've got to be in the right environment, and then you've got to be in that right environment for a sustained period of time. The welfare recipient in our example stayed in that poor, unenriching environment over a long period of time, so, odds are, when they flew the nest that their parents provided for them, they went on welfare themselves. And then, they have kids who possibly do the same thing with their kids. Why do you think we have third- and fourth-generation welfare recipients? Because the assistance isn't freeing them from the need for assistance. It's incredibly difficult to break out of your environment because you're fighting everything you've learned for 18 years.

That being said, if you know what you're doing, and you actually do it step by step, you can climb out of an environment like that. You can set yourself free from that environment. Just understand that it's not going to happen overnight—not if you've been in that environment for 18 years or even 10 years of your life.

Now the welfare environment may not be relevant to you, but there are other negative environments that can affect you just as much that you might not think of right off the bat. Maybe you were raised in an environment where people were always talking over one another, or people were very judgmental, or family members were in constant conflict. If that's your environment, you become a product of that. It's a law that you and I are all governed by, whether we are aware of this or not. But remember, we can take actions to consciously change our environment. Once you are aware, it is a choice.

Another way in which you can consciously work with this law would be to decide what it is you really want to have manifest in your life. And then ask yourself, "What would be the type of environment that if I was to put myself into, and keep myself there for a while, would naturally produce the very thing that I really want to have manifest in my life?"

Let's say the decision that you are about to make is based on the desire to transform some aspect of your life. Then, if you were to really put this law to work, you would be asking for an environment that naturally produces transformational experiences. Assuming this is a real transformational environment, if you were to simply immerse yourself in that environment for a sustained period of time, then according to this law, your transformation, maybe not all at once, but over time, would manifest. Because at some point, having been in this environment, you would eventually become a product of this transformational environment you had been immersed in.

LAW #11: The Law of Process

The Law of Process says that everything we do, we do by process. It can be no other way. Doing something by process means there's a step-by-step sequencing that needs to take place.

Maybe we're unconscious towards this because we haven't heard anything about this law and don't know anything about it. Or maybe—and this is something I sometimes see with my students—intellectually, we know about this law, but we don't have it down experientially (at least just yet). Meaning we're still in some sort of internal fight with this. We're still afraid of something. We're perhaps afraid to confront something inside ourselves that we perceive to be ugly, or disgusting, or even scary.

I have seen so many people pretending like they're so far along in their journey, but then something dramatic happens, and they find themselves in the hospital hanging on for their life. Yet, months before that, they had it all worked out.

That, my friend, is an unconscious manifestation. That is somebody that is thinking they're conscious, but clearly, they're not as conscious as they thought they were. Because only months later, they've got a manifestation that's so loud that it manifested in physical form.

Let's say someone loses $39 million in the span of a year and a half. Now, if you can't relate to that figure, think about the last time you lost $2,000... How did that feel? You made a choice, and it went south, and then bam! $2,000 gone. It evaporated. Poof. How did it feel? So now, if you can, imagine losing almost $40 million in a short period of time. That is a manifestation. Now was the person who lost the money conscious of it? Of course not. Who in their right, healthy, well-balanced mind would ever go and consciously lose $39 million? Exactly. No one.

> *The Law of Process indicates that there's a step-by-step sequencing that needs to take place.*

Did you catch the key words there? Did you really catch the operating part of what I just said? Who in their *right mind*, who in a *balanced mind*, who in their *healthy mind, who consciously* would do this? No one.

It's only the people who are not in their right mind, who don't have a balanced mind, who are possibly the servant to their mind that could potentially manifest something as unpleasant as the loss of millions of dollars.

When something manifests from the unconscious that is coming more from the negative side of things, there's a good likelihood it is going to be something unpleasant, something shocking, or something that's going to possibly wake you up—or something that's potentially going to shock you into waking up.

Now, when this happens, the last thing we want to do is go back into the unconscious. In other words, we want to work through this energy. We want to get to this part of our unconscious that's manifested whatever the unpleasant experience was and trace that back to its point of origin.

When somebody comes to me who has broken a bone, or has lost a bunch of money, or had something bad happen with one of their children—whatever it might be—I go through its timeline sequence.

Before I do that, however, because I'm very empathetic for people in this regard, as they're in a lot of pain when these sorts of things happen, I connect with them on an empathetic level. Then, once I connect with them, I'm constantly checking in to see, okay, where are they really at? Do they really want to know what part of them actually manifested this? Are they in a place to even accept responsibility for this part of it? Are they ready for this? And quite frankly, sometimes the answer is no. Some people just aren't ready.

If this is the case, I just zip it up. I don't say a word. Back in my younger days, I would sometimes get myself into some major trouble by sharing what it was that I knew was happening to somebody when they clearly weren't ready to hear it. I learned the hard way, so to speak, that sometimes I am not supposed to be sharing what I know just yet.

And I'm glad I learned that because it is not helpful for me, and it is not helpful for the person I am trying to help.

That said, now when I see that this is something they've manifested, I might give them a little teaser. I might ask something like, "If there was a 'why' for this happening, what might the 'why' be?"

They may place blame elsewhere by replying, "Oh, the guy ran the red light," or something else that removes the responsibility from themselves. I listen to hear the victim language, and if I do hear it, I know to say nothing more, as they are not ready to look within themselves yet.

The victim can come out so quick, stating what's been done to them with no personal responsibility whatsoever for this creation, this manifestation, even though I know that manifestation is coming directly from them—from some part of their unconscious. They're just not quite willing or ready to go there—to that part of themselves that they've been unconscious towards that has created or manifested their unpleasant experiences.

Now on the other hand, the unconscious could also manifest something that becomes more pleasant and positive that you might not even be aware of. Of course, you are aware of the positive manifestation, but how aware were you when the positive manifestation was in process of happening and where that manifestation was coming from within your unconscious mind?

So, let's say a true love manifests in your world. Do you know where that came from? And if the answer is yes, then you are conscious of that process in having that true love manifest in your world. If, however, the answer is no, then you were not conscious or were unaware of where this beautiful manifestation known as a true love was coming from within your unconscious mind. Yet you see something in front of you now known as whatever or whomever this true love has manifested into.

So, whether we manifest a positive, pleasant experience or an unpleasant, negative experience, one of the master keys here is to become conscious of this process in whatever it is that we are currently manifesting here on this physical plane of existence. So that ultimately, we rise to the level of manifesting with precision like a master.

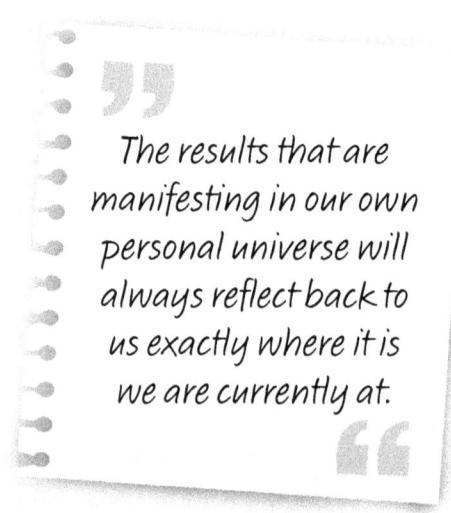

The results that are manifesting in our own personal universe will always reflect back to us exactly where it is we are currently at.

One of the best gauges for us to determine where the manifestation is coming from is obviously to remain conscious because if we're unconscious, how would we be able to spot it? One of the most practical ways to spot where a manifestation is coming from is to literally put up that gauge on the dashboard of our life that gauge being our results. The results that are manifesting in our own personal universe will always reflect back to us exactly where it is we are currently at in the exercising of our natural ability to manifest on a conscious level.

LAW #12: The Law of Growth

The Law of Growth is one of the easiest Universal Laws to comprehend. It exists to ensure that something always grows. Everything in life has been set up for evolutionary growth. One of the biggest transformations I made in my own life is when I began to realize that with everything that happens, there lies an opportunity to advance my growth.

This is one of the gifts that I give people I coach and mentor. No matter what they bring to their coaching session, no matter what they bring to the next conversation we have, whether they're aware of it or not, I'm already looking for the opportunity where their growth lies, and then I'm going to help break it down for them in a way they can comprehend. And once I do this, they start to get excited about it. They start to feel hopeful again. They start to feel a little more inspired again. This is because evolutionary growth is what we're meant for!

The Law of Growth also states that we're either growing and expanding or we're contracting and dying. This law is clear and easy to comprehend because there is no in between. You're either growing on the inside or you're dying on the inside.

Everything happens on the inside first. People will say things to me like, "I found this skin cream that reduces the aging process. What do you use?"

Well, the only thing I use externally is an oil called squalene because if I cut myself shaving, it stops the bleeding within 60 seconds. I will tell them that, and they'll say, "Well, don't you use a moisturizer?"

And I tell them, "No, I don't. Not that I am opposed to it, but up until now, I haven't. And that's because I've known about this law that whatever happens on the inside will express itself on the outside. If I'm improving myself on the inside, the outside will reflect that level of improvement, and if I'm hurting myself on the inside, the outside will express that as well."

In my view, one of the biggest, most painful mistakes a person can make is when they say, "I don't want to learn anymore." When they say this, what they really mean is, "I want this growth to stop. It hurts too much. It's too painful. It's too inconvenient. It's too uncomfortable." You can live like that if you want, but if you want your life to be different, then at the very least, it will require you to explore this idea of where you are at in having a genuine desire and even commitment to that of your growth at soul level. Remaining resistant, or even stagnant, to this natural process of growth could literally accelerate the aging process.

You could be 75 years old, but if you are really growing on the inside, you'll never feel like you're 75. Someone who's dying inside will always think they're older than what they really are physically. Someone who is growing inside and who has turned this into a lifestyle will always resonate with a more youthful state, no matter what body they currently have.

My handyman is the handyman of all handymen. I really like this guy a lot. He's super skilled and incredibly pleasant to hang out with. When he met me, right away, he thought I was a young man. At some point, I asked him why he assumed that. He said, "Well, I know how old I am, and I know you're younger."

I asked him, "How old are you?"
He said, "Guess."
I said, "I guess you to be somewhere in your early sixties."
"Wow," he said. "I'm 63. Well, how old are you then?"
"How old do you think I am?" I asked.

Let's just say he massively underestimated my age. I contemplated whether or not I should tell him my age, because, as it turns out, I'm actually older than he is. Well, I chose to tell him, and at first, he was really shocked. And then he asked me, "Do you have a secret to staying young?"

We were in my house at the time, and I had one of my books nearby on a table. I pointed to it and said, "If I had a secret to share with you, it would be found in the pages of that book, *Being Called to Change*."

> You're either growing on the inside or you're dying on the inside.

One of my first mentors recently passed away at the age of 88. He was a man who loved to grow. He was always learning, and this kept him youthful in spirit up until the very end. I remember when he was in his seventies, no one would have guessed he was in that age range unless he chose to tell them. He literally had the energy of a 27-year-old. And no one could keep up with him! His love of learning and growing kept him young.

Most people learn when they're younger and then they drop the learning as they get older, implying once they drop the learning, they literally become older. This was not the case with my first mentor, however, as learning and growth clearly became a lifestyle for him.

The average person thinks they're the age they see when standing in front of a mirror. And yet, nothing could be further from the truth. We're either growing or we're dying. There's no such thing as staying the same. And ultimately, you get to choose which side of the coin you're going to live your life from.

If you're looking for the external thing, and you spendyou've been spending all kinds of money on creams, procedures and surgeries, that's your choice. And I'm not saying you should or shouldn't, but if you live more externally,. There are some amazing products, specialty companies and practitioners out there that can improve your skin. No question about it.

The message here is what you are going to attract. that if the focus is on the external for the next better cream, procedure or surgery that will hopefully be the magic fix, it will just continue on and on with no end in sight. Because the internal issue is not being addressed.

If, on the other hand, you're really dialed into what's going on inside of you, you'll start to realize you have a whole inner life happening and you can change up, you can level up, that inner life anytime you wish. And should you choose to do it, then that leveling up of your inner life must get reflected in your outer life, in your external worldin your external world, which also includes the radiance or vibrancy of your skin and body. In other words, when our inner life is healthier, richer and fuller our outer life and external world will be as well.

My first mentor was one of those few people on Planet Earth who knew this, and quite frankly, he'd known this since I met him when I was 20 years old. I got to watch him from time to time over the next half century, and he was a walking example of this principle.

If you knew about his early life... talk about someone who was willing to do the work and rise up! But most people either don't want to know how to do this or aren't willing to do the work on their inner life that's necessary for them to exist like this.

So, what direction are you going in? Are you growing or are you possibly dying? And what direction do you think we're going in as a human race?

When I present this question in my seminars, most people respond that as a species, we're going backwards—and I would have to agree. At first glance, because of our technology, it looks like we're going forward, but we haven't gone forward in a long time.

This is almost a repeat of what happened in the Atlantean civilization. Now does that mean we have to complete that trajectory? I don't think so. I don't believe we will because there are a number of us on this planet, as individuals, who are truly growing and really evolving.

Those of us who are growing are doing so because we feel the inner promptings of our Souls—the desires of our Souls to mature, evolve, and expand.

So, if you personally want this evolution, this expansion, and want to be a part of this global evolution, then find an environment for that growth and turn it into a lifestyle.

On a much deeper level, this is where our work must be focused. This is where our service must be—those of us who are interested in not just helping humanity but helping the earth, helping the true essence of the Mother Earth, who has served humanity for thousands upon thousands of years now.

Some have taken advantage of her and contributed to this heavy weight that she's been carrying. This is a whole other problem, of course—one that needs to be solved and eventually will be solved because it's part of our greater destiny to help solve it. However, we've got to get more individuals to take a new level of responsibility and accountability to rise up to a new level of conscious awareness around themselves as Souls.

John Maxwell, a business consultant in the corporate world, has something very interesting to say about growth. He says, "We don't just grow by accident. We must be intentional and deliberate about it."

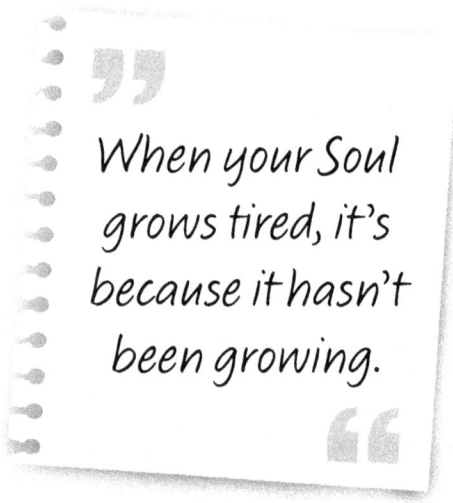

When your Soul grows tired, it's because it hasn't been growing.

I couldn't agree more. What I've noticed with those that I've helped grow the most, whether it's an individual, a company or an organization, is that the ones who go the furthest become intentional. They become deliberate about growing their own consciousness or the consciousness within their organization that they are serving and/or leading.

Growth doesn't show up accidentally. If it did, all of the individual Souls here on Planet Earth would be thriving. But I assure you, the majority of the Souls on Planet Earth—both the Souls that are in incarnate form, as in a physical body, as well as the Souls that still haven't crossed over since dropping their last body, are growing tired. And, as I pointed out earlier, when your Soul grows tired, it's because it hasn't been growing. If you want your Soul to get energized, start helping your Soul to achieve this growth. You must become enthusiastically involved in this process.

Remember, the reason you are manifesting the things you don't want is because you don't understand, on a deeper level, what's really at stake. Do you really want to live out the rest of your life and find out, once you have full remembrance of yourself as a Soul, what your intention really was? Talk about missing the mark. And now you have a tired Soul.

Your Soul has been waiting to grow for who knows how long. You might have gone through a series of lifetimes completely unconscious. During these lifetimes, you more than likely forgot yourself as a Soul. To which you lost consciousness around that of your Highest Self, which is a significant part of your overall Divine Soul Essence Self. You would have then started operating out of the ego–thinking that the ego was your Soul. In turn you as a Soul haven't grown much.

Once your Soul starts to get what it signed up for, everything in your life changes for the better. Your day-to-day life improves, and all of a sudden, you could be 70 years of age but feel like you're 35 because you've genuinely connected to your Soul in a very real way. You're helping your Soul to achieve the growth, the expansion, the evolution that it signed up for at the very beginning.

No one knows when the beginning of your life was. It could have started when you came into this life, and it might have started a hundred lifetimes ago. If that's the case, talk about a golden opportunity in this life to get it right! If you could get it right in this life, the implications for your Soul are huge.

LAW #13:
The Law of Perpetual Transmutation of Energy

The Law of Perpetual Transmutation of Energy states that energy in and of itself does not die, it simply changes form. This law is one of the master keys to manifesting on and from a higher level. So much so that we've devoted a section later on in the book to where you'll be given a few examples around applying this law to your desires of what you would like to manifest in your life.

We'll explore later how this law relates to most of the Inner Powers, principles, and laws that we'll be learning about throughout the book. If we are going to get better at manifesting on a conscious level, one of the things we need to learn how to do is transmute energy. And to succeed at this, we need to create a newer, higher, better, faster-moving vibrational State of Being.

As our understanding deepens this becomes quite empowering, as it will show us exactly where we're at around the power level of our current State of Being. And then more importantly to recognize the power level of our future State of Being that we're being called to rise up to, by that of our Highest Soul Self.

Transmutation is a process of ascending where we are literally shaping upwards towards its pinnacle. When we expand into a new level of consciousness we're expanding because we're transmuting the energy at the level in which we've been in, up to an even higher State of Being. This changes everything for the better in our personal, professional and/or spiritual lives each time we rise up in which we become the embodiment of this newer higher State of Being.

We'll also take a look at the Law of Perpetual Transmutation of Energy and how it relates to the Law of Attraction on a much deeper and more expansive level.

Making These Laws Work Together

Now we are going to connect these and better understand how they all work together at a higher level, operating within this network of Universal Laws. In the pages that follow you will also be able to see where you are in your own process of aligning and operating your life with or by these laws. Now let's dive into Chapter 3....

CHAPTER 3

MANIFESTING FROM THE CONSCIOUS/UNCONSCIOUS SELF

I n the 1989 film *Field of Dreams*, there was a wonderful quote, "If you build it, they will come." A lot of people resonated with that powerful, divine message and tried to bring it into their lives.

Keeping in mind what you learned around the Law of Consciousness and the Law of Vibration, once we start to tap into a couple of your Inner Powers, you will begin to see what it is you are going to be building, and then, if you do it correctly, it—"it" meaning your dreams, your truest heartfelt aspirations—will come.

Build the right consciousness for what it is you would like to have manifest in your day-to-day world, and it will come to you. Once you deepen your understanding around this, and you begin to build it properly, you'll no longer have to work as hard, struggling to make something happen. Doesn't that sound refreshing?

One of the most amazing discoveries I've made with regards to manifestation is that you can use it to transform your life into a heavenly experience. Truly, your day-to-day life can feel absolutely heavenly. Moreover, anyone can pull this off—even if you start out with the odds against you; even if you've come from an impoverished or uneducated background. Whether this takes a few years or a few decades is entirely up to you, but it's within the realm of possibility and is available to everyone on Earth. If somebody else can do it, so can you.

> *When we're transforming our lives, we're either moving in one direction or another, but we can't go in both directions at the same time.*

You're constantly transforming your life—transforming your reality. Now, if you're not currently transforming your life into a heavenly experience, then what kind of a life are you currently transforming it into? I'll make it simple for you, even if it comes off as blunt. You've probably been transforming it into a hellish experience, because those really are the only two options. I'm sure you know or know of somebody right now who has literally turned their life into a hellish experience, and perhaps you know somebody who has literally turned their life into a heavenly experience. When we're transforming our lives, we're either moving in one direction or another, but we can't go in both directions at the same time.

So, what is really going on here? Is the person who has turned their life into a heavenly experience just lucky? Is the person who has turned their life into a hellish experience just unlucky?

If this is your perception—if you attribute everything in this world to luck—then I'm sorry to say that your perception is faulty. When you change the way you are looking at something, that something you're looking at... will change. This is a Universal Law that is completely impersonal. Once you start to embrace this law, you will be empowered to change and transform your own life.

There are a lot of people who will try to go up against these Universal Laws. Some of them even act like they're the General Manager of the Universe. Perhaps you've met a few along your journey. Now, what's happening with this type of person is that they more than likely have a deep-seated control issue—and perhaps they are among some of the most controlling people on the planet.

It's not really their fault, however. You see, they haven't gotten the full memo yet on how this has all been set up. And until someone gets that full memo, they're not going to understand it. And if they don't understand it, odds are they will remain in their own continuum experience, repeating variations on the same theme and wondering why nothing has changed. That same experience will play out over and over on repeat unless and until it is addressed with consciousness.

The Continuum Experience

Just so we're clear, within this looping continuum dynamic, you could still have one part of your life where you are thriving. For example, maybe your business is doing well, but your relationship part of your life could literally suck, and you can't seem to make it not suck—no matter how much you push. Well, it will continue to suck as long as you are in this continuum.

You are doing nothing more than repeating a manifestation. The manifested experience of that part of your life is playing out over and over again. That's all you're doing. You can color it any way you want in your head, but at the end of the day, it won't make a difference for you in *your* life experience.

Another way to perhaps recognize this is when somebody you know personally is in their own continuum experience—where they are literally repeating the same thing over and over again. An example of this might be where they go and put their money in a piece of stock or real estate—so convinced at that time that they've done the right thing. And at some point later in their journey, they wonder how they got here. Here being where they have lost a good chunk of money once again, whether it was that stock going south on them or choosing to hang on to that real estate investment instead of letting it go when they had the opportunity to do so.

How do we know this? Once again, we look at the result. You see, the result never lies. We don't have to look far to see the results of our manifestations. They've been staring us in the face. So, it might be our time to really look closely now and get brutally honest with ourselves about manifesting the life we truly want.

When we bring consciousness to our experience, we can begin to defuse and wind down the undesired manifestations instead of reinforcing them to continue.

Let's say we have a problem in our world that's been repeating itself. It could be a shoulder problem. It could be a heart problem. It could be a hip problem. Think of someone who has already gone through say four surgeries, including two on each side, for their hips alone. They can't do anymore hip surgeries, and the person let's say in this example is now confined to a wheelchair.

How the heck did that happen?

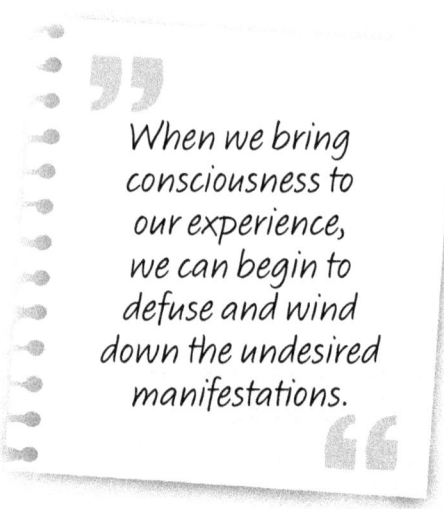

When we bring consciousness to our experience, we can begin to defuse and wind down the undesired manifestations.

Well, in this scenario due to this possibly being the continuum experience, it's more than likely all energetic. In other words, it's coming from their subconscious. Think about it. Four? It's one thing to have one hip surgery. It's another thing to have two hip surgeries... but how many hip surgeries do we have to have before we get the memo? How many times does our body have to hurt in the exact same place before we get that memo?

I've had people come to me and say, "Dale, I just, I'm way beyond headaches."

"Oh really? Tell me more."

"I get these migraines and I'm at the point right now where the migraine's coming on, I get really afraid, like really anxious, it's excruciating."

To which I would ask, "What do you do for the migraine?"

They always tell me about some medication they use—whether they've purchased it over the counter or picked up a prescription from their doctor.

"Does that help?" I'll ask.

And they'll say, "Well...sometimes it does, but many times it doesn't."

I'll ask them, "Have you ever asked *why* it doesn't help?"

And their usual reply is, "No."

I might then say, "Over the last seven days, how many times have you thought about the exact same thing, trying to make something work over and over again? And here you are, seven days later, and the needle hasn't moved forward one iota?"

They start to think really hard. It's all over their face. They're trying really hard mentally. Sometimes their brow starts to wrinkle. Where are they going? They're going right to their sixth energy center and they're applying pressure on it. Well, they're speaking volumes to me at this point. They're not aware of it, but that indicates to me where they've been spending most of their time: *in their head.*

When you spend a lot of time in your head, and if you turn this into a lifestyle where you pretty much spend all of your time in your head, you must now know that at some point your head's going to really start to hurt. Without making a conscious change, you're going to keep on doing whatever you've been doing. Then, instead of just getting a headache, eventually, the headache will turn into a what? A migraine. You don't just get a migraine out of nowhere. It's like anger. You don't just get anger. That's an impossibility. Before you get anger, you've gotta get a lot of frustration.

Frustration is part of the equation of what's going on when someone gets extremely angry. Anger is like a branch off the tree of frustration. If you're not dealing with your frustrated moments properly, correctly, responsibly, the writing is on the wall. The frustration eventually grows into anger. If you still don't deal with your anger, eventually the anger is going to morph into resentment. If you still don't deal with the resentment, it's going to morph into rage. These unaddressed emotions accumulate to the point where the rage is so intense that if someone comes along and frustrates you, next thing you know, you become unhinged with rage. Then there's a real possibility that you'll do something that unconsciously sabotages some part of your life that you really value.

That's the bigger picture that's at play when someone comes to me saying, "I've got this pattern of migraines, and now I'm fearful. I'm terrified of the next migraine." That's some serious stuff. If you're on the continuum in some aspect of your life, that's your gauge to know something is seriously off.

Sometimes, we need that unnecessary pain to tell us that we've gone way off course. Sometimes we need pain that becomes so excruciating, so alarming, so shocking that it is simply unavoidable. It's that pain that gets our attention—because in these scenarios, that's what it took. Did it have to be that way? No, of course not. But with some it appears it does have to be that way. As that seems to be the way that helps them the most in getting whatever it is they are to be getting from all of this.

In fact, as you look out into the world right now, at our external world collectively, isn't that so true with our race? The only way that the majority of people are going to change is through this completely unnecessary pain. Spirit knows this. God knows this. The Universe clearly knows that the majority of people on Planet Earth just don't like change. They resist it like the plague. And so the majority of them need a crisis event. They need something to happen in their world that becomes so loud, so painful, and even so scary.

> Sometimes we need that unnecessary pain to tell us that we've gone way off course.

Study human nature, and you'll see this pattern go back hundreds of years. A unified response only happens when there is a real, loud, impactful, dramatic crisis. That's what has gotten humanity to actually change. We as a race have been so lazy when it comes to change, and yet our Souls—both the individual Soul and the collective Soul on this planet—are clearly continuing to do their part in coming into our worlds, knocking at our doors.

The question is, can you even recognize it when your Soul is knocking on your door? Saying to you, "Come on! Better change this! Change this now. Or a year from now, there's going to be an excruciatingly painful mishap." Your Soul, the wiser part of you, knows what's coming well in advance. If you ignore the call of your Soul, this mishap might bring you to your knees. You might end up in a hospital or bedridden at home. But if that's how it plays out, that's perhaps what you needed for the change to happen.

Let's remember, whenever a change happens, it needs to happen within us because everything that happens outside of us is governed by the inside of us. This is governed by Universal Law. On an energetic or spiritual level, when you ignore the urging of your Higher Self—your Soul—you're bound to walk into a powerful experience that's going to change your world. And when I say powerful, I mean this experience is going to have power *over* you.

This could play out where you fall down, and you break an arm. Or, next thing you know, you go and bend down, pick up something, and tear a muscle. Or you go and invest some money because you're hellbent that this is the be-all, end-all. Meanwhile the Soul, your Soul, is giving you subtle signals. "Stay away..." But you go ahead anyway and drop $8,000 into the pot, and four months later, it's gone.

When you start to look around, you see this happen all the time. Misinterpreting this as luck, or fate, or destiny conveys a lack of understanding. A lack of understanding of who it is we are to become. You can never get full-on understanding because this is an evolutionary process. There is so much to you. Even when you get a handle on all the lower parts of you, then you've got to get a handle on all the higher parts of you.

That's why I know there is no quick fix here. It doesn't exist. You have to show up. You have to really embrace those things that you might not feel ready to embrace. While all of this isn't easy to do, it is clearly worth your time, and ultimately, you will do this, if not in this life, then in the next one. It's governed by Universal Law. You are destined to do this. We are *all* destined to do this.

Within that destiny, you do have free will. Now you might be really good at exercising your free will, or you might be terrible at it. Wherever you fall on this spectrum, the Universe couldn't care less. The Universe is completely impartial.

The impersonal Universal Laws that govern our experience were set forth long before you and I ever came along. They work 100 percent of the time. Every time, all the time, period. These laws don't get emotional. You could be on the floor screaming, tears streaming down the sides of your cheeks because you're in so much pain. The Universe just does not care.

The fact that the Universe has been set up this way is a good thing for humanity, even if it can be difficult at times. These impartial laws support a humanity that is to be rising up, raising and deepening its consciousness by learning more about itself. I'm sure you've seen the evidence in your own country, wherever you are, that humanity has temporarily lost itself. As of this writing, it's become somewhat painfully obvious that some of our nations have abandoned their own Souls.

The way back of course from this scary state is to better understand these Laws of the Universe and rise up collectively once again to our higher and greater selves. This is possible for us both individually and collectively.

Continuous Creation

Whether what shows up in your world is a new friend, a soulmate, a bunch of money, or a hardship, you or some part of you has manifested that. Whether you believe in this or not, at night, when you go to bed, some part of you is manifesting something. Your dream space is a manifestation. That's why in my *Dream Course*, I teach on the importance of developing a practice for remembering your dreams and effectively working with them.

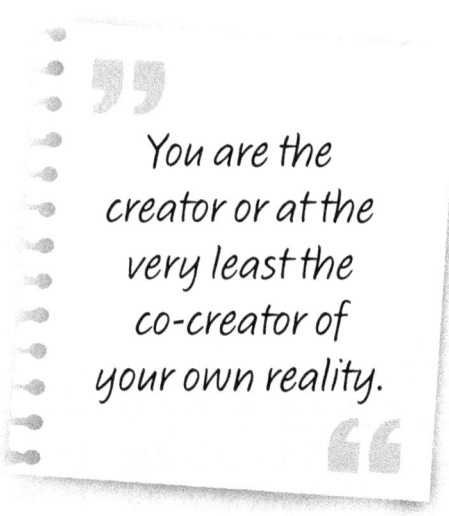

You are the creator or at the very least the co-creator of your own reality.

Both you and I are manifesting something every single day, 24 hours a day. Remember, it's governed by law, so it doesn't matter if we believe in it or we are aware of it; we are working with this law every single day. Regardless of whether we believe in the Law of Gravity or not, if we decide to walk off of a 12-story building because for some reason we believe we've become God-like overnight, and we can now fly with our physical vessel, well, you probably already know what's gonna happen next...

Not only are we always manifesting, but we are also, at the very least, co-creators of our own reality. You see, you are the creator of the reality you are currently living. Now for some people, this has been a really tough thing to accept. If someone is experiencing a lot of negative manifestations, it can be tough for them to even consider that they had a hand in their creation.

So now you might be thinking, *Wait a minute. You mean to say I manifested that accident?* Yeah. If you really want the truth—you did. Or at the very least, some part of you did. Now the key here would be to take the accident and trace it back along your past timeline where you started making choices that were not in your highest and best interest. So much so that those choices eventually led you to what's known as this accident—whatever that might have been. Once again, whether you believe in this or not, you are the creator or at the very least the co-creator of your own reality.

Let's say, for example, that you know someone who has been believing they are a victim for quite some time. They think like a victim. They act like a victim. They walk like a victim. They speak like a victim. I'm sure you have at least one person in your world like this or did at some point. Maybe there was even a time when this was you!

This is probably one of the biggest ego tricks because if you start to resonate with that idea—if you start to believe you are the victim and identify with this idea that you are the victim—then because you are the creator of your reality, you have been transforming your reality operating from this place of the victim with this belief. In this case, the victim within you has been allowed to grow and strengthen over a long period of time. In other words, you have not been transforming it. You have not been healing it. In fact, you've been going in the opposite direction.

Remember... we're manifesting 24/7. Imagine what happens when someone has this victim mindset. Imagine what the individual who believes that they're the victim creates in their reality from that place of thinking like the victim, acting like the victim, speaking like the victim–all from a complete state of resistance around the truth that they are the creator of their reality. When you understand the gravity of this, it then becomes a powerful teaching, because that's when you can begin to change this reality and shift from the victim state to the victor state. More on the Victor later...

Bruce Lee, the legendary martial artist, became a master of his craft, the master of his mind, and the master of his physical vessel. Now, yes, his life was short, but during it, what did he accomplish? What did he produce? How many lives has he impacted, to this very day—decades later—since his passing?

Back in the sixties, when television was only in black and white, he had something to say on this very subject on a national television show. He said, "Thoughts create your reality." He really got a lot of flak for that statement back then—lessons like this weren't taught in that era. But he knew something most did not.

Why would he say such a thing? What was he offering? Clearly, Bruce was a teacher. He wasn't just a master; he was a teacher, and a very skilled teacher at that. He also was an example of his teachings—a very powerful man with a very powerful energy.

"Thoughts create your reality." What the heck was he talking about when he said that? Think back to what was going on in the 60s. What was happening? If you were around in the 1960s, where were you? Where were you at in terms of your consciousness? Where were most people at in terms of their awareness, in relation to what was going on in the world? If you were alive back then, were you considering how your thoughts were creating your reality?

Fast forward all these years later, to present time, and people still aren't doing this. They can't, or refuse to, wrap their brains around this concept that they are creating, or at least co-creating, their reality with their thoughts. They're still doing that victim thing, which says, "I'm being done to." And when we're being done to, what happens is we become enslaved to that circumstance. Talk about a painful and hellish way to live your life that constantly promotes more suffering... Talk about being out of alignment with Universal Law...

In all fairness, this type of person has no freaking clue at all when it comes to their rightful responsibility in their personal world, along their personal journey. They believe that what they are manifesting—what they are experiencing—is *happening to them.*

> *We're either creating more of what we do want or more of what we don't want.*

Here's another part of this truth... We're either creating more of what we do want or more of what we don't want. It's one or the other, period. Now this week you might create more of what you do want and next week possibly create more of what you don't want.

I'll bet if you've broken your leg, you probably didn't want that. I'll bet if your body developed heart disease, you didn't want that. I'll bet if you lost $2,000 because of a poor choice you made six months ago, you didn't want that. And I'll certainly bet that if you chose a relationship that went south, you didn't want that either. Yet somehow these are all things that you or I manifested.

Are you seeing my point here yet? We've either been manifesting something that we really do want, or we've been manifesting something that we really don't want.

Conscious and Unconscious Manifestation

These manifestations are coming from two different dynamics. One is a dynamic that you're conscious of—this is your Conscious Self, or the part of you that you are currently conscious of. When you're in the process of manifesting from this Conscious Self, you're aware of what it is that you're manifesting.

If we go back to that initial exercise that I gave you around selecting something that's easy to manifest—whether it's ten quarters, three $100 bills, a new refrigerator, or a new paying client—whatever it is in that designated period of time—this is you now being conscious. And if you follow this to the T as I've laid it out—meaning you will choose to stay conscious through this process of manifesting whatever it is you want to manifest—it will work for you. Then, you can begin to see and feel what it's like to manifest with awareness on a conscious level.

Now there's another area, another dynamic, where manifestation also emanates from, and that is from the Unconscious Self. Or you could say from your subconscious—specifically, it's the part of you that you've been or perhaps are unconscious towards.

Many of our great teachers that have gone before us have touched on this—the unconscious, and how at the beginning, until you start to wake up, most of your manifestations are coming from your unconscious world. In other words, you are not conscious of what you're manifesting. When you manifest a nasty, toxic, abusive relationship, you can be assured there is no way you are consciously manifesting it. Because who would do such a thing to themselves consciously, right? If you are truly a creator of your own reality, then why on earth would you ever manifest a serious, toxic, dysfunctional out-of-balance, Jekyll-and-Hyde type person in your world? Why would you manifest a business or romantic partner who comes into your bank account and literally robs you of your money that you spent 10 years saving? Why would you do such a thing?

Were you conscious of that? Now you might be thinking, *Well, I think I was...* But I can assure you that, no, you weren't. When you stay conscious of what you're manifesting, you begin to actually see what you're manifesting. And if you don't like what you're manifesting, you can do a rewrite—you can course correct. We touch on this in the second book in the trilogy, *Transform Your Destiny*. Course correction is a skill that most people have not yet developed. They don't know when to course correct, let alone how to course correct. So, they go down this path that's leading nowhere; it's a rabbit hole—a deep, dark, dense, dysfunctional rabbit hole. They're not conscious, because the only way they're going to manifest something like that is by staying unconscious.

And when we're in that place, it can be too freaking painful to look consciously at what we've been manifesting because it's possibly another toxic, dysfunctional, abusive person in our world. Of course, we would never do that if we really had conscious awareness of it. This is what the master teachers have shared with us over thousands of years.

Let's go back to the 97 percent of the population who has yet to manifest/create the life of their dreams. Where do you suppose they've been manifesting from? Exactly. They've been manifesting mostly from their unconscious.

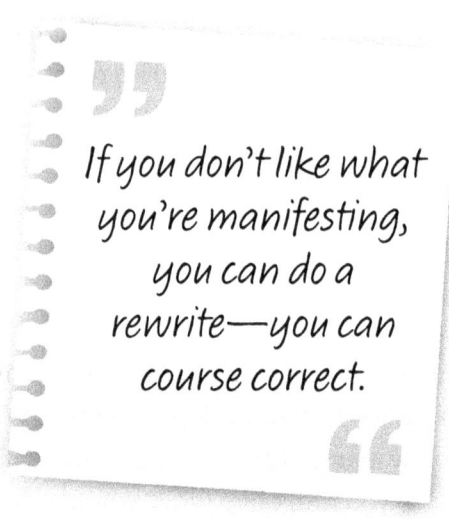

If you don't like what you're manifesting, you can do a rewrite—you can course correct.

The biggest trick that your ego will play on you when you manifest from your unconscious is that it will try to get you to blame it on somebody or something else. I've had people blame it on the weather, blame it on the economy—blame it on anything or anybody but themselves. And yes, these types of things can happen. The economy can go up; it can go down. The weather can be really nice, and the weather can be not so nice. That is true. But understand that when something happens in your world that you don't want, you might be the problem. You have to understand who you are, and maybe you don't really know who you are just yet. But here's the deal. Until you are willing to become conscious of what you've been manifesting unconsciously, you'll never *Manifest Like a Master*. It's an impossibility. It will not happen.

Now I'm assuming that you are reading this book because you want to learn how to *Manifest Like a Master* so that you can create the life of your dreams. Now, to accomplish that, you've got to get a handle on this. There is no way around it. So, when something unpleasant manifests in your own personal environment, or your physical vessel, take ownership that you created that. Or, at the very least, some part of you created that. Boy, if you can just wrap your brain around that and take ownership of it—become responsible for it—that in itself is so huge. Why? Because it's a truth.

The actual manifestation, or the process of manifesting, cannot be stopped. It cannot be hindered. It cannot be blocked. That which is manifesting is manifesting because it's coming from inside of us.

Becoming more conscious of what you've been manifesting unconsciously is a game changer. One of the goals here during the course of our journey through this book is to make the unconscious conscious—for the benefit of and on behalf of your Soul. You are to be bringing what was unconscious to a conscious reality. You are to be bringing that which is in the dark into the light.

Quite frankly, if you really want to know the truth, you have been attempting to do this for every single lifetime you've had on this planet. So, if you aren't very conscious of the manifestation process so far in this life, it is more than likely you've had a lifetime or two prior to this one where you've done the exact same thing that you've been doing in this one up to this point. You've refused to become conscious of what was unconsciously manifesting on your behalf in your personal universe.

If you really want to know what's going on in your unconscious reality, the best gauge is the results that manifest in your world. The results never lie.

A woman I knew had a tumor manifest in her brain. It got pretty serious. She came really close to dying. In her case, I saw the manifestation at play before it was detected in physical form, and I attempted to bring it to her attention. I shared with her that this could all be traced back to a pocket of hatred that she was holding inside. She didn't want to hear it. In fact, she got really angry at me for even suggesting such a thing. You see, she thought—given her spiritual path at the time—that she was only about love. So, when I suggested there was a certain amount of hatred inside of her, she just couldn't accept that as a possibility.

And then, only a few months later, she was being rushed into one of the best hospitals in our country to have surgery because they found out she didn't just have a tumor, but the tumor was taking over her brain. And yet, only months prior to that, she believed I was talking gibberish.

Reflect on that for a moment. And now might be a good time to do some journaling…

How conscious was she of what was manifesting in her physical body? She couldn't see it. She couldn't connect with it. And then somebody comes along to attempt to bring it to her attention, and right away, she makes the messenger wrong. How about that? Do you know of anybody who's done that before? Or possibly, have you done this before?

Our Life Force Weakens When Manifesting from the Unconscious

Another dynamic that I've noticed through my many years of observing this is that when someone is manifesting more from their unconscious than they are from their conscious—meaning they're not really aware of what they're manifesting—then, over time, their life force gets weaker and weaker.

You know what happens when your life force gets weaker? You age faster. I'll say it again... one of the ways you might be able to spot that your life force is getting weaker is that you start to notice that the aging of your body has accelerated. This is a symptom of your life-force energy being depleted.

> *Until you are willing to become conscious of what you've been manifesting unconsciously, you'll never Manifest Like a Master.*

Thus, you're not going to be very good at consciously manifesting because to become skilled at consciously manifesting, you're going to need your life-force energy. A strong life force will support you tremendously in manifesting whatever it is you truly want to manifest.

Having a strong life force means you're going to punch through your fears. You're going to punch through your struggles, resolve your issues, and clear up your blockages. This is big stuff.

Now most people on the planet are enslaved. This concept—that very few of us have been unplugged from this conditioning—was portrayed so well in the first *Matrix* film. And to that, very few have been unplugged from their past programming.

So more than likely, the rest of us do need to be unplugged—we need to rise above this. And here's the truth... Anybody can be unplugged, and anybody and everybody can rise above this conditioning and programming.

Finding the Right Mentor

You're probably going to need a teacher, a coach, or a mentor. You're going to need a guide—not a best friend. You're going to need somebody who's further along on their journey than you are. I'm not saying you shouldn't have friends in your life that are at a similar place in their journey, but if you're going to do this and do it well, it will serve you to have someone who is more advanced. This more-advanced mentor should have already freed himself or herself completely from the lower matrix. Ideally, they will have completely freed themselves from their mundane problems, their unresolved issues, their past wounds, and their unresolved karma. To have this freedom is absolutely huge. You just have to get a guide in place who is most right for you to help illuminate the pathway.

Now, of course, the other option is to do this all by yourself. But as I often say to people who are attempting to do this alone: how has trying to do this all on your own been working out for you? How effective has it been for you to try to do this alone? This is especially difficult when we're addressing those deep-seated fears inside of you. Yes, those fears can be cleared, and, in fact, it is part of your destiny to transform your fear. Is it easy to do this? Of course not. It's going to challenge you, and it's going to challenge you to the core of your being, big time.

But by the time you are done—by the time you complete your work in really transforming that deep-rooted fear that's been in your consciousness for who knows how long—your greater truth will be revealed, and everything will change for the better forever.

The Music Inside

When Oliver Wendell Holmes was alive, he said, "I will not die with my music still inside of me." This is one of the last things that he imparted to all of us. He also said in his experience of the people he encountered in his life that the majority of them went to their graves with their music still inside of them.

One of the most painful ways for your Soul to die is to go to your grave with the music—with your greater truth—still inside of you, meaning you never touched it; you never became conscious of it. You didn't connect with it, and ultimately, you didn't embody it to bring it all the way through and become the expression of it.

Eventually what happens when we get better at consciously manifesting is that we will truly have a happier life. I know as we look out at the world, for some it might not appear that way. If we look at the conditioning that the world has in place, we can see that it is set up so that we're all to be afraid, scared, stressed, anxious, miserable and unhealthy.

However, part of our destiny is that we have divine birth rights. And in the second book of the trilogy, *Transform Your Destiny*, we learned what those divine birthrights are—and one of them just so happens to be happiness. Believe it or not, it was divinely meant to be for us to find our happiness… for us to create a happy life. How about that?

Earning It to Keep It

What do you suppose it will feel like for you to know in your bones that you've actually done the work once it has been done? Do you have any idea what that's going to do for you and the way in which you experience your life? Do you have any idea what that accomplishment might feel like?

I've been teaching and leading people for a long time, and when I say a long time, I'm going back to when I was a boy. I've been doing this pretty much all my life. And there's nothing better than knowing that you've earned your way. I know there are a lot of other teachers out there that are giving you the seemingly quick fix. They might say something like, "All you've got to do is this, and you're going to have all this. And you're going to have it in a few days." If you hear this, my advice is to turn around and run for the hills. Because that is just not realistic.

You've got to earn it… if you're going to keep it. That means you've got to do the work rather than go for the bypass or the quick fix. When you earn it, you get to keep it. If it's given to you, odds are you will lose it. And just so I'm extra clear here—before you lose it, you might even abuse it.

I've coached countless parents over the decades. Some of these parents, who are somewhat wealthy, have given their children everything, but in doing so, they've possibly robbed their children of the opportunity not just to learn but ultimately to come to appreciate what it's like to actually earn something.

Earning your way... What that really means is that it's yours and you get to keep it versus it being handed to you. Sometimes in my past, my kids would get frustrated with me because I lived by this—that they had to earn what they had—but I couldn't have cared less because I knew what the real deal was. I loved them way too much, as I would often tell them. I helped them to earn whatever they received because I knew in my bones that when they earned it, they'd get to keep it. And as a parent, I didn't want that to be taken away from them. That's what's at stake here.

> *It was divinely meant to be for us to find our happiness... for us to create a happy life.*

Now, earning it is the longer way. Absolutely. I'm sure you might be thinking, *This is probably going to take a while.* Exactly. It will. But I'd much rather something take a while, and I actually get it, than attempt to bypass or speed up the process only to realize I never really got the thing I intended to—because if you don't actually get it, you have to repeat the process all over again. Talk about one big waste of time!

When I do something, I'm going to do it right. I'm done repeating things and wasting my time. I've seen so many people, even some in my current classes and coaching programs, who constantly create more suffering for themselves because they're so desperately trying to bypass—they're so desperately trying to avoid doing the work. There's tremendous value that comes from actually doing and embracing the work—staying true to the work all the way through to completion.

So how long is this going to take? I get this question often, and the truth is—I don't know. I know how long it's taken for others and for me. How long will it take you? Nobody knows the answer to that question. Rather, what I do know is this: how to go the distance is to get resolved in this idea that it will take however long it takes. And that you will do whatever it takes for however long it takes in order to complete this—-period. That you will do whatever it takes for however long it takes in order to reach the point of knowing (in your bones) that you actually earned it, which means you now keep it forever... that it's now in your Soul—the part of you that lives on and on. Once you earn this, it never goes away because you've now become it.

Why Manifest What We Don't Want?

Why would we manifest what we don't want? Why would we do such a thing, even if it is unconscious? Now this is a huge question, and obviously a deep question. It can even be a dark question because to find the answer, you're probably going to have to go into pockets of darkness within your own consciousness—your lower levels of consciousness—in order to uncover whatever this is.

But rest assured that when you or I manifest something we really don't want to manifest, there is a why. Quite frankly, there's a why behind everything–every single thing.

Now, you may not be willing to get to the why—at least not just yet. Or maybe you're only willing to get to 30 percent of your why, not the full 100 percent. And why do you suppose that is? Because it's possibly too painful, it's too uncomfortable, or maybe it's even too scary. Many times, to get to your why, you're going to have to confront something inside of you at the core of the way you've been living your life. And a part of you might be really afraid of that. Or you might have the why in a lot of a judgment as a way to protect yourself—to make sure you never have to go face to face with it.

Two Common Denominators

Now we're going to hone in on two very specific areas. These are common denominators among every single person I've worked with. These are also common denominators from my personal work on myself that I've been very engaged in for many decades.

#1 – Past Programming

Why would we manifest something we don't want? The number one reason why we manifest things we don't want has to do with our past programming and/or conditioning.

Our past programming can be programming from this life—as in our earlier days in childhood, adolescence, or even young adulthood. It can also go back even further into a previous lifetime.

We've all been exposed to past programing, and this past programming, as I mentioned when I was doing the overview of the Universal Laws, probably makes up 90 to 95 percent of what we end up manifesting in our world when we're manifesting from the unconscious reality.

So, the question is, do we need to know all the details of where this past programming is coming from? No, thank God, because that would take you forever.

However, we do need to connect to the energy that makes up the past programming, and quite frankly, we need to do it in present time. Remember the Law of Energy? We need to connect to that energy in order to transform it.

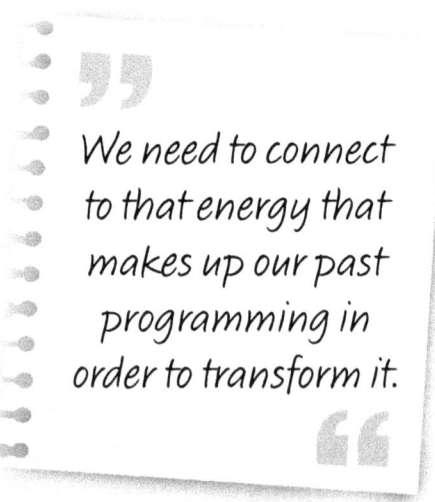

We need to connect to that energy that makes up our past programming in order to transform it.

Now that's on an individual level. I highlight this in my course titled *Freedom from Fear*. In that course I break this down and talk about the individual programming that affects us, which I refer to as conditioning. The individual conditioning is whatever experiences you're bringing forward with you from a previous time.

And there's no one that can escape this. Everybody gets conditioned and/or programmed. Even before we came into this life, we were being conditioned. Months before we were born, the conditioning began, whether we like it or not. Whether we believe in this or not, again, it doesn't matter. This is governed by law as well.

The other level of conditioning and/or programming is from the collective. Now the collective has a couple areas to it. The collective would be the family that we've chosen to be born into. Whatever the dynamics are in that family; whatever the conditioning is that our family has been exposed to and are further reinforcing, there's no way around this... we are going to take on the conditioning of that collective family unit.

Then the third level of conditioning that I highlight in the *Freedom from Fear* course is the collective conditioning that we take on in the lower energy realm, which I refer to as part of "the matrix." I also taught on the matrix in my last book, *Transform Your Destiny*. Should you wish to refresh your memory, you can go back to that section in book two, and I also encourage you to check out the Freedom from Fear course if you want to learn more. In this course, we go in depth on the collective conditioning that's been happening on this planet long before we were born into this current lifetime.

That collective conditioning of the matrix is beyond the conditioning of your family or your ancestry line. It's important to be aware of because it can also influence what you are unconsciously manifesting. The question might now be, will you like what it manifests? Will you even be paying attention that day? Will you take the time to make the connection to where that particular manifestation is actually coming from? You're going to want to understand this and become conscious of its potential influences as well.

So, on the collective side, you've got your family—your birth family, your ancestry—and then, of course, you've got the greater part, which has been controlling humanity, controlling Earth for thousands of years, which again could be referred to as the matrix. Regardless of what influences are acting upon you, you have all of this inside of you, and as long as that conditioning or programming is still inside of you, you're going to have to clear it up. And you can clear it up. It is part of your destiny to clear up that past programming and conditioning.

#2 – Lacking Understanding of the True Self

The second of the most common denominators that I've experienced through the thousands of coaching sessions that I've done, seminars I've given, and the work I've done in my own life is that when somebody is manifesting something that they don't really want, they lack understanding of their true self.

Now, I know you might disagree with this. You might think you know who you are. But if you continue this work and continue to follow these teachings, it's only a question of time before you'll see—just like those who have gone before you have discovered—that you do not know as much as you think you know.

I do not say that to put you down. I say that because it is an absolute truth. In the movie *The Matrix*, Morpheus said to Neo, "Once you take the red pill, all I'm gonna do is show you the truth." This is what a true and authentic teacher is always going to do—bring you back to the truth—no matter how much you complain, whine, or groan or try to blame it on somebody else.

See, here's another part of the truth… If you are still manifesting things that you don't want in your life, you likely don't know how remarkable you actually are, how powerful you are, and how truly intelligent you are. One of the biggest tricks of the ego is that it keeps you in the intellectual side of learning, rather than the full embodiment of intelligence. It wants to keep you in your head rather than letting your intelligence move down into your body, where it can settle into your cells and create a memory of feeling to be built upon.

To understand yourself in the deepest and most profound of ways, this would mean that you've been experiencing yourself at those deeper levels in your physical body, in every one of your 70 trillion cells that make up your physical form.

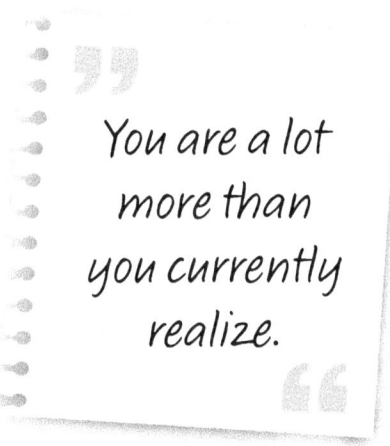

You are a lot more than you currently realize.

Now, this is not the stuff you learned about when you were going to grade school. It's not the stuff you learned about when you were going to college. It is not even the stuff you learned about when you were going for your master's degree. And yet this is the very stuff that can literally change your life in the best, brightest, and greatest of ways.

When was the last time you discovered something truly unique, special, or powerful and dynamic about yourself?

I will go on record saying to everyone reading this book that you are a lot more than you currently realize. There's much more for you to understand about yourself that you just have not yet accessed.

Remember, you are remarkable. You are powerful. You really are magnificent. You just don't know it yet, or at the very least, you don't know the whole of it yet.

There's a reason why those who have reached mastery of themselves up to this point in time—who have become the master of manifesting whatever it is they genuinely desire to manifest in their personal universe, and who, depending on who they are at soul level, potentially have enough power to be able to serve tens of thousands, possibly millions of people, at a given time—have taken approximately 25 years to develop this.

Now I'm not suggesting it's going to take you 25 years. That's not the point of mentioning this to you. The point is there's much further to go and you have more to discover about yourself. Unless you can honestly say that you have become so skilled that you can manifest on a conscious level with precision, then you've got more to discover about yourself. Which means you've got to deepen your understanding.

This is another one of the many reasons why it's so important to have a teacher or mentor, and more specifically, the teacher or mentor that's most right for you. That's why it's so important to have this type of individual in your world, not just for a month or two but for a sustained period of time.

I suggest you be very selective when it comes to who you choose to call forth to come into your world to serve in this role of helping you to deepen your understanding. Because when you have the right person in that role—a person who gets all that you really are and can guide you—then you're going to get to a point where you're no longer going to manifest those things that you really don't want to manifest.

Another way of saying the same thing is this: you're going to get to the point where you're literally going to manifest and create the life of your dreams. How about that? Is this something you want to sign on for?

Manifesting What We Want

Everybody is manifesting 24/7. We're either manifesting what we really want or manifesting what we don't want. It's one or the other—period.

Most manifestation that we do on a day-to-day basis requires no creative input. It's like how the weeds growing in your garden require nothing from you. There's no care—no conscious effort involved. Like the weeds in our garden, this type of manifestation is usually what we don't want. What we want to start doing is manifesting with our creative power—with intention. This is called the *creation*.

When I was a young man and I started my first series of manifestation seminars, they were called Goal Achieving Seminars, and we'd spend three to four days setting goals with the intention being to achieve them. That was it. This was a very powerful course. A lot of the people who attended did achieve many of those goals, all while creating excitement together, supporting each other, and cheering each other on.

What I had learned back then, and it holds true to this very day, is that one of the toughest things to do when it comes to manifesting what you want is to *decide what it is you actually want.*

With some people, in a matter of minutes, this question just starts to bring up stuff. It starts to activate things like doubt. It starts to activate the inner critic. The inner critic might say, "Who do you think you are? You can't have that."

I've also come across people who won't put their responses down on paper. It's like they're afraid to make their desires tangible. This implies something, and what it implies is going to be different for each person, but I've noticed that even when these people finally do put something down to paper, their answers are shallow. They are experiencing a block.

The opposite can be true as well. Some people's answers are incredibly thoughtful and deep. There's a contrast that can be quite stark between the person whose answers are disorganized and only skim the surface and the person who can go deeper and really answer the question.

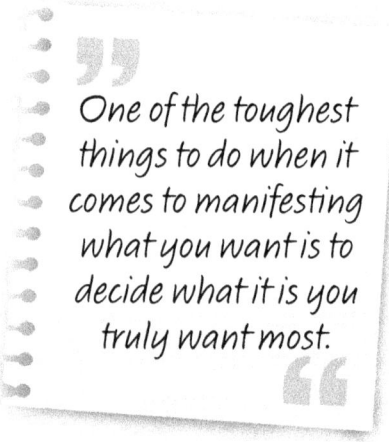

One of the toughest things to do when it comes to manifesting what you want is to decide what it is you truly want most.

I point this out not to criticize the person who has a tough time with this question—it is simply to recognize that for some of us, this seemingly basic question is actually a tough part of the journey.

There are also people with whom I've worked with over a long period of time whose lists will completely change. This is all part of the process!

Exercise #1:

If you want to start manifesting what you want, instead of what you don't want, then you need to start somewhere, right? When it comes to any complex project, one of the most helpful things you can do is to create a list.

> It begins with reflecting on the question: What do I want? Now this question may seem basic—it may seem elementary—but it turns out it's not elementary at all. Reflecting on this question turns out to be a very powerful practice.
>
> So, right now, take out the notebook you have chosen for doing the exercises in this book and write down this question and then reflect upon it: What do I want?
>
> Write down your answers as they come to you—not just today, but perhaps also in the days that follow. As in, you could be in your kitchen cooking dinner when another answer comes to you as to what it is you want. Go ahead and jot that down in your notebook as well.
>
> Return to this question periodically and note any changes as you progress through this journey.

Exercise #2:

> Let's drill down a little deeper. With your notebook handy, take a moment and reflect on this question and write it down: "If your Soul or your Future Self wanted you to have something, what would it be?"

To answer this question, a good starting place is to get connected with your Soul—to think about your future. Your Future Self, at the very least, is an inkling of your Soul Self.

Another way to approach this question would be, "If your Future Self could speak to you out loud, right now, one year from today, how would it answer this question?" (Write down any additional thoughts or feelings that come to you when approaching it in this way.)

If you don't connect to your Soul when looking at what you want, then there's a likelihood that your "want" will come from your ego and/or some aspect of your lower self. Then, if your ego or lower self wants to sabotage this process, all it needs to do is either undervalue the want or overvalue the want. For example, your Soul Self might say, "I want $100,000." Your ego, on the other hand, might say, "I want $1 million." So, if you listen to the ego, you're listening to what turns out to be a false want. Maybe you're not ready for $1 million, but you are ready for $100,000.

Remember that battle that goes on within? If your ego can trick you, you can be guaranteed that your ego will trick you—right from the beginning part of this process of creating your list. Your ego is a magician. It's the ultimate trickster. It can even try to convince you that its voice is your Future Self and/or your Soul Self. It can imitate flawlessly, especially if you have a strong ego. So, if this happens, you'll possibly overshoot it. I've watched and trained a lot of coaches and consultants over the years, and they'll constantly overshoot their goals. And in doing so, they'll literally shoot themselves in the foot. They don't have the experience yet. More importantly, they don't have the right self-concept yet. They overshoot it because they've been fooled by their ego. Their ego took the want of their Soul and amplified it. The Soul said, "I want this for you." The ego takes the want of the Soul, amps it up, multiplies it by 10, and says, "This is your want." It could very well be a setup. And if it's a setup to fail from the very beginning then that's what will happen. I learned a long time ago that the closer I can get to the wants of my Soul—the closer I can get to the wants of my Future Self—the better off I will be. Period.

> *Our Soul has a whole other set of wants that we likely haven't gotten in touch with yet.*

In all aspects of my existence, this has proven to be true over and over again. When I was younger, when my ego was running the roost, I would overshoot. I didn't know it at the time, of course, but nonetheless, it was running my life. I would spend all this time going towards something that I was never intended to have in the first place. Think about that for a moment...

Talk about a waste of energy. I watch people in my life right now waste their precious energy going for something that either, number one, they're not even close to being ready for, or number two, they're never going to have because that was never the design of their Soul. Their Soul has a whole other set of wants that they haven't gotten in touch with yet.

So, when you go off path, what happens? You push your Soul aside. Now your Soul goes into a waiting pattern, and once again, you're on your own. This is why many people often feel like they're completely on their own—because in a sense, they are. They've temporarily separated themselves from their Soul because they're thinking their Soul's not thinking big enough, when, in fact, their Soul is thinking exactly the way it needs to be thinking.

You can create your life from these smaller, lower places, under the influence of the ego, or you can create from the higher, greater, and far more powerful places. One way to know that you're on the right track is that you don't have the stress, you don't get the struggle, you don't have the anxiety when you're creating from these higher places. Things are just smoother. There's more grace. Everything works easier. Things fall more effortlessly into place.

> So, connect with your Future Self and reflect on your responses to this exercise. You'll get the answer. It might not be as big as you want just yet, but you'll get the answer. And just go with that, whatever it is. You'll be amazed at how easy your life can become over time when you deepen your listening to that of what your Soul truly wants for you.

Exercise #3:

All right, so now let's move on to the creation of the List of 12 Things You Want to Manifest.

> Take out your notebook and write down the numbers 1 through 12. This will be your list of 12 things (or 12 desires or 12 wants) you

would like to see manifest within the next year. It's important to keep this process simple for right now and not think too far into the future.

When you make your list, I suggest you go into complete silence and connect with your Soul. Listen to the voice of your Soul or your Future Self as you create your list of 12. Do this by focusing on the questions from above and reflecting back on your answers. This will help you get connected and stay more connected to your Soul during this process.

List up to 12 things that you want in any area of your life—relationships, career, business, finances, health, recreation, spiritual advancement, and so on. All areas of your life are now on the table.

Just remember, when you're making your list, this is your Future Self speaking to you, saying, "I want this for you." Ultimately, you're becoming that Future Self. You're becoming those wants or desires that your Soul wants for you.

Again, there's this battle going on within us. The ego might try to get in there and encourage you to go after something that has nothing to do with your Soul whatsoever—something that has nothing to do with what your Future Self really wants. So, once you get to the point where you are your Future Self, you're going to say, "What's this? I never really wanted this."

This is why it's key to connect with your Soul on a conscious level during this process. Your Future Self not only knows what it wants, but it also knows what it has. It already knows this is what has been scheduled. Your Soul knows which results come from who you truly are. This is the big difference when it comes to manifesting at a conscious level.

Remember that your Soul communicates through feelings, images, or impulses. Your Soul will utilize your mind as a creative instrument, but it doesn't live there. Your 12 wants or desires will feel meaningful to you at the level of your heart space—your fourth energy center. That's where your Soul ultimately resides. Your Soul's desire will literally fill every cell of your body.

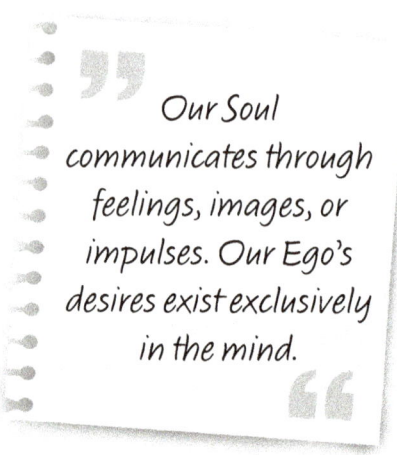

Our Soul communicates through feelings, images, or impulses. Our Ego's desires exist exclusively in the mind.

Another way to think of this is that when you're tapping into your Soul's desire, it is one that you're discovering. It's not something that you're coming up with because it's already there.

Your ego's desire, on the other hand, will exist exclusively in the mind. You will not get the same meaning or fulfillment from a goal created by the ego. Your ego might surface when you're writing this list. It might say, "What will others think about this? What will others think about me?" That's a sign that your ego has been activated and something to look out for. Don't let your ego thwart your desires, and don't let it steer them either.

The crossover between the ego and the Soul is the biggest battle you're going to face here. And it's all happening within. You'll know when the battle is over because you'll feel inner peace. There's no more anxiety, no more stress, no more resistance. Everything will calm down. When you get to that place and it's sustained, you'll know the battle is won.

> For each item that you're exploring from Soul level on your list, you could also ask yourself, "Is this a genuine desire? Is this something I really want? If my life was ending at the end of the year, would I even care about this thing?"

This puts each item on your list to the test. All of a sudden, it puts things in perspective. It will help you discover if this desire is really coming from your heart... or if it's merely coming from your mind, meaning your personality that is run by your ego.

Ultimately, everyone has the ability to connect with their Soul, but we've all developed this ability to varying levels. This may be something you need to practice a bit. Maybe you'll discover *this* is something you want—to have this ability to connect to your Soul with more ease and consistency.

> You might need to return to this list in a few days and see what you feel then. You might come up with an entirely different list that comes from that feeling place. Everyone is different, and this process takes more time for some than others. You might wake up three mornings from now, emerging from your sleep, and your cells are flooded with a knowing of exactly what to put on your list—knowing exactly what your Soul wants for you. You may have had this feeling of knowing before.

That's the higher part of you telepathically communicating with you. The truth that you feel when this happens is incredible.

This process of creating from your Future Self is quite different from anything you may have done up until this point. We're used to creating from our present selves and even our past selves. In a sense, you're helping your Future Self by connecting with it. You're helping yourself to become your Future Self.

So, take your time, connect within, and come up with your list. This isn't about driving forward or figuring it out. If you feel pressure, pull back. That's a function of the ego. Make sure every item on your list feels right. Feel into the sensations or impulses from your heart.

Keep your list within reach so you can see what you've achieved in a reasonable amount of time by referring back to this.

A Final Question to Ponder...

Before we move on to the next chapter, I'd like you to think about what it would be like if you were to actually get better at manifesting on a conscious level. HoldGo ahead and hold that in your mind and as you do, go with whatever answer thiscomes up for you...

What would it mean to you if you were to get better at manifesting what you truly want on a conscious level with precision—whether that's personally, professionally, spiritually, and/ or financially, and relationally?

CHAPTER 4

THE THREE SELVES

Whether we're conscious or unconscious during the creative process of manifesting, we are creating from one of three different places in our timeline. These are our Past Self, our Present Self, and our Future Self.

Just out of curiosity, where would you say most people are currently creating their life from—their Past Self, their Present Self, or their Future Self? If your answer is from their Past Self, then you are correct.

#1 – The Past Self

The 97 percent on the planet who have not yet manifested the life of their dreams have been creating from their Past Self. This means that whatever their past programming or past conditioning was—whatever their unresolved issues are, whatever those wounds are that have not yet been healed, whatever their unresolved karma still is—all of that is impacting their manifestations that are being created by their past selves. Again, look for the result. How you'll recognize this is somebody who creates from their Past Self repeats the same manifested experience over and over again, and once they get to round four or five of that same repeated experience, it begins to get louder with an increase of intensity.

This is the continuum experience we described in Chapter 2. To refresh your memory, the continuum is like Groundhog Day. You just basically spin around the exact same creation on a repetitive cycle. What could make this repetitive experience even more perplexing is the person believes that as they go through this repeat cycle again, it is actually going to create something new. And yet nothing could be further from the truth.

Someone who creates from their Past Self repeats the same manifested experience over and over again.

Now they are truly destined to create something new. But here's the deal... if I'm creating from my Past Self (whether its conscious or unconscious), and this is the only place I know how to create from, then all I'm going to get is more past repetitive experiences, period.

You might recall, at the beginning of *Transform Your Destiny*, I wrote about what really drove me to create that book. *Transform Your Destiny* is really a compilation of teachings that I›ve discovered, practiced, and embodied over a period of more than 20 years. It›s deep, powerful, and very potent, and if you haven't read it yet, or it has been a while since you have reviewed the material, I invite you to do so.

In that book, I describe how I had a number of people in my life that committed suicide, dating back from when I was a young boy.

I remember the very first time somebody dear to our family died by conscious suicide. I woke up one morning, was getting ready to go to school, and got the news that our dear family friend had killed himself the night before. This sent a huge shock wave through my nervous system that left me stunned for weeks, given we just saw him two days before this all happened. He was in our house having dinner with us.

I was just a kid of maybe 10 or 11 years old at the time. And this news traumatized me. From that point on, I ended up knowing a number of people who committed suicide, and I know that a few of my students in our network have lost dear friends or family members in this way as well.

Now, whether a suicide is committed consciously or unconsciously, I have an inner prompting to help more people on this planet become better educated and to better understand suicide. Why? Because it does not have to go down this way.

I have not proven this scientifically, nor do I know of anyone else who has (though they might be out there), but I've had an awareness for many years that suicide can be traced to the problem of creating from one's Past Self.

Think about this for a moment… If you were only creating from your Past Self, what might happen to your hope? What might happen to your belief in yourself? If you were to spend 53 years basically repeating the same experience over and over again, would you still want to be here? What would your limit be?

Now, of course, we also have kids and teenagers that are committing suicide left, right, and center these days. I mean, it's a real problem. And again, it's a problem that I'm committed to helping solve on the planet.

Creating from the Past Self could be potentially deadly. Over the years I've watched people destroy their life or destroy some part of their life that they truly value—like a really good relationship, friendship, or business partnership. Or maybe they started off with great health, but they became very unhealthy. Or let's say they had a wonderful talent, and they were in expression of that talent, yet they could not get beyond a repetitive experience and truly progress in mastering that talent.

So here they are, this phenomenal artist, just overflowing with incredible talent, and yet they recreate the same thing over and over. Again, it's the continuum. When we're creating from the Past Self, we turn this into a lower energetic pattern or a set of lower energy patterns. I might mention that doing so is usually done unconsciously—quite frankly, nobody in their right mind would do it this way if they knew what was really going on here. And I'd say that most on the planet do this, and more than likely are unaware that they are—which eventually produces the lower energy pattern that simply repeats itself. What that means is they are now in the experience of the continuum and basically repeating the same thing over and over again. How long can they go on before they give up? How many rounds will it take?

We can hope that once they finally tire of getting the same result, they will seek out a way to make new and better choices rather than giving up altogether or possibly ending it entirely. There will be those tiny feathers dropped in front of them in various ways to lead them to a support group, or to teachings like these that empower them to begin to choose differently in order to get a different result in terms of which self they are to be creating and manifesting from. All they need to do is choose to make that new choice, and they can begin to turn the rudder of their ship the one tiny degree that will take them in a new and different direction. But remember that we are all at choice. And we never know how someone else will ultimately choose.

> *When we are creating from our Past Self, it's usually coming from the negative part of our ego or some lower aspect of us.*

When we are creating from our Past Self, it's usually coming from the negative part of our ego and/or some lower aspect of us. One of those lower aspects could be our inner child. And if it turns out we have a seven-year-old inner child stuck, trapped, frozen inside of us, then much of what we've been manifesting in our day-to-day world is coming from that inner child who is under the influence of our negative ego.

Now if that's where our manifestations are coming from, then the result is going to reflect that. This is the Law of Reflection at play—our outer landscape is a direct reflection of our inner landscape. So, next thing we know, we're going to find ourselves in a relationship. Of course, we're going to tell the whole world that we've met our dream partner because at the beginning of any new relationship, everyone wants to believe they've met the person of their dreams. But then possibly 10, 12 months later, or however long it might take, all of a sudden, where did that dream partner go? That person is still standing in front of us, but they've become something else. Or were they the same all along, and we just couldn't see it because we were creating from our Past Self?

When you're creating from your Past Self, it's impossible to see the entirety of what's at play. You can only see a sliver, a splinter. And then, if your ego's really strong or clever, it can convince you that the little splinter of truth you're seeing is the whole of it.

That's a trick. It's your ego influencing your thoughts to get you to believe you know exactly what you're doing, when, in fact, most are only conscious of about 10 percent of what they're doing. The other 90 percent of what they're doing is unconscious. When you're operating like this, you might go nine months before you come to a painful realization about your physical manifestation: *Oh my gosh. How did I get here? How did this happen?* Well this happens to us when we are creating from some lower aspect of ourselves, such as our inner child (aka our subconscious) or maybe even our shadow side, all under the influence of our limiting, sometimes overprotective and negative ego.

#2 – The Present Self

Now, your Present Self is a very different place to create or manifest from. When I'm creating from my Present Self, I am more conscious than I am when I'm creating from my Past Self.

That simple exercise that we engaged in at the beginning of the book could have a profound effect on you. That little exercise might not be as little as you may have thought it was. It is my hope, however, that you take it seriously and that you really go for it. Because that exercise will show you, believe it or not, where you're at in creating from that of your Present Self.

In order to go the distance and actually get a victory on manifesting those three $100 bills, or manifesting that new paying client, or manifesting that new refrigerator, or manifesting $10,000 or more in 30 days—whatever it is that you put down on paper that's most right for you—you're going to utilize your Present Self.

If most of your creating has been coming from your Past Self, you're about to have an experience. And that experience is gonna go something like this... your Past Self, like a powerful tractor beam, is going to pull you back to it (like a magnet) because this is where you've been doing most of your creating and/or attracting from up until now. And perhaps you haven't been aware of this. But now you are.

Even though it's a simple thing that you're out to manifest, if the Past Self is where you've been doing the majority of your creating from up until now, this will challenge you—because you've been wired to create from it, which at some point along your past timeline became a lifestyle for you. And this happened, again, without you possibly knowing it had occurred.

On the other hand, you're going to have an experience with your Present Self. Your Present Self is you being exactly that—present. As you've got to be present if you're going to remain conscious of what it is you are in the process of attracting or manifesting. Can you see the magic here?

Now, what's so cool is you can choose this. You can choose this any time you wish. The illusion says you're locked in. You believe inside yourself that this is where you create from, even if it's not a conscious thought.

This is the Law of Belief in action (which was described earlier in the chapter on Universal Laws and again in more detail later in the chapter on Beliefs). However, the belief inside you that this is where you must create from is not based on any truth at all. It's 100 percent false.

The Past Self is completely ruled by the lower parts of you. It is often ruled by your negative ego, but it can also be ruled by an unhealed inner child or a subconscious that is still mostly being run by old, negative programming. You may not have fully connected with your inner child, or you may not even have an awareness around it yet. In other words, that inner child has not been healed or transformed yet to its greater potential.

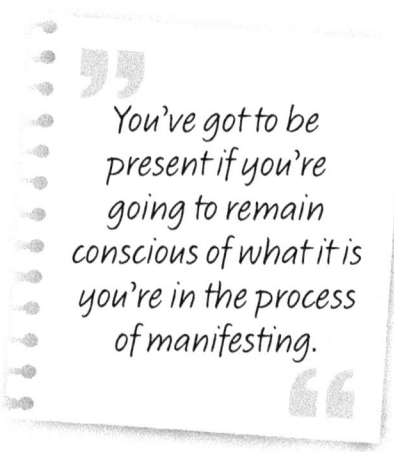

> You've got to be present if you're going to remain conscious of what it is you're in the process of manifesting.

But here's the deal: if that's what's going on inside of us, then we can be assured it's going to be easy to suck us back to creating from our Past Self. Because our ego, our inner child, or subconscious have been in charge of our creative process for so long. And the lower parts of us do not want to give up this level of power—at least not just yet, as they've been programmed to continue doing whatever it is they believe they're to continue to do. Of course, until we get in there to change it.

If and when you're able to create from the Present Self, it's now going to be a little different. There's going to be some crossover. You're still going to have that negative, limiting ego involved somewhat—especially if you have a really developed ego that you've been empowering, building up, and strengthening for years.

In book one, *Being Called to Change*, we cover ego worship—this is where the ego takes the place of God. People can unconsciously worship their egos. This is done completely unconsciously. Often people become disgusted by what they've been doing on an unconscious level once they become conscious of it.

So, you see, the negative ego, at any point, depending on its strength level and its power level within us, can cross over from the Past Self to the Present Self. And this is where the ego will battle with another part of us—our Soul.

Now this is where your Soul comes into play when you're creating from your Present Self. When you're fully present, when you're in the here and now, when you're in your body, this is the most direct way to fully connect with your Divine Soul, aka your Higher Self.

The negative ego does not like the idea of us getting connected with our Soul. Why? Because the limiting ego is afraid it's going to get stripped of its power. And quite frankly, it is going to get stripped of its power. However, the ego takes this belief further—it believes that if it is stripped of its power, it is going to die, which, in reality, it won't.

What actually happens with this part of your ego, if and when you go the distance along your spiritual journey in ultimately transforming yourself, is that the best parts of it will integrate into your magnificent Divine Soul Self.

If you want to learn more about this, check out the *Transcendence* course in our Online Learning Center. This is an entire course on the transcendence of your ego and the raising up of your inner child and your subconscious to a higher level of functionality.

So, when you are creating and/or attracting from your Present Self, you're now in the moment; you're consciously aware of whatever it is you're out to manifest. To this, you could still be experiencing this internal conflict, which you might or might not be aware of, between the ego and the Soul. This is where the Soul will either get its way, or perhaps the ego will get its way.

Ego Pushback

When you're getting closer to being present more consistently, the part of your ego mentioned above can get very intense. As you know, your ego has all kinds of tricks up its sleeve.

Now remember, your job is to learn how to actually work with your ego. Your job, first and foremost, is to get to a point where your ego is not in charge of you anymore—where it is not a major influencer.

Take a look at your personal network or community, and you'll see all kinds of people who are being hoodwinked by their own egos. They just perhaps don't know it. And, of course, when that's going on, your ego learns how it can best create or produce another trick—very much like a magician. Over time, your ego can end up accumulating countless tricks that it can then utilize whenever it wants you to do something on its behalf.

What this means is that as you're getting closer to creating from the Present Self, this part of your ego could very well get louder. And more than likely it's going to get trickier. It might even back off on purpose to get you to believe that it's no longer there—that you no longer have to be concerned about it; that you no longer have to be aware of it.

> *Your ego can accumulate countless tricks that it can utilize whenever it wants you to do something on its behalf.*

When the powers that be (also known as the Illuminati, the Elite, the Kabal, or the dark forces) are pulling a trick—when they want to get something done without us noticing—they create a disruption, a distraction. They get us to focus over there so that nobody's looking over here. Now, without anybody watching, they can do whatever it is that they want done. Quite frankly, they're absolutely brilliant at it. They've been doing it for a long time. We might just not be aware of it. Similarly, though not at the same level of power, our limiting, negative ego will get us to look over there while it's operating over here. It's setting something up that we can't see, as we've temporarily lost awareness and likely are not even fully present.

It's never a great strategy to lose awareness of our own ego because that's when we become unconscious. And when we become unconscious, all bets are off. At this point, our ego really has us—so whatever is going to happen in our world is going to happen under the influence of our untamed, negative ego.

As you become present, as you come closer and closer to connecting with your Divine Soul Self, there's going to be a battle from your ego. No doubt about it. As the ego begins to sense that the connection with your Soul is coming back online, it will push back. And you want to be aware of this. Because when it does, this is where it becomes your responsibility to yourself to get better at consciously working with it—which also includes learning how to actually tame it.

Once you start to touch the Soul, the Soul's going to continue to want this contact.

Now, when touching your Soul, I'm not referring to just thinking about your Soul or entertaining the idea that you have a Soul, or that you are a Soul—all of which is true. Rather, what I'm bringing to your attention is actually touching your Soul, touching the pulse of your Soul and being fully aware that's what you're doing. When that happens, you have a visceral experience that you're not just aware of in your head but throughout your whole body at a cellular level.

So, once you make that first serious touchpoint with your Soul, as you're coming more into the Present Self or creating more from the Present Self, the ego's going to ramp up its trickery. Simultaneously, the Soul is going to become a little more intense with its inner prompting as well. In other words, the Soul isn't going to just leave you alone anymore.

It's possible that up until this point of making conscious contact, your Soul has left you to your own devices. Perhaps it has given up hope temporarily that you're going to come into the truth of who you really are in this lifetime.

So as this connection is being established, when you are creating from your Present Self on a more regular basis, this battle is going to increase—at least for a little while.

In fact, this battle, between the ego and the Soul, might be the greatest battle that you will ever personally experience—and it's all happening within you. We have fought battles and wars on this planet for thousands of years, but these are nothing compared to this battle between the ego and the Soul that will occur within, once you consciously make contact with your Divine Soul Self.

While your Soul doesn't want to back down at this point, your ego does not want to give up the power you've given it over time. The ego could be compared to some of our politicians. Once they get a certain amount of power, good luck trying to strip them of that power.

The thing is, it's not even real power. Come the end of your life, you'll realize none of this type of power is real, just like all who have come before us have realized this. And yet you can embody your own real, authentic power. You can. I can. We all can.

This battle between the ego and the Soul is not only intense, but it can go on for some time. I don't know anybody—including mentors in my past and in my own personal experience—who have had the fortune of having this battle resolved over the course of a weekend, a month, or even a year.

Can it be resolved? Absolutely. Is it to be resolved? Absolutely. Is it a part of your greater destiny to resolve it? Absolutely.

Managing Resistance

One of the first and most important things you can do when it comes to taming, teaching and ultimately transcending your ego is to get in the habit of checking your ego for resistance. If you're unconscious to subconscious resistance, the odds are you'll hold the energy of resistance in place, which will only make the limiting, negative ego stronger. For those who want to learn more about unconscious resistance, the negative ego and/or the taming, teaching, and transcending of your ego, I invite you to refer back to book two of the Trilogy, *Transform Your Destiny*.

The ego is going to use that resistance as a way to push back on us. Remember, everything's coming from inside of us, so when we're ready to really begin disarming our ego and dismantling the power that we've given it over time, we need to start to clear out this resistance.

This process isn't a one-time deal. It's a major process that's done incrementally.

You can tell if you have resistance by noticing if, or when, you're pushing on someone or something, if you're pushing something away, or even if you're pushing something down. Maybe you're pushing down unpleasant feelings or pushing away something you don't want to do—such as an action step that you've been avoiding actually doing. People who have procrastination as a lower energy pattern don't realize this is an extreme form of unconscious resistance. If this is something you do on a day-to-day basis, check to see if you're resisting something or someone.

You might recall the Hidden Law of the Universe (The Law of Opposition) from book one of the Trilogy, which says, "That which we oppose strengthens." So, whatever it is we are resisting, this would be the equivalent of us giving our power to it, whether we are conscious or not. And whatever "it" is, by this hidden law, this implies that it will get stronger.

To soften up this energy of resistance, it could begin with something as simple as taking a moment and getting in touch with yourself, such as taking a couple of deep breaths through your nostrils with your mouth closed and just breathing deeply. This really helps to calm your nervous system. Then, ask yourself, "If there was someone or something that I was resisting right now, who or what might that be?"

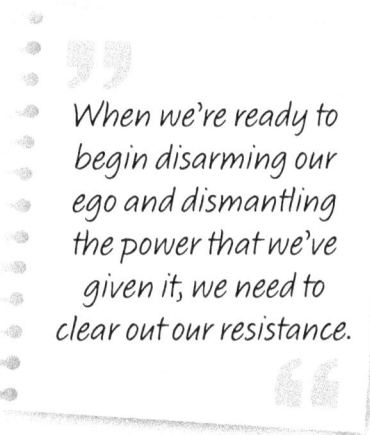

When we're ready to begin disarming our ego and dismantling the power that we've given it, we need to clear out our resistance.

If you are resisting someone or something, then by law you must get an answer. Not because I say so. Remember, I work with the exact same set of laws that you've been getting better at working with. This is another Universal Law: Ask and You Shall Receive. So, when you ask, you're going to get an answer—and then you'll need to ask yourself: "Do I want to release this layer of resistance? Do I want to clear it?"

By the way, that could be a yes or a no answer. Maybe in current time we're a frightened little boy inside of a man's body. Or a terrified little girl inside of a woman's body. This might be our truth, or our reality, at that moment. To this, we might not want to let go of this resistance just yet.

Why would someone want to hold on to resistance? Because they have it hooked in. Because they've got it wired into their brain, under the influence of their ego, that the resistance is somehow or in some way protecting them. That resisting someone, or something, is going to protect them. Or if the resistance is going on within, it's protecting them from confronting some uglier part of themselves—perhaps it's a shadow aspect of themselves that's been living in the dark and has been cut off from the light for some time. This part of them might very well look like an ugly, dark, or even somewhat distorted version of them. When somebody looks at this part of themselves for the first time, it can be very scary—as it may appear contorted and unrecognizable.

Believe it or not, if we've been living in this pattern of holding our resistance in place, we've been doing so because we've been hoodwinked by our overprotective ego into thinking that our resistance is actually protecting us. This resistance is like a wall. And it's not uncommon to build an energetic wall of resistance. Of the people I have coached and mentored, in about 85 percent of the cases, when they began their transformational work with me, they had an energetic wall of resistance that had been built up over time—and they were not even aware of it. In other words, this was all done unconsciously.

How did that happen? Well, the ego created it as a shield of protection. We then believe that shield is somehow going to protect us from everything ugly, harmful, dark, or negative. But it's just an illusion. Quite frankly, it's been a brilliant trick of the limiting part of our ego that has been set up over a long period of time.

So, you're going to have to dissolve that internal wall of resistance. And it can be done. Others before you have done this, so you can do it too.

This is where it starts to become a regular practice. You have to check yourself every day for this resistance until it becomes a lifestyle. Of course, your ego is going to fight you on this—which is another form of resistance that your ego is in with you, in wanting to dissolve this energetic wall. It's going to try to trick you and manipulate you because its survival is being threatened. What could be helpful here, of course, is to teach your ego that you really are safe—that it doesn't have to protect you in this way anymore.

#3 – The Future Self

When you are creating from your Future Self, you get a very different experience of the manifestation process. First of all, when you're creating from your Future Self, in order to do that, you've got to be present. You've also got to do something else. You've got to let go of your past.

When you are creating from the Future Self, what that means is that you've blended the Present Self into the Future Self, and you are only creating from the Soul. The ego no longer has any jurisdiction over the creation. When you create from your Future Self, you are completely present—completely in the moment—but you're literally projecting out into your future timeline.

When it comes to your destiny, you've got a lower octave of destiny, and you've got a higher octave of destiny, or a Lower Destiny and a Greater Destiny. When you master manifestation from the Future Self, what this looks like is you are basically accessing your divine humanness. In other words, you become the Divine Human.

When you're manifesting from your Past Self, on the other hand, you are manifesting from the level of the Basic Human. For more on the

Divine Human, the Basic Human, and your Greater Destiny, check out book number two.

You get to choose which one you're ultimately going to be—the Divine Human or the Basic Human—and which place you're going to manifest or attract from. In the course of this life experience, you can remain at the level of the Basic Human, which means, for the most part, you'll continue to create from the Past Self. You might however, dip your toe into learning how to create from the Present Self, which now means you're going to start to access your Soul—your Divine Soul Essence Self—at least to some degree.

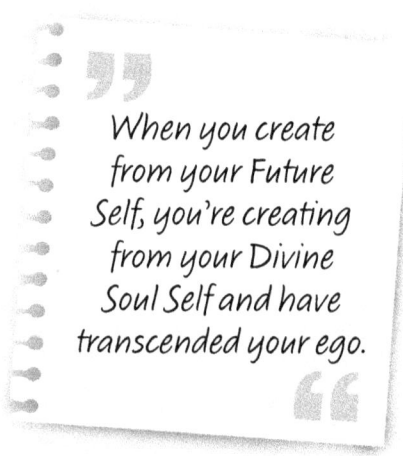

When you create from your Future Self, you're creating from your Divine Soul Self and have transcended your ego.

Will you move all the way to the Future Self and really begin to embody this, to master this? Maybe, maybe not. This too gets to be your choice. If you've been working through the last two books in the Trilogy, it's likely you've already started to access this, little by little, slowly but surely. In all likelihood, at least some of your creations and/or manifestations have already been coming from your Future Self. Though some of them are probably still coming from your Past Self, as well, and most certainly from your Present Self.

Later on, we're going to go through an exercise around how to create and attract like a magnet from your Future Self. We'll also highlight a timeline that works best for manifesting from your Future Self so that you don't overshoot it or self-sabotage it.

Remember, your ego is in there, and quite frankly, whenever it sees fit (for its own reasons), it can sabotage good things in your world—including higher teachings and newfound wisdom. It likes to sabotage these things because of what they imply. Once you start to really embody these teachings, it's going to rock your world—it's going to change your world. And your ego doesn't like that because, remember, it doesn't want the power that you've given it to be stripped away.

When you create from your Future Self, you're creating from your Divine Soul Self. This is your most authentic self and what your Soul has wanted for you from the very beginning—it wants you to become that Divine Human. It wants you to become the embodiment of your Divine Soul Essence Self within your physical vessel. This is very dynamic, life-changing stuff.

In order for this to happen, your ego must be transcended; its best parts must be integrated into the true essence of the Soul. When that happens, you become a Divine Being in physical form—a master at conscious manifestation. The Divine Human, just like the Basic Human, is manifesting 24/7. The only difference is that the Divine Human is conscious every step of the way—it never loses conscious awareness. It is the Soul Essence of the Divine.

Reflection Question

Based on your current results, what "self" have you been creating most of your life from, up to this point in time? Be as honest as you can here. Honesty is one of the master keys.

So, if you haven't already, pull out your journal and write down your answer.

Why did you give the response you did, and explain why you feel this is the self you have been creating from?

Your answer might involve multiple selves. For example: "I'm usually living from my Present Self but when activated, I slip into my Past Self."

Remember, if you're creating from the Past Self, there are going to be certain symptoms. There are going to be giveaways. When you're creating from the Present Self, there are also going to be giveaways. Remember that gauge on the dashboard of your life? All you have to do is examine your results, and you'll have your answer.

If you are creating from the Past Self, nothing of significance changes, and you can't see a vision of your Future Self; you have a difficult time making contact with it, as there is more than likely a blockage. This is one symptom that gives itself away. That's a gauge on your dashboard. Another one is the continuum—where you have experiences that just keep repeating.

There can also be a crossover between the Present and Past Selves. Just like the ego and the Soul, there's a crossover that exists in the Present Self. In the Past Self, there's no crossover at all, however. It's all under the influence of the ego and the inner child, or the current programming of the subconscious.

Then there's the Future Self. There isn't any crossover here either. It's your Soul—your authentic self, your Divine Self.

When you are going from past to present and present to future, you're going to experience these crossover points—where you can see where you're operating from and when the shift occurs.

> *If you take steps forward, and then are pulled back, that means there is some past issue that hasn't been healed.*

If you feel like you take steps forward, and then are being pulled back, like a tractor beam pulling you backwards, that means there is some past issue that hasn't been healed, or you might be dealing with conditioning from your childhood, your ancestry, or the collective. So, if that's the case, you need to explore a couple things in order to determine what, specifically, is keeping you in your Past Self.

Sometimes just having an awareness of these teachings is enough to wake you up so that you can punch through. Sometimes, knowing the truth is the nudge you need to elevate your consciousness. If you're ready to make these types of shifts internally, it can happen rather quickly.

All of a sudden, once you have the knowledge, you can make the choice to remain as aware as possible when it comes to where you're creating or attracting from. You might even find yourself thinking, *Boy, that was definitely a Past Self creation...* Or you might find yourself thinking, *Whoa! I think I just created something from my Present Self.* Or, *Oh my gosh, I think I'm actually creating something from my Future Self!*

It's all about having awareness of these teachings, then choosing to work with them, all while having a little fun with them. This process will help you to get better at manifesting on a conscious level.

One of the things you'll want to do is get better at recognizing repetitive experiences so that you can start learning from them. The only way to grow from those experiences is to learn. One of the reasons we have repeat experiences is because there's a lesson that's been encoded in them, and we haven't yet fully learned the lesson.

Once you learn a lesson from that experience, it begins to melt like a pound of butter on a hot summery day. A weight is lifted. The experience is resolved. It's a really cool experience, and it's also empowering because now you're making that transition from creating from your Past Self to your Present Self.

Sometimes these repeat experiences can be traumatic events. And whenever we're repeating a traumatic event, it means the trauma is still sitting in our cells that make up our physical form—our brains, our nervous systems. The trauma is still there, and it is still charged.

What we want to do is get to whatever that trauma is and start discharging it. Discharging the trauma means getting to the stuck emotions that are literally residing within the pool of the traumatic experience that impacted the cells of your physical body or the cells of your physical brain.

Remember the Law of Energy? Everything is energy. So, what you need to do is help loosen that energy so it can start to do what it already knows how to do—which is to move. And it will move. And more specifically, it will move through you and from you. Now, this might not happen all in one sitting. You might have to do this incrementally, depending on how strong that emotional energy is that's trapped within the cells of that traumatic experience that you had.

Trauma is unique because if a person has a lot of trauma in their cells that they have not discharged, then this trauma becomes its own energy force. It creates its own set of patterns. Then, we start to unconsciously behave in a way that's consistent with that energy, known as the trauma. And, of course, this is all based on the Law of Attraction. As in, like energy attracts like energy. So now we attract yet another traumatic experience with someone else because the trauma in our cells hasn't yet been discharged.

If and when you discharge this trauma properly, you'll no longer attract traumatic experiences to you. Similarly, you'll no longer be creating from the Past Self. Addressing and discharging your trauma will help you to make the transition to the Present Self. You'll be able to stay and operate within and from that Present Self on a more regular basis when it comes to creating whatever it is you're creating. Which then also sets the bridge for you to get better at connecting to and creating from your Future Self as well.

All trauma is rooted in fear. So, the Past Self, at its core, is 100-percent fear based. The root of fear can run very deep within our unconscious, and then, that root will make its way into the trauma. It sounds strange, but this root of fear actually feeds off of the trauma. If you get enough trauma suppressed in your cells, over time, that fear will grow.

The key, once again, is to clear up the trauma that has been suppressed in our cells, for as we do this clearing, we're transforming our fear as well.

CHAPTER 5

BELIEFS

All limited beliefs are rooted in fear, and all unlimited beliefs are rooted in love. Fear is a very powerful force. It can be downright destructive—it can hurt people, destroy people, murder people. Fear can cause people to commit suicide.

Love is powerful, but powerful in a very different way, in a higher way, in a brighter way, in a more radiant way, in a more spiritualized way.

Remember from the Law of Consciousness that within our consciousness is a system of beliefs, some of which are rooted in love, and some of which are rooted in fear. Now, some of these beliefs are weak, and some of them are very strong. The ones that are very strong are the emotionalized beliefs. These beliefs are made up of thought forms, and thought forms are structures which are rooted in emotion. This is what makes a belief emotionalized within our consciousness. Both limited and unlimited beliefs are beliefs that have been emotionalized. A limited belief is rooted in fear, and an unlimited belief is rooted in love.

Think about it... When you're in love with someone or something, are you feeling limited, or are you feeling liberated? Now, when you're hating someone or something, when you're judging someone or something, how are you feeling? Are you feeling unlimited and free, or are you feeling limited, stuck, blocked, or restricted?

One's coming out of the root of fear, and the other's coming out of the root of love. When you have a belief that's truly coming out of love at its root, there are no blockages or restrictions. What you end up with is freedom, which uniquely enough happens to be another one of your divine birthrights. How about that?

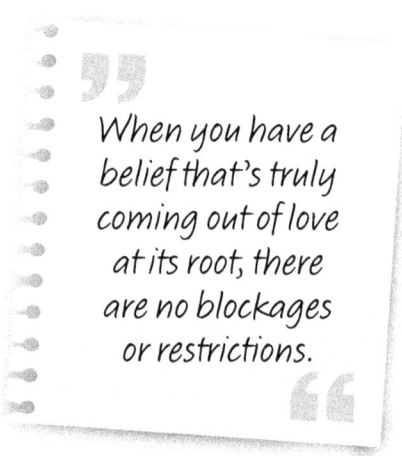

When you have a belief that's truly coming out of love at its root, there are no blockages or restrictions.

When we look around us, however, we don't see many people who are free... I mean really free. And yet we could all be free, every single one of us, because inside of us all, we have freedom as a divine birthright.

Now, to be clear, this birthright doesn't entitle you to your freedom. Your divine birthrights are part of your destiny to uncover so that you can experience them in your day-to-day world. It doesn't matter if you're a man, woman, teenager, young adult, or wiser person.

I say wiser because there are people who have lived more years in this lifetime, but they aren't elderly. They don't look like they're elderly. They might be 70 years of age but don't look a day over 50. How the heck did that happen? The opposite can be the case too. We have people who are 45 years old but look like they're in their sixties.

Age is reflected in these concepts of fear and love. The person who appears more youthful is coming more from love, and the person who appears older is coming more from fear. One has more unlimited beliefs, and the other has more limiting beliefs. A limiting belief will accelerate the aging process. An unlimited belief will do the complete opposite, or at the very least, it'll slow it down dramatically. This is how powerful these beliefs are.

You can think of these emotionalized beliefs like self-fulfilling prophecies. According to the Law of Correspondence, if you have a strong emotionalized belief, it must, by law, produce a reality in your external world. And because it's in your external world, you'll be able to spot it. If the belief is rooted in fear, that's going to look like and feel like a restriction or a blockage. You might even feel like someone or something is holding you back.

Belief Systems

Everyone has a belief system. If your belief system leans heavier on the limited side, the restriction will be seen in your life, and it won't matter what you do. It's not because you are doing something wrong, or someone is cursing you or you have bad luck; it's governed by these laws.

If you're unsure and you want to know what your beliefs are, become good at skillfully examining your results. The essence of your beliefs will clearly show itself in the character or in the texture of the result that's being manifested in your own personal universe. That's that corresponding reality. Again, the essence of the Law of Correspondence is "as within, so without." Whatever's inside of you must play itself out. It must produce itself somehow, some way. This may happen over a short period of time, or it may happen over a long period of time, but, by law, it must produce a perfect reflection of the beliefs you are holding within your consciousness.

The goal is to have an unlimited belief system inside of you, and my suggestion to you here is to transform your belief system into one that is going to produce the freedom for you to create the life of your dreams.

In my twenties, I heard a particularly captivating story that clearly showed the power of one's belief. There was a switchman who was working on the railroad. He had been working there for a couple of decades. His work had to do with the refrigeration units, or reefer units, within the box cars. The box cars on the train had refrigeration units in them so that they could haul produce, meat, and frozen goods from one side of the country to another.

This man had lost a couple of his friends at the job. A worker would be inside one of those reefer units, and sometimes the box cars would collide as they were being joined back together. When this happened, the doors would slam shut. Because the reefer unit was well insulated, for obvious reasons, it was impossible to get the attention of somebody on the outside of the box car to open it back up, as the box cars could only be opened from the outside at that time. If they were left in there long enough, they would either suffocate or freeze to death. So, there were a couple of instances in which this guy had coworkers who were found lying dead on the floor of one of these reefer units.

Because of this, this switchman had been traumatized a few times, and he told some of his family members and his close friends how afraid he was that one day, on that job, someone might find him frozen to death on the floorboard of one of those units.

Well, a number of years passed, and one day, he found himself working inside a reefer unit, and the door slammed shut. He couldn't get out. Days later, he was found in the box car, dead.

> *If you want to know what your beliefs are, become good at skillfully examining your results.*

But that's not where the story ended...

When they performed his autopsy, they determined the cause of death was that he froze to death. However, they discovered something else that was even more revealing. Upon investigation, they found that the reefer unit had never been turned on.

So, what does this story tell us?

It tells us the power of someone's emotionalized belief. If it turns out that an emotionalized belief has been rooted in fear, it is going to reflect itself in reality. It can be extremely dangerous to have an emotionalized belief about the worst-case scenario—as this story portrays.

Now, are people whose beliefs that are rooted in fear even aware of this on a conscious level? They might be, or they might not be. In today's time, more and more of us are becoming conscious of our emotionalized beliefs. That said, many could still be unconscious of their own emotionalized beliefs, similar to the story above of the switchman working on the rail lines. As this scenario clearly depicts, the power of our beliefs shapes our physical reality, and it would behoove us all to continue the work on bringing our unconscious to light so we can impact our present reality in the most positive of ways.

EXERCISE: Other's Beliefs

Here's a simple exercise that you can do with your family to illustrate others' beliefs.

Go ahead and ask a member of your family, "What is a belief?"

And then listen to what they say. Pay attention, and don't interject.

Next ask them: "How was that belief created? How did it get developed?"

Then, just for the heck of it, throw in one more question. Now remember to just listen. Don't facilitate or coach. Just observe what this other person, whom you love, sitting before you, has to say about these three questions.

Ask them: "Who created this belief? Where did you get this belief from?"

Now, you would think everybody would be able to answer these three questions with some deep, rich answers, but you might find that when you ask these three questions, there is a serious lack of education on what a belief is, how a belief gets developed, and where a belief comes from.

Once complete, consider documenting in your journal what this exercise revealed to you.

How Belief Systems are Developed

Now this is where the Law of Attraction comes into play. Remember, like energy begets more of its own; like will always seek more of its own. None of us can stop this from happening.

A limited belief will produce a restriction in some aspect of your life, whereas an unlimited belief will produce freedom to manifest a true desire in some aspect of your life. How about that? Can you see what's going on here yet? Are you starting to connect some of the dots? Are you starting to light up a little bit like a Christmas tree right now?

This is big stuff. This is life-altering stuff.

If you want to see what someone really believes—whether it's your beloved, your teenage daughter, or your 35-year-old son—one of the ways to determine this is to see how that person shows up. This will give away whether their underlying beliefs are mostly limited or unlimited.

The challenge most parents have in uncovering their children's beliefs is that they haven't yet connected with their own beliefs; they don't know what their own beliefs are. So, clearly, they aren't going to be asking these types of questions to their children. And yet, if they were to become aware, if they were to just become conscious enough, if they had access to these types of beliefs, it wouldn't take them long to see what their children believe.

> *A person will give their beliefs away through how they're behaving, how they're acting and how they're speaking.*

A nine-year-old boy already has a belief system. By the time that boy turns 13, that belief system is getting well rooted into place. By the time that boy turns 16, good luck trying to change those beliefs. By the time that boy turns 18, and most certainly no later than 20, you're not going to change those beliefs, at least not anytime soon because that young man is now going to have to play out those beliefs and have experiences with them, for at least the next three to five years of his life or possibly even more. If he doesn't have an experience with them, how else is he going to connect with them and then ultimately transform them?

We always act in a manner consistent with our strongest beliefs. Quite frankly, even the way we speak, our language patterns, will give our beliefs away.

I notice these things when I'm around people because it's something I've been learning about and practicing for years. I don't judge anyone, and I don't comment on my observations. I have a lot of compassion for people who clearly have a lot of limited beliefs—especially when they're older, because at age, say, 50, it is a tough go to pluck those beliefs from their system. They're well rooted. Now, they still can be changed, but that person has their work cut out in order to do it.

A person will give their beliefs away through how they're behaving, how they're acting, how they're speaking—especially the way they speak about themselves. This can be seen in limited beliefs, as well as beliefs that are rooted in love.

When a person's beliefs are rooted in love, you're going to have a very different experience with them. You're going to notice things about this person. You might start thinking things like, *Wow, she is the real deal. I love being around her. When I'm around her, I feel more secure. I just love being in her presence.* Or you might think, *what a breath of fresh air. He doesn't waver at all. He's so solid and grounded.*

Here's another truth for you. When it comes to the Law of Attraction, we don't attract what we want. As long as we keep wanting, as long as that's our recipe for manifestation, it isn't going to work. You see, we get what we believe. We attract in our lives what it is we believe most, whether limiting or unlimiting. In other words, our beliefs that we carry inside, whether we are conscious or unconscious of them, carry more weight and power than that of our wants.

Let's say you have a belief that feels restricted or dense. This heavy, dense belief could be something like *"Life isn't fair,"* which is nothing more than a thought form.

You might even say these words out loud sometimes: "You know, Jack, life isn't fair." You're broadcasting that life isn't fair out into the world.

So, if I believe in my consciousness that life isn't fair, then according to the Law of Correspondence, what that means is my external world is going to reflect what's going on internally. So, in my life, how is the external world going to reflect this?

With unfairness.

Now, here's where the big trick comes in from the ego. Now you've got evidence that life isn't fair—so you get on your soapbox and tell everybody in your family about how life isn't fair. You might even teach this to your kids.

This all comes from your thought that "life isn't fair" that you've emotionalized; that you've brought from a thought form to an emotionalized belief. This belief is one of the beliefs within your system of beliefs in your consciousness. Now you've gone out into the world and spoken this belief aloud 105 times, convincing others in your life that life isn't fair.

Then, you get some evidence because the belief must by law attract its like. So now you start to get unfair experiences, so to speak, that show up in your world. But you don't see it as a gauge telling you it's a limited belief. Rather, you see it as evidence for your belief. In fact, you're going to mount up this evidence possibly for five years—or even more.

But it doesn't have to be that way. You could spend those five years evolving, becoming a new version of yourself. You can see your results as evidence, or you can see them as a gauge. You can see your results as an indication that you have a belief that's been emotionalized. This is how you can change your life. This is how you can change your path of trajectory.

Another limited belief I've heard often is "I can't have what I want," and when people say this to me, they'll bring out the evidence. Some people have a garage full of evidence to prove their little thought form that says, "I can't have what I really want," when, in fact, it's not the truth. It's just a belief. Once they've gathered all of this evidence, however, they're absolutely convinced that this thought form is one of their truths.

> *Victim mentality is a big trap that will keep attracting victimization.*

In all fairness to these people, they obviously don't know this yet, and maybe they don't even want to know it because some people can get really invested in their stories that they've been concocting along the way. They've been building up and exaggerating this "poor little me" story. What they don't realize, however, is that this victim mentality is a big trap that will keep attracting victimization.

Unlimited Beliefs and the Law of Correspondence

Back in the eighties, I took a great liking to this gentleman named Arnold Patton. He was a walking example of an unlimited belief. His belief was the exact opposite of the previous example. It was "I can have it all," and he proved that to the world.

I feel so blessed because I've had a number of these people in my world over the years. These people just had wonderful lives. They truly did have it all. They had beautiful relationships. They had wonderful businesses. They had dynamic careers. They were making good money. They were healthy. They had all kinds of energy. When they were 60, they looked like they were 40. When they were 80, they looked like they were 55. They did, indeed, have it all.

One belief says, "I can have it all," meaning, "I can have what is right for me to have," and the other belief says, "I can't have it all," meaning, "I'm never going to have what is right for me to have. I'm never going to get it." A belief like that means you're going to go through an entire lifetime and never experience what was originally destined for you to experience in this life; to never actually have the beautiful things you were meant to have in this life. A person like that is never going to have true love, or wealth, or at least the type of wealth that gives them a degree of freedom, where they're no longer enslaved to their bills.

Me, on the other hand, I'm going to have some vibrance. I'm going to have some radiance. When I'm 70, my life is just beginning, baby. My life is not ending at 70. It's just getting started. I'm just getting warmed up. It's just beginning. This is an unlimited belief, rooted in love, which is one of the most powerful emotions in the Universe.

Fear, on the other hand, is one of the most crippling, one of the most paralyzing, emotions in the Universe. So, if you're feeling paralyzed, if you're feeling crippled, if you're feeling restricted, if you're feeling held back, if you're feeling limited, guess what? Exactly. You've got some limited beliefs. You've got some beliefs in your consciousness—at least one or two, that are restricting you. They've been holding you back, and more than likely, you've gathered all kinds of evidence somewhere along the way to further support those beliefs.

Before we move on, here's another common limiting belief, just for the heck of it. This is one of the greatest hits—we've all heard it. "I can't trust anyone anymore." This one is a prison sentence. If you have this limited belief, you've set yourself up for a lonely path. This means you can't trust your best friend, your kids, your parents, your lover. Also, more than likely, it means you can't even trust yourself.

I've had so many people try to convince me of this fear-rooted belief over the years. If you hold onto this belief over time, you will start to feel a restriction. You will start to feel confinement. You will start to feel some form of handicap or some form of crippling in some aspect of your life, whether that's in your finances, in your relationships, with your health, or, quite frankly, just with your own physical energy.

On the other hand, the unlimited beliefs are going to feel lighter and freer. When they're in play, they're going to produce a corresponding reality in which you can feel yourself moving forward. Your life is going to be moving onward and upward. It's going to be getting better. It's going to be expanding. You're becoming a nicer man or woman; a softer man or woman. You're becoming a more powerful man. You're becoming a more confident woman. You're becoming a healthier parent. Everything starts to improve, little by little, slowly but surely.

Our beliefs influence the quality of our consciousness. A lower-energy belief can feel like a prison sentence, whereas a higher-energy belief can feel like we've been set free.

The Two Places Our Beliefs Come From

Before we move into the exercise for this section, we need to review where our beliefs actually come from.

The majority of our beliefs come from one of two areas.

One is earlier past programming. By the time you reached age 12, no matter how you cut it, you ended up with a belief system, and it's pretty obvious where it came from. Good old Mom and Dad.

Now, before we get too tough on Mom and Dad, please remember that at one time, they were also a little girl or a little boy who had their own mom and dad. We've been doing this thing for thousands of years. We've been basically passing on our belief systems in current time to our children. In fact, we do this quite skillfully without even knowing that is what we are doing. If you've had children, you've done this too. It's almost impossible not to. That's why you've got to be super, super conscious, which entails clearing out your own lower-energy beliefs.

The second place where you can get a belief is from a past-life experience. When someone comes into this world and has a very strong belief at a very young age, such as when they are a toddler, it can be a carryover from a previous lifetime. They're coming into this life with the remnants from previous conditioning and programming. Around the age of seven, this belief is going to make itself known, and most parents aren't even aware of this happening.

When you come across a belief that's really strong, that belief is going to come with some complexity. It's been around for a long time, either in this lifetime or possibly the last lifetime or two leading up to this one. In other words, it's got some deep, deep roots. It's going to take a little time to pluck it.

There are beliefs that can come up later in life, too. Maybe at the age of 16 you're madly in love with your high-school sweetheart, and you find out they've been cheating on you. That could crush you. That could be a traumatic experience. And when that traumatic experience happens, a new belief can be formed. And now, at age 54, you're having a repeat of that experience from your teen years, because a belief was created around betrayal, and that belief is manifesting itself in your external world.

> *Limited beliefs that exist in our consciousness can be transformed and replaced with unlimited beliefs rooted in love.*

In addition, if you were abused as a child in your younger years—physically, sexually, emotionally, psychically—then odds are limited beliefs were created based on your experience.

Now, the great thing is that all of these beliefs can be healed. Every single one of them can be transformed. There's work involved, of course, but we can all do this as long as we are disciplined and determined enough.

Whatever limited beliefs exist in our consciousness can be transformed and replaced with unlimited beliefs that are rooted in love, the most powerful driver in all the Universe. That could be your reality. In fact, you can create a whole new system of beliefs that are truly unlimited. Those are the beliefs that set you free.

Social Media and Children's Beliefs

There is another place where children pick up limited beliefs nowadays. I think it's apparent that a lot of children are struggling right now, and that is because they have more than just their parents' limited beliefs influencing them. Children are absorbing many other beliefs with their newfound access to social media.

Children are very impressionable, and they are being bombarded with information. They are not just absorbing all the beliefs of their caregivers but also the beliefs of any social media influencers that they regularly watch or listen to.

As a kid, if you're being bombarded with messages and opinions and others' beliefs online, it's going to create a sort of energetic scattering. This is simply unhealthy and affects the brain chemistry of that developing child.

If I had young children, I would have a lot of guards in place around social media. Technology can be risky because it is a place where these beliefs can be curated, and unless, as a parent, you have guards in place, you don't have any control over this. Basically, if this door is left wide open, and your child has full opportunity in this world, it can turn into something that's very unhealthy. I often hear parents let their kids play games online, and sometimes into the middle of the night. This is an issue that is growing out of control in today's society. And long term, it can have consequences.

Kids have to deal with struggles at home, at school, and now online. It's too much for their nervous systems. These online stressors are ones that they don't even need to be experiencing, so it is up to the parents to step up and take charge of the situation to protect their children from these outside influences.

> *Children are absorbing many other beliefs with their newfound access to social media.*

It's one thing to have an influence, and it's an even better thing to have a really awesome influence on someone or something in your world. But, when there are a whole bunch of influences on a child, and they are scattered, and they are potentially limiting beliefs that are being repeated, it becomes a whole other thing entirely.

The messaging that children get from these social media giants amounts to collective programming. It needs to be taken seriously. If you're a parent, I'm not advocating for becoming a control freak, but if you're able to put your foot down and do the thing that's most right for you to be doing for your child, it's the best solution for your kids in the long run.

Generational Beliefs

Sometimes we are influenced by generational beliefs. One belief that a student brought up to me, in the context of family matters, was "Keep everything inside." This deep, hidden belief around not speaking out and not acknowledging the limited beliefs that she inherited from her family was something this student grew up with. She felt like this belief was buried deep within her programming and she might bring disrespect to her family if she explored her beliefs.

A belief like this is a biggie—no doubt about it—because this idea that you're going to disrespect your family or you're going to get in trouble for speaking out puts this constant external pressure on your psyche.

It also turns out that the opposite is actually true, meaning it's far more respectful to just let these beliefs come to the surface where you can see them and become conscious of them. This is actually a form of respect towards your family and your ancestry.

When we keep beliefs inside, we're attempting to trap that energy. Remember, beliefs, like everything else, according to the Law of Energy, are made up of energy. And according to the Law of Vibration, all energy must move.

When you go in there and attempt to interfere with energy and try to stop it from coming to the surface to be acknowledged, that is your ego interfering with it. If you allow the energy to move and you acknowledge it, then you have the opportunity to clear some of it. But up until this point in time, you may not have been able to do that.

That energy inside ultimately wants to move. It wants to manifest. According to Universal Law, it has to—even if you try to hold onto it.

Now, when you are first bringing up these beliefs, are you going to do it in a way in which you might embarrass or humiliate your family? Of course not. This is something that you can do privately, away from your family, at least for a period of time. Maybe you get a coach in your corner or a mentor or guide so that you can start to call up these beliefs, exposing them to the light instead of keeping them hidden.

Start to develop a relationship with the things you kept hidden.

You don't have to do this all at once, or all in one setting. In fact, you can do this one at a time. You can start to develop a relationship with these things you kept hidden. You can learn about them without making them or yourself wrong. You can even develop a level of fascination about these beliefs that have been limiting or restricting you.

Once you make contact with a belief, you can share it out loud with this one person—this coach, or guide, or mentor. At some later point, if you feel inspired, you can then share it with your family if the setting is right for you to do so.

There are a number of different ways to go about that. For example, at some point, when you're now aware of one of these beliefs that had been hidden in your consciousness, you might be having a conversation with your parents, and maybe you come up with a couple of questions to get Mom or Dad to open up a little bit around certain things that happened earlier on in life.

For example, maybe the belief is "Life always has to be a struggle." This is a pretty common belief that people inherit, and it's a tough one. I know of a couple people who have been working on clearing out this limited belief, and for the longest time, they wouldn't even touch this thing. It was like a hot potato! In fact, they were constantly gathering more evidence to prove that their life has to be this hard.

So, if you're having a conversation with Mom or Dad, you might ask, "On a scale of 1 to 10, when we were little, how hard was life?" Or you might ask, "How easy was life back then?" You can take it whatever direction you want, but in all likelihood, they will answer you right away because this is a relatively non-threatening question. Then, it might spark a conversation where you can check in with how far they want to go. You might be pleasantly surprised with how much information they offer you from that period of time.

Then, one of your questions could be, "Did you ever express it out loud, that life was a struggle?"

And they might respond, "Oh gosh, that was almost my mantra back in those days. I always seemed to be saying that."

Now, this is all good information for you to have—not to punish your parents but to answer the question of how you came to this belief and why this belief has become so strong. This process can be incredibly helpful, and it can be done in a very respectful way. But, before you even get to this point, you need to be willing to touch one of these beliefs.

Allow one of these beliefs to bubble up into your conscious awareness so that you can see it. Then, you can speak it out loud, to just one person to start. There's something wonderfully transformative that happens when we acknowledge, through spoken word, what we want to clear. It is then that we're coming to a place to ultimately resolve, heal, and transform these types of beliefs.

This is a higher strategy, a greater strategy, than keeping it all inside. Now you could keep these limited beliefs inside until the day you die, and you have the free will to do that, but it isn't the best strategy. It isn't even the healthiest strategy.

If your parents are no longer with you, it can be difficult to uncover these things and bring them to the surface. However, at any point, you can speak to your parents, deceased or not. At any point, you can acknowledge the beliefs that you've discovered with them in a loving way.

Again, this is not about placing blame on your parents, so therefore, you aren't disrespecting them. You can address these family beliefs while choosing to be respectful of everyone involved—in other words, you're not out to expose them; you're not out to make them wrong, or give them a hard time, or make them pay for the next 10 years of their existence. You can do this in such a way where you're just letting this come to the light so that it can be viewed clearly, for exactly how it is.

You might be pleasantly surprised to uncover that by doing this, you get deeper into this belief with the intention being to clear it, transform it, and heal it.

By you doing this, you're potentially also helping your parents, even if they're no longer with us anymore. You are connected to your ancestors on an energetic level. So as you shift, heal, and grow, you can not only affect your future lineage but your past as well. Your parents are a very real part of your ancestry, and they always will be. Whether they're here or not, energetically and soulfully, they can potentially benefit from this work that you find yourself inspired to do.

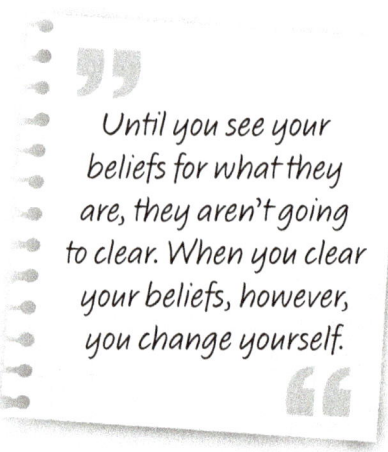

Until you see your beliefs for what they are, they aren't going to clear. When you clear your beliefs, however, you change yourself.

Until you see your beliefs for what they are, they aren't going to clear. They will follow you wherever you go in this life and the next, because they're inside of you. When you clear your beliefs, however, you change yourself. And you can even potentially change your ancestry and future lineage—they might just get the wonderful benefit of you accomplishing or achieving these types of changes.

Making these changes is a beautiful thing. It's an act of bravery to recognize our beliefs and transform them, and its benefits extend outward, into the past and the future.

EXERCISE: Uncovering Our Beliefs

In this exercise, you're going to begin to examine some of your beliefs. Here I'm inviting you, I'm encouraging you, to be as real as you possibly can be. Don't worry about disrespecting anyone; this exercise is intended for you to have an experience with yourself. We're going to try to accomplish a couple things here.

One is to bring your limiting beliefs to the surface so you can see them more clearly. Maybe you'll just want to focus on one to start. The second thing is that you might even jar an old belief loose that, as of this moment, you don't even know is inside of you, meaning you've completely forgotten about it. You've tucked it away so deep somewhere within your psyche, somewhere within your consciousness, that you possibly don't even know of its existence just yet.

So, there's a chance that one of these beliefs could get jarred loose during this exercise, or even later in this book, or at night while you sleep.

Uncovering your limited beliefs is so important because once you uncover them, you can begin the work to transform them. It is also important to uncover any unlimited beliefs that you have in order to strengthen them. Or to begin the creation of an unlimited belief.

Remember, the limited belief will create a restriction, whereas the unlimited belief will create freedom. The feelings are like night and day. So, start looking at your life and ask yourself, "Where do I feel restricted?" Then ask yourself, "Where do I feel free to be me?" If there are areas where you feel free, there is an unlimited belief somewhere.

So, take the following questions one at a time, and write down whatever comes up for you. Just put pen to paper and refrain from judging, editing, or evaluating your answer.

Exercise Question #1:
What did your father believe about life?

For this first question, we're going to give some energy to or attention to your father. This could be your biological dad, or, if you were raised by an adoptive father or another caregiver, write about this father figure. The key word you need here is "father."

What did your father believe about life? Was life hard? Was life easy? Was life complex? Was life simple? Was life misery? Was life fun? Was life good? Was life bad?

When answering this question, you can look for the results, but your father probably let you know, at some point, through his words, as well as his actions. Maybe when he was really angry or he was really down or depressed, some belief he held about life just rolled off the tip of his tongue. Or all of a sudden, he had a violent reaction to you or someone else around you. Now this reaction of his may not have even had anything to do with you, it was coming from inside of him, yet his explosion on you or onto someone else that you were witness to caused you to take this on as a belief.

Now the same can be said if he indicated what he believed about life when he was happy or relaxed or just enjoying himself.

Some of the examples of emotionalized limiting beliefs that parents might share include: "Children are inferior and don't deserve respect." "I can't win for losing." "People are out to get you." "Everyone else comes before me." "This is my life. I just have to accept it." "Money doesn't grow on trees." "I can't acknowledge my accomplishments."

As you write, make sure to check your breathing. It's important to keep breathing while you're engaged in this exercise.

Exercise Question #2:
What did your mother believe about life?

Repeat the previous question with your mother—either your biological mother or a mother figure. What did your mother believe about life?

Exercise Question #3:
What did your last partner believe about life?

For this exercise I'd like you to think of a previous partner, a current partner, a business partner, a lover, a close friend, or someone whom you were relatively close to in your past.

Now that you have a person in mind, consider: What did this person believe about life?

Again, check your breathing.

Now I would like you to take a few moments to reflect on this question and the previous two before you move onto question number four, which is what we are building up to.

Exercise Question #4:
What do YOU believe about life?

> What do YOU believe about your life right now, in present time? Write down your responses in your journal.

Some responses that I've received in my seminars include: "My only value is in what I can do for others." "I have to earn everything." "Love is conditional." "I don't deserve good things." "I get in my own way." "You have to do work that you don't like."

Some unlimited beliefs I have heard include: "I have no limits." "The purpose of life is to grow and become enlightened." "I can transcend collective programming and be safe." "Every day is a new day for growth." "I am blessed with abundance." "I have a destiny I am meant to fulfill." "I can attract anything I want."

> Now, for whatever particular belief or beliefs you've just written down, I want you to take this one step further and look for the evidence, both for your limited and unlimited beliefs.
>
> Remember, as within, so without. This means that if it is truly inside of you, especially if it's a strong belief, meaning it's fully emotionalized, you're going to spot this belief all over the place. You won't have an issue in coming up with evidence.

Now, your ego might trick you into thinking that you have a particularly appealing unlimited belief. But if you don't have any results to back that up, or if you have very few results to back that up, then that belief has not been fully emotionalized. You are just intellectualizing it. It's a belief that sounds good to you. Or your ego is tricking you so that you don't do any work for that belief to become fully rooted.

Remember, we don't get what we want; we get what we believe. So when that belief is strengthened in the root of love, meaning it will work for you, it will just automatically produce its corresponding reality 24/7 for you.

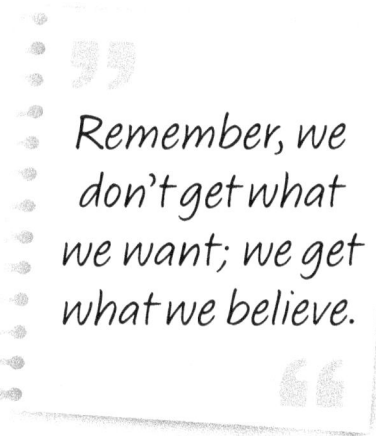

Remember, we don't get what we want; we get what we believe.

Examining our results is where we put this to the test because our results never lie whether they are pleasant or unpleasant for us to look at. We can lie to ourselves, but our results will reveal the truth.

Until you become the master of yourself, fully and completely, you'll want to take this to that testing-ground place. Your ego will try to hoodwink you. And looking at your results is a great way to put your beliefs—both the limited and the unlimited ones—to the test.

We have certain unlimited beliefs inside of us, in our consciousness, that are so well rooted that they produce a corresponding reality while we sleep at night. Our unlimited beliefs will do the same for us, if they aren't already. But we've got to put them to the test to see if they are rooted. If they are, they'll naturally produce. This is the Law of Correspondence in action. Our unlimited beliefs, once rooted, have the potential to free us to have a richer and more expansive experience in our day-to-day world and in all facets of our life..

In addition, it's important to uncover your limiting beliefs—especially those which have become emotionalized to the point of driving your results because these beliefs have the potential to block you; to hold you back from your own higher and greater good.

> So, evaluate which beliefs are producing evidence—producing a corresponding reality—to determine which beliefs are real. In the case of a limited belief, this could be an illness, an imbalance, or some discordant energy in your physical system.

A result is something that just happens naturally. In other words, you don't have to do anything. It's like a program on your computer that's running all the time. Whether you're aware of it or not, it will continuously produce an external reality that corresponds with it, and then it will repeat, and repeat, and repeat.

> So, check them out and put them to the test. If you think you have an unlimited belief, but you don't have the results to back it up, it could just be you have to do a little more work in order to root it more deeply. Once that happens, you'll have all kinds of experiences that show up naturally, organically, and effortlessly.

You'll want to check in with your results on a regular basis—at least once or twice a month. If you don't want to get hoodwinked by your ego anymore or if you just simply want to course correct, this is one of the most practical things you can do.

Now, I want you to look back at the first three questions again. What did your father believe about life? What did your mother believe about life? What did your last partner believe about life? And then, I'd like you to look for any connections between your answers to the first three questions and your answers to question number four: What do YOU believe about life? Are there any connections between what you now believe about life versus what your mother believed about life? Versus what your father believed about life? Versus what your last partner or your last closest friend believed about life?

Exercise Question #5:
Discoveries I've made are...

In this section, I would like you to write about any discoveries you've made. Whatever these discoveries are, go ahead and write them down in this section.

Maybe you've taken on some of your dad's beliefs to be like him in order to secure his love and acceptance. Maybe your beliefs are synthesized from your mother, your father, and/or your previous partner. Maybe you've discovered that you have, in fact, reprogrammed some of your old beliefs. There are huge discoveries that can be made here.

If you discover that there are beliefs that were impressed upon you by your mother, father, or partner, ask yourself, are these limited beliefs or unlimited beliefs?

If you can make the connection between your beliefs and those of your mother, father, or partner, it will help you in your process of transforming that limiting belief or possibly strengthening that unlimited belief within your own consciousness.

I've done this exercise with students many times over the years, and most commonly, people will connect with beliefs of all three of these individuals. When people start to connect the dots, it's an incredible revelation that these other people were so impactful on their psyche or their subconscious.

You might even have realized that your very beliefs are the ones as a child you swore you would never take on. Maybe you had a judgment against Mom or Dad. Fast forward a few years, and you've turned out just like them in many ways.

Sometimes we take on beliefs that are the opposite of what our parents had. And other times we have possibly adopted their beliefs on an unconscious level. We make the ultimate sacrifice in order to retain their approval; in order to be a part of the tribe. Some of us are terrified of losing a parent's approval or losing the approval of our tribe. We might even find ourselves making day-to-day choices based on this fear, in relation to that person or that tribe.

We may inherit both positive and negative beliefs from our parents. For example, we may have unlimited beliefs about finances but limited beliefs about relationships. For instance, you could have a belief from your father that investing in property helps to secure a better future. This belief may manifest in your reality of knowing which properties to invest in at the right time. Through this belief, you might even attract great opportunities.

On the other hand, you may have inherited a belief from your mother about not being able to trust men. Obviously, this belief is limited and will create a reality that corresponds with it. In this case, one of two things can happen. The first thing is the type of men who come into your life that were not even worthy of your trust from the very beginning of that relationship. You were just trying to make them worthy of your trust. That is until you realized, and more than likely had a painful realization, that no matter how hard you tried, you were never going to make them worthy of your trust.

> *We can lie to ourselves, but our results will reveal the truth.*

You were possibly then forced into seeing the ugly reality of what it was you cocreated with this other person. Now this all stems from the limited belief that you've been running around with in your own consciousness that says you can't trust men.

This belief is going to attract the type of man that you can't trust because he has his own issues with trusting himself. You're not going to attract a man who has cleared all that up—a man who really knows himself; is strong, solid, well centered, and well balanced; a man who doesn't need you to give him your trust right away and is a-okay with being willing to earn your trust.

There's another option here… Throughout the years I've come across a few women who had gotten stuck in another dynamic in order to escape this one, because it was so painful. This is when they went into isolation and basically became single for the next 15 to 20 years of their life. (Now please understand that this is not what they wanted. They would sometimes share with me that they wanted to be in a new relationship—and yet that seemed to escape them.) This type of a limited belief was imposing a restriction on their desire to be in a new relationship.

If you were to clear out this limited belief, however, and replace it with an unlimited belief that says, "men are trustworthy," then you will be able to spot the types of men who have cleared up their own issues around trust. One of the ways in which you will be able to spot them is that they will not ask you to trust them completely with your bank account within the first month of you meeting. In fact, they may never ask for the keys to your bank account. Once again, they will be a-okay with earning your trust.

Now, they probably won't want to have to take the next ten years to prove their worth to you, but more than likely they'll be happy to embrace this process of earning your trust for the first year or so.

How will a man like this prove he's worthy to you? You'll have plenty of experiences with him to look at and plenty of situations to observe. Take a look at how he lives his life. Take a look at how he is with other people in his life. Do other people who are already in his life trust him? And when situations arise in your life together, how does he show up with you?

Another way to examine these beliefs that have been passed on from your parents is to examine the results in your parents' lives. If your mother doesn't believe that men can be trusted, examine your mother's results. This can be done lightly and without judgment of your mother. Simply ask yourself: What type of men does she attract? What kinds of experiences does she have? Are they light? Are they fun? Are they joyful? Are they fulfilling? Are they meaningful? Are they deeply connected?

Explore it. You'll see it, and you'll know for a fact that this belief is limited.

Now the second thing is that if you can see these results in yourself, too, you've got a double whammy. So, what does this mean? It means you've got to roll up your sleeves and clear it. It might take a little time to pull this off, but it will be worth it because as the new unlimited belief comes in, remember that it equates to freedom.

If you have issues with trust in your relationships, just ask yourself: How free would it be to genuinely and totally trust my partner? Really think about this. Think about what it would be like to totally trust the person you're with and to have them trust you.

This doesn't only apply in romantic relationships but in business partnerships, friendships, parent-child relationships, and even employer-employee or customer-salesperson relationships. Trust is liberating across the board.

The important thing to remember here is that all of these are just beliefs. Beliefs, like everything else, are made up of energy. They can be changed. They can be healed. They can be transformed.

The process of ultimately transforming a belief entails going into that unpleasant feeling, that unpleasant experience, and really confronting it, taking ownership of it, and starting to work with it consciously. It needs to be acknowledged and purposefully brought into the light—so that you can ultimately learn the lesson you need to in clearing it.

So, through this reflective exercise you may have uncovered that you've taken on some of these beliefs from Mom and Dad. And, deep down inside, you may feel like you're going to disrespect or dishonor them if you let this belief go. Now, you might identify with this right away, or this might sound really weird—but there is a reason why this happens.

Since you were a child, you have shown unconditional love to your mom and dad, and part of this was taking on their stuff. It's like what a dog does with his owner—a dog will take on his owner's stuff. Why? Because the dog loves his owner without condition. And when you're a kid, you typically love your mom and your dad without condition. And this is where that transference clearly, at the very least, can happen and often does. If you can, identify with this without judging it. Do remember, these are just beliefs—all of which can be changed and transformed.

Freedom Beliefs and Prison Beliefs

In your journal, create a two-column chart. Title the right column "Freedom Beliefs." Title the left column "Prison Beliefs."

Freedom Beliefs	Prison Beliefs

Now, write down up to five beliefs in each column. The Freedom Beliefs are your unlimited beliefs, and the Prison Beliefs are your limited beliefs that you have right now, in current time.

As you are coming up with these, you can go back and forth. Or maybe you start with one column and then move on to the other. There is no right or wrong way of doing this.

The freedom belief is always in alignment with your greater truth, as it's already in alignment with the person YOU REALLY ARE. These freedom beliefs are potent. They're powerful. They're literally earth-shattering. When you begin to line yourself up with an unlimited belief, and that unlimited belief gets well rooted into your consciousness, it gets stronger over time.

The prison beliefs are the opposite of the freedom beliefs in that they are falsehoods. They are illusions. That prison belief, no matter how hard you try, come the end of your life, will never be a truth. Now, that said, you can believe that limited prison belief as truth. In fact, 97 percent of the people on this planet who have not yet created the life of their dreams are living in accordance with belief systems based on limited, prison-oriented beliefs that they have come to accept as true. The power is not just in the limited belief; rather, it's in the act or the choice of them believing that these types of limited beliefs are actually real and/or true, when, in fact, they are not.

Collectively, humanity has been struggling with this for thousands of years now. We've been trapped in this lower energy system of beliefs. The problem is that we don't understand what we got trapped into. Once we come to a conscious awareness of this and then become willing to change and are courageous and brave enough to work at this, we can change it. We are all destined to change this, and some of us already have.

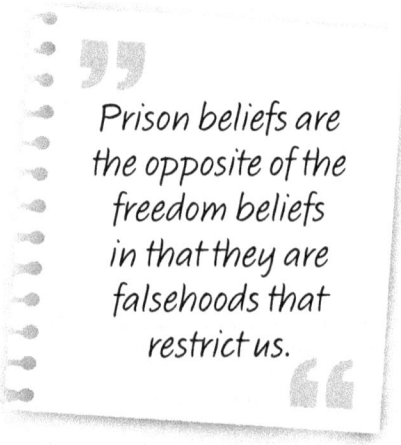

Prison beliefs are the opposite of the freedom beliefs in that they are falsehoods that restrict us.

This was never how life was intended to be. This was a fall from grace. We have been hoodwinked into a system of beliefs which have been doing nothing more than keeping us in an energy of limitation—restricting us and holding us back from our higher and greater truth, both individually and collectively.

In order to access that Greater Destiny, it's critically important that we get a better, deeper, richer understanding of this belief system that's inside of our consciousness.

Once we do, we can begin to intentionally, consciously pluck out those beliefs that are no longer serving us—those prison beliefs, those limited beliefs. We've got to pluck them out, just like you would a weed in your garden. Maybe you've got a garden full of nasty weeds that have been growing there for the last 28 years. You might literally have to pluck them out one at a time because they're so well rooted into the earth. Maybe these weeds are entangled into the roots of other weeds that have been growing in your garden for the last 28 years. This stuff takes work! But as we do this, we create the space to have a beautiful garden—a system of freedom beliefs, of unlimited beliefs, of beliefs designed to liberate us and empower us. These beliefs will bring us into alignment with our greatest truth, our highest truth.

It is your time, it is our time collectively, to really get this, to comprehend this, to understand this—and to be willing to see this, to be willing to work through whatever we need to work through in order to have something better, richer, more alive, vibrant and radiant.

CHAPTER 6

THE CREATIVE STATE

In order to consciously manifest, we need to set up our creative state. There are four areas of life that we want to be aware of, as they influence this creative state. To evaluate where you're currently at and where you can improve, we're going to explore some questions. Take out your journal and a pen and come up with a number, on a scale of 1 to 10, where you feel you're currently at in these areas:

AREA 1: Wanting Your Life

So, the first question we are going to explore is: How much do you want your life? Rate this on a scale of 1 to 10, 10 being a lot, 1 being very little. If you really want the life you have, for example, you will answer 10. If you completely hate your life—if you think it utterly sucks—then you will answer a 1. Maybe you'd rather have someone else's life, but yours will do for now—your number might be somewhere in the middle. Now reflect on your number... and as you do, answer this, "Why did you come up with this number for yourself?"

If you gave your life a score of 8 or higher, you more than likely see your life as sacred. You see your life as a gift. You see your life as something that you greatly value. You cherish your life.

Even if you didn't give yourself a higher number, rest assured that there was a time you did. And believe it or not, it was prior to your conception that you really wanted this life.

Consider all of the Souls lined up for their very next lifetime experience, waiting to possibly incarnate. All of these Souls want a life, and then, 20, 30, or 40 years later, all of a sudden, some of them no longer want it. In fact, they may want someone else's life, or they may simply not value life at all.

There's a reason for this… After our conception, after our Soul becomes a human child, we might find ourselves in a family of darkness, a family of dysfunction, a family of imbalance, a family of negativity, or a family of aggression. And no matter what kind of family we're born into, at some point, upon entering into that family, the ego gets created again.

Once your life gives birth to that ego, all bets are off. Now the ego creates from a level of survival and separation—which are a couple of the reasons as to why the ego can resist change and forward movement. As learned about in book number one of the Trilogy, the ego can be easily threatened and does all that it knows to maintain status quo. As the ego starts to get stronger, it begins to take center stage and basically bumps the Soul out of your lower field of consciousness. It then takes over your lower field along with the other aspects of your personality—as in aspects of your shadow side and of your inner child.

At this point, we're basically at the whim of our ego, which is also at the whim of the collective ego of our family. Once we're at the whim of all of that, if our family is overtaken by dark energy and/or a dark family history, it's going to result in a dark life for us. This could become the point at which we begin to think, *I could care less if I die.* We think in order to survive through this experience, we have to be tough. We develop a hard exterior and shut down from others. We possibly have to stop caring.

> *We can't create a new reality based on a life of our greatest dreams when we are still focused on our past failures.*

However, your Soul or an aspect of your Higher Self isn't completely silent. And odds are, at some point, you're going to start listening to your Higher Self or Soul. Your Soul might prompt you to attend an event, spend some time with a particular person, or go to a particular place. Your Soul will likely guide you to something that will help pull you out of this experience of not wanting your life. Your Soul will bring you back into alignment—back to where you were prior to being conceived, when your desire for life was true, strong, and genuine. You get a taste of this remembrance—remembering what it was like to enthusiastically desire this life. This doesn't mean that you're embodying your Soul or Higher Self just yet, but you are experiencing an aspect of truth at soul level.

These remembrances can stack up and get stronger over time. Your Soul will guide you towards the right people, experiences, and places—if and when you get to the point of self-realization, which is where you really get connected to yourself as a Soul. This is when you completely remember your genuine desire for life and from this point forward you follow through on the inner prompts of your Soul or Higher Self without question. You will have deeper, richer moments where you feel, *I really want to be here. I am very glad to be here. I really want this life.* As we begin to have these moments, we come to realize that, unlike the ego that is creating from the level of surviving and separation, the Soul creates from the level of thriving and unification. You see, we can't create a new reality based on a life of our greatest dreams when we are still focused on our past failures, losses, mistakes, or even trauma from some previous time—which is where the ego can influence us to stay. This means we're no longer present at least in that moment.

Now to create the life of our dreams, it is best done from the level of our Soul—which is already wise and whole. From this place we can draw in the help we genuinely need, for whatever it is we need to assist us in achieving our greater goal. When we're operating at and from Soul level, it's automatically recognized that whatever it is we genuinely desire to see manifest in our own personal universe will and does require the assistance from the Divine or the Universe.

This self-realization is also a significant step towards complete embodiment. Embodiment of the Soul or Higher Self may or may not happen within this lifetime. Each individual Soul decides if this is the case. However, every single Soul does strive to be in this state of remembrance. Your Soul wants you to desire your life. And as our desire for life remains strong and steady, it helps us to remain more present in our own day-to-day life.

When we truly want our life, we then see it as sacred. We naturally cherish it as a gift given to us by God, the Universe, and/or our Higher Soul Self—whatever term we'd like to use. It doesn't matter. What matters is we continue to remember and even acknowledge our life here as a divine gift. Genuinely wanting our life is one of the key essentials for actually being more present in our life. This idea of being more present in our daily life is what empowers us to become better at manifesting on a conscious level. You might recall in a previous chapter where we learned the best place to create and manifest from (which is the Present Self). One of the biggest lessons for us as individuals to ultimately learn is how to live our life in and from the moment of NOW.

Some people struggle left, right, and center when it comes to this area. They're in this internal fight where they don't really want this life they're currently in. Or they want their life today—as in this moment—but as soon as life presents a few challenges or problems, they don't want it anymore. As soon as they get stressed, they don't cherish their existence. As soon as they become anxious, they place little value on their life. As soon as something negative happens, so to speak, they sometimes want to run away from their life. They attempt to push their life away. This is where the person can become non-present. And when we're not present, we're not able to create anything new.

This is also where we can potentially hurt ourselves. Just ask the person who took a fall as they were walking down the street, or stubbed their toe on something, or took a misstep in ascending or descending a flight of stairs. When someone becomes non-present, they typically fall into what's known as repeat mode. If they're doing this on a more regular basis, they might even begin to feel at some point, like they're having a Groundhog Day moment. Remember, to create the life of our dreams, we need our creativity. To be in touch with and in flow with our creativity, we need to be present in the here and now.

If this is where you are right now. You're getting a personalized snapshot of your perspective. There is no right or wrong perspective, of course. Your perspective, however, might be distorted based on a limited, restrictive belief system, lower energy patterns, or shadow aspects of your personality that just haven't been cleared or transformed yet. Now even though one's perspective regardless of where it's currently at is not wrong—it just IS. It would be helpful to recognize that it is also changeable. Meaning it can be changed, healed, and leveled up.

> Acceptance of your current reality here is key. The more honest you are with these questions, the more opportunity you'll have to advance your own personal growth and your Soul's evolution.
>
> This book carries great potential for anyone and everyone who is committed and dedicated to helping themselves really get better at creating the life they most desire. To do this we want to rise to the highest vibratory state within ourselves to create with. Now this might take a while to get there. Be patient and persistent in your learning process, or if you're an older Soul in the process of remembering how to actually do this.
>
> Your answers in our opening question in this section and the three that follow are just indicators of your current vibrational frequency. A higher number—a number, for example, that indicates the current desire you really have for your life at this time—will indicate where you're at in present time. If you want to change or raise the vibrational frequency you currently have for your life... you can. We all can. To assist us in doing so, it would be helpful to purposely return back on a regular basis to these questions to simply check in with ourselves to reflect on the state we're currently in.

AREA 2: Gratitude for Your Life

> The second question is related to the first, with your pen and notepad, write your answers to the following: How much gratitude do you feel for your daily life? And how much do you express it? On a scale of 1 to 10, 10 being you're constantly expressing gratitude multiple times a day, and 1 being you never express gratitude, how much thanks are you expressing for your life? Look back over the past 30 days. Maybe it's hit or miss—some days you do, and some days you don't. How much gratitude do you feel today? Whatever your number, there's no right or wrong answer as long as you're being honest with yourself. Now reflect on why you gave the number you did.

Gratitude, or more specifically, the feeling of gratitude in our body, is what can elevate us to that higher vibrational state mentioned above. For gratitude is a state. A state of being that is. When we feel gratitude for our life as it is... it rather quickly can lift us up to a higher octave where we feel better about ourselves and our lives. One of the master keys here is: to live from an attitude of gratitude for that of *what it is we've already been given*. Whether it's the pain, the healing, the victory, the positive, the negative... we are grateful for it all. For every what it is we need, begins with being grateful. In book two of our Transformation Trilogy, we learn about one of our divine birthrights, GRACE. To experience more grace in our life has everything to do with how often we are grateful for our day-to-day life.

Can we practice gratitude when our life throws us a curve ball—something that we we're not expecting and yet, there it is? Can we practice it when something or someone gives us a problem or there's some hiccup or roadblock presenting something to us that challenges us? What do we do then with our gratitude? And yet, whatever that is that's challenging us more than likely has some kind of a message that we're to be giving attention to, or a lesson that were to be learning, or perhaps a test we're being presented with by the Universe to see how far we've come along in our transformational journey. Hmmm, might this be something to be grateful for?

Is there a possibility of a miracle manifesting if you were to truly get the message that the Universe or your Higher Self is sending, or actually embrace and learn the lesson, or pass the test that your life is presenting to you? Well, first of all, do you believe in the possibilities of miracles happening in your life? Albert Einstein said, "There are only two ways to live your life. One is as though nothing is a miracle. The other is as though everything is a miracle." So, which is it for you? You get to choose.

> Again, your number indicates your vibrational state, which can change and shift, so be mindful of what lowers your number. Maybe you're doing great and practicing gratitude every day, and then something negative happens and you stop the practice for a short while until something else happens that reminds you to return back to living in gratitude. Being mindful of this and reflecting on these factors will help keep you on track.

AREA 3: Loving Your Life

> This third area has to do with love. Now this is a biggie. The greater truth of our existence is that we're all destined to be in an abundance of love. At a subatomic level, we are made up of love particles. It's who we fundamentally are. So, this question differs from the first question because it considers that love energy: How much do you want your life?

So, on a scale of 1 to 10, in current time, *how much do you love your life?* Now, if your answer is 10, you're completely in love with your life. If your answer is a 1, maybe you're not sure if you can even love your life. If you're somewhere in the middle, perhaps you've been going back and forth when it comes to the love you feel in your own life. Another helpful question to consider in examining this area of your life would be, is when the last time was that you heard these words come out of your mouth? *"I love my life... I just love my life."*

Now whatever your number is, consider why you gave yourself that number. Again, you're going to want to be as honest as you know how to be with yourself because more than likely there is going to be an experience that will possibly test that answer. Your Higher Self and the Universe are going to co-facilitate an experience that tests your love for life. This might sound cruel, but it's actually an awesome thing that we have those tests, because if we didn't, we wouldn't have a measure of how well we're doing! The challenges that arise become blessings—these are wonderful gifts or even miracles for our Soul's evolution. Oh, perhaps this is possibly something else to be grateful for?

Loving life is equivalent to living our life in joy, as they go hand in hand. Living in joy is how we can use the Law of Attraction powerfully in consciously manifesting our heart-felt desires. Next to gratitude this is also one of the highest points in state when we're living our lives in joy or with joy. Sanaya Roman channeled a book with a timeless being of love and light named Orin in the nineties. This is where I first experienced and remembered, thanks to their book *Living with Joy*, that when we're in the higher state of joy, we are naturally aligned with our Soul... our Higher Self. This state of joy automatically raises us to a higher octave in working with the Law of Attraction. Our life just flows better when we're operating at this octave. In other words, when we're experiencing our life as a wonderful thing versus a dreadful thing, it strengthens the positive side of one's electromagnetic field. This is where things that need to come together for our higher, greater good in the overall process of manifesting our desires, dreams, intentions or goals simply fall into place with more ease and grace.

Here's a little tip: happiness within us naturally increases as we become more grateful for everyone and everything in our own life. It's the heartfelt gratitude that leads to miracles and more blessings. More is given to those who live in gratitude—therefore, giving us more to be grateful for. Like attracts more like to itself. That is the Law of Attraction.

> Are you in love with the life you currently have? Give your answer a strength level: between 1 to 10... 1 representing not at all, 10 representing very much so. To successfully create the life of one's dreams, we would be at a place along our journey where we can honestly say we love the life we now have. It's another one of the master keys: which is to first create the life we love. This is what truly sets the stage for manifesting the life of our dreams. It's the loving of the life we currently have... AS IT IS.
>
> If you haven't yet fallen in love with your life, or if you don't know how, you might view it as starting a love affair with life... your life. Now if there are parts of your life that you don't love, then know you can change it. It might not be easy to do so due to what might be required for you to confront, clear, and perhaps let go of in your life personally and/or professionally, whether it's a situation, a person, or an old way of being (such as a behavioral pattern or even addiction). You may possibly need to re-organize or re-prioritize something. Whatever it is, it's a wise choice to purposely monitor your progress in this area of giving attention to this powerful and transformative question: *How much do you love your life?* Loving your life is equivalent to loving

yourself. As you learn how to love your life, you're also discovering how to better love yourself, as these two love dynamics further complement each other.

What we're looking for with this question is your answer in the present moment. The present is very important because that's where your power for manifesting at a conscious level is the strongest. The present moment empowers your creative state, bringing it to a higher octave or level. And as you rise to that higher level, it will be clear—as you'll have the results to back it up. The type of results that manifest in your day-to-day world will be of that higher, greater level.

AREA 4: Feeling Good Naturally

I would like to preface this question with a discussion on productivity. This "good feeling" has a lot to do with productivity, because true productivity is produced from higher-vibrational feelings. When you're able to naturally feel good and sustain it, you'll become a powerhouse of productivity. In fact, I designed an online course entitled Productivity Powerhouse that goes much deeper into this amazing topic.

Productivity is an art. It's also an aspect of mastery. For example, when you look at, for example, in salespeople, there are some who produce ten times what their sales colleagues produce, and they do it like clockwork. Why is that? It's not because they're stressing themselves out. It's not even because they're trying extra hard. In fact, it's the complete opposite.

It's because they know what to do and they just do it—which makes them feel great. It's second nature for them. These high-vibration feelings are so powerful that not only will they level you up to a whole new state of productivity, but they will also open the doorway to ascending to a higher state of creativity.

> So, for this question, get out your pen and notepad and think about the past seven days, and ask yourself: How much of this period of time did you naturally feel good? Naturally being without stimulants, alcohol, marijuana, prescription drugs, or other chemical inputs. In this case, giving yourself a 10 would mean that over the last seven days, you've felt completely amazing, and a 1 would mean that you've felt extremely heavy or negative over the past seven days, and perhaps you've needed chemical inputs to even feel OK. Then, consider the reasons why. If you did, why did you need these chemicals? What perhaps kept you from naturally feeling good?
>
> What was it that helped you feel good naturally? Maybe you're feeling good because you've finally solved a problem or healed an old issue. Maybe you're feeling resilient and energized. Maybe you've had some frustration—but running, dancing, or listening to music has kept your spirits up. Maybe you've been prioritizing your self-care, or you've found yourself seeking out ways to laugh more, cook more, or to connect and have good conversations with more amazing people. Maybe you've been devoting time to helping others or taking care of your body.
>
> Or maybe you need two or three more caffeine-based products to get you through the day, or perhaps alcohol or marijuana to get to sleep at night. Maybe you feel depressed or have low energy and can't remember the last time you felt good naturally. Whatever your answer, the most important thing here is to be honest with yourself.

Feeling good means that we're vibrating at a higher frequency. Sometimes, when we're feeling really good—naturally and organically—for days or weeks at a time, there could be a lower frequency within us that has been suppressed, that activates from our subconscious and comes to the surface, directly opposing this higher frequency. This is generally a negative or heavy emotion or a restrictive thought pattern.

Here's an example... You'd think that other people would be attracted to that high frequency—that your higher frequency would help to lift theirs up. Sometimes, however, that isn't the case. Say you're naturally feeling good, and you have been for the last five days. Your frequency is high, and the higher frequency you're experiencing is continuously propelling you up—and keeping you there. You walk into a meeting with a group of friends... Say, there are four friends there, and two of them normally don't feel good. The only way they feel good is if they get buzzed or even completely drunk, and then they feel good for a short while. But once they come down off of the high from that alcohol, they're feeling the hangover. So, then they might feel a little nasty, or even miserable. Maybe these two friends have been feeling like this way for weeks.

And, not thinking about their state, you just walk in, being yourself. You're feeling good, and at some point, they start to pick up on it. How are they going to react to you at this point?

Do you think they're going to respond to you with: "Your energy is so contagious. You are a life saver. Your happiness is so inspiring to me—it's helping me turn my day around. I've been in a funk for the last three weeks, and just by you walking in this room, I'm feeling better already!" Is that how they're gonna show up with you?

Probably not... at least with the two of them that have been living their lives in that lower energy for a while.

And why is that? Well, they've been stuck in this negative vibration for the last three weeks. The last thing they want when in this place is to walk into the energy of somebody that's in a feeling state of a higher vibration. So, what are they gonna do? More than likely, they're going to resist you. Heck, they might even react to you with their negative energy. They might say something nasty to you. They might condescend. And if they don't do it with their words, they may well do it in their thoughts. You might see it in their body language, or just feel it in your own body. In a matter of minutes, you might feel a truckload of judgment come off them.

> *More is given to those who live in gratitude—therefore, giving us more to be grateful for.*

Now you're experiencing an energy that directly opposes you as you walk into this room. If you're not aware of this, then that in itself could be devastating to you—it could take you down. You entered the room in this higher-vibrational feeling state, and by the time you're done with this get-together, you're practically crawling out of the room! Clearly something's happened to you that's very different than what was going on with you before you joined your friends. That good feeling you had is gone—at least temporarily.

Now you are feeling something that's more in alignment with the vibrational frequency of those two individuals who were stuck in that negative state of feeling for the last three weeks. It might not be the exact same, but at a frequency level, it's similar.

Why do they have the power to bring you down?

Well, remember that what happens on the inside will happen on the outside. This is the Law of Correspondence at play: as within, so without. Maybe you get to the point where you're actually starting to feel good about something or someone, or maybe you just accomplished something. Maybe you just completed a big project you took on, and you're feeling so amazing to be on the other side of this thing. Or maybe you just had a wonderful experience with somebody you really respect, like, or care for. As in, something went really well for you, and you're feeling good, and then something else happened that keeps you feeling good. And it goes on like this for two or three days.

If you have a lot of resistance inside of you, if you have anger inside of you, if you have sadness inside of you, if you have depression inside of you, if you have jealousy inside of you, if you have insecurity inside of you—these lower frequencies can surface and directly oppose that higher frequency of feeling good. Something on the outside will trigger these feelings, if, in fact, they're there.

And yet, if you're going to operate from this higher, more powerful creative state to manifest from, you're gonna need to maintain that naturally good feeling. Obviously, this isn't easy to do. If it was easy, everybody on Planet Earth would've already done it! They'd be living in this good-feeling state 24-7, nonstop. And they would be living there without the devices or substances they once needed to numb themselves out with, to keep from feeling the suppressed feelings or emotions that they hadn't allowed themselves to feel yet.

If we don't become conscious of these suppressed feelings and process them through, this is one of the many reasons as to why we are not able to sustain that good feeling state. To this, we don't understand that what is on the inside of us will eventually surface. And when it does, it is more than likely when we least expect it.

> If you're going to utilize your creative state in a higher and greater way, you've got to get to the bottom of these feelings that surface and ultimately heal or transform them.
>
> So, once again let's revisit this question: as you reflect back over the past seven days: *How much of this period of time did you naturally feel good?* A 10 would be that over the last seven days, you've felt completely amazing, and a 1 would be that you've felt extremely heavy or negative over the past seven days. Then answer, why did you give yourself this number?

Maintaining the 4 Areas:
Your Baseline for Manifesting on a Conscious Level

In order to have regular access to a higher creative state, we would have mastered or at least be well on our way to mastery of all four of these areas—wanting life, having gratitude for life, loving life, and feeling good. This is where we would have consistent, high numbers in these areas—which would have become sustainable.

You have to want your life, even when it isn't convenient—even when your world is turned upside down. In fact, it's when your world is upside down when you can really evaluate how strong and steady your desire is for your life. It's like being in a committed relationship or partnership with someone that you truly love and respect. What happens to the love when a challenge or issue presents itself? Do we take our love away from the other? Do we stop loving them for a week when we become challenged in the relationship? Probably not... We still love our partner or friend while we go through the challenge or consciously deal with the issue at hand.

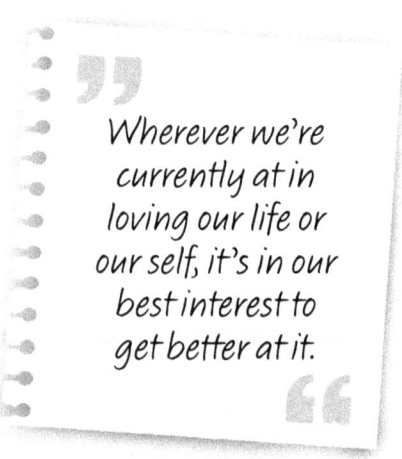

> Wherever we're currently at in loving our life or our self, it's in our best interest to get better at it.

We want gratitude to be a lifestyle, even if it's unfamiliar to us. We probably have people in our life right now that we've done some really nice things for, or consistently do really nice things for, and they haven't thanked us, or when they do, it's insincere or the gratitude is doled out sparingly. Because they don't live in gratitude. Somebody who lives in gratitude expresses it often and genuinely.

For many of us, we have to practice this powerful thing called love and we have to apply it to our life. There'll be people that will come into our life that we'll love, and then they'll go. But come the end of the day, we have our self—we have our life. Wherever we're currently at in loving our life or our self, it's in our best interest to get better at it.

The goal could be to literally fall in love with our life. When we're in love with our life, we naturally feel good about our self. When we are feeling good, our life simply works better. Things become a little easier, lighter, and happier. It's the gift of feeling good that keeps on giving. Boy, if everybody on our planet took the time to learn how to do this, and actually did it, there would be no more wars on Planet Earth. People all over the world would be creating wonderful things and beautiful, life-enriching experiences.

There is great significance in our *state of being* when it comes to manifesting at a conscious level. It's an understanding of the way the Universe works. It simply responds to our thoughts, feelings, and actions that are repeated over and over again. There will be much more on thoughts, feelings, and actions as we dive into the powers and principles later on in this book.

All States of Being vibrate at different frequencies. All of which the Universe just responds to. All manifestation (conscious or unconscious) is first preceded by vibration. We could say our current reality is nothing more than the vibrational state of frequency in which we've been living or operating at.

This also implies that if we want a better, richer, healthier reality, we can do so by raising our inner frequency to a higher State of Being. This is where our state of feeling comes into play—as in feeling in love or being in love. Or feeling joy as a result of engaging in a kind act or bringing joy to someone else. Or living in the feeling of gratitude for what it is that's already been given. These are all powerful feelings or emotions, as they simply elevate us to Higher States of Being when we are actually feeling these powerful emotions in our body.

In conclusion, begin evaluating these four areas on a consistent basis. And continue to practice the aforementioned ideas, working with the exercises based around the questions, as a way to increase your awareness of these key areas. Once you get really high numbers in all four areas, you'll be consistently vibrating at a higher frequency and your creative power will be primed for intentional conscious manifestation.

CHAPTER 7
THE INNER MANIFESTING POWERS

In addition to Universal Laws, there are specific Inner Powers that are going to assist you on your journey to manifesting at a conscious level. Remember, consistent application is what is important, as well as a depth of understanding.

An Inner Power is much like an inner muscle... We aren't able to see the inner workings of the Inner Power just as we aren't able to see the inner workings of our muscles. We can see the development of our physical muscles on the outside—just as we can see the development of the Inner Power on the outside in how that power is being utilized, or possibly even being suppressed. An Inner Power such as those listed below are aspects that make up your overall personal power. This is the power you are going to need if you want to get better at consciously manifesting whatever it is you genuinely would like to see manifest in your own personal universe.

POWER 1: The Power of Imagination

The first power is the Power of Imagination. Now everybody has an imagination. Everybody. It is another Inner Power that you were endowed with from the very beginning. Albert Einstein once said, "Imagination is everything. It is the preview of life's coming attractions."

This is another power that we've been likely misusing. I'll give you an example. Let's say you're in a loop of negative thinking, griping, complaining, judging, being overly critical and angry. You're really angry at somebody, and you've been in this place for a few days. You're feeling bitter, and you've decided you're going to give this person the silent treatment for the next week.

Thoughts go around in your head, like, *"They'll be sorry they did that."* Or *"I'm going to make them pay for what they did."* And to that, we can even start building the case in our mind of what we are going to say to them or how we are going to be toward them when we are with them next.

Obviously, you haven't gotten the memo yet, or you've lost the memo. Because here's what you've been doing: You've been using this Inner Power that you were endowed with in a negative and possibly even a harmful way.

As you live this way, whether you are aware of it or not, it automatically activates that Inner Power of Imagination. You can't stop this from happening. So now you're imagining the worst. You're imagining the worst about that individual. This can be applied to all sorts of situations outside of personal relationships. Maybe you're imagining the worst about a project. Or you're imagining the worst about a business or career direction. Wherever it is or whoever it is that you're imagining the worst possible outcome with, what you're really doing is imagining the worst about yourself. Remember we are the center of our own universe. So, whatever I'm thinking or feeling about you, I'm also thinking or feeling the exact same way about myself. I just might not be aware of this yet.

What do you suppose happens when you get really stressed or anxious over something that's going on in your world? What do you suppose happens with this Inner Power of Imagination then? Are you utilizing this power correctly when you're all stressed and anxious? Probably not.

> *Whatever I'm thinking or feeling about someone, I'm also thinking or feeling about myself. I just might not be aware of it yet.*

Rather, you're utilizing it incorrectly. In fact, you're utilizing it to hurt yourself, or possibly hold yourself back from something that could be beneficial for you. This innate ability is so powerful that you have the potential to damage yourself beyond repair in this life. Einstein also said, "Your imagination is so powerful. It's more powerful than any piece of knowledge that you'll ever come across."

And yet people have been misusing their imaginations for lifetimes. Talk about a lack of understanding. It's huge. Most of us don't even know we're doing it. We've got to get a handle on this one because when it comes to manifesting, how we use our imagination can determine what manifests next.

If we've been manifesting things we don't want—lack, scarcity, stress, anxiety, broken relationships, financial despair, etcetera—and we want to stop this, it's simple... Just stop using our imagination incorrectly and start using it correctly.

Years ago, I developed a course for a company that became a huge hit. Four hundred people took this course, and it rocked their worlds. The title of this course was Life Is a Do-It-to-Yourself Project.

There were a few people who were upset about it, however. They only attended because it was their boss who told them they had to.

Now the boss was completely on board. All of their executives were on board. All of their high-level managers were on board. They could not wait for me to deliver this seminar because at the time they could not get through to their people. The amount of blame and defensiveness that was going on in that company was destroying their productivity. It was a serious problem that I was asked to come in and help solve. And we solved it.

As I already mentioned, there were a few people there who got upset with me and with their employer. There were a few that didn't stay with the course, and a few people who even quit working for the company (which turned out to be a blessing in disguise).

I learned some time ago that life really is a do-it-to-yourself project. When we are using this Inner Power of Imagination incorrectly, we are literally doing it to ourselves in the most negative, most harmful, and the nastiest of ways. And then if we are really unconscious, we're likely going to blame it on somebody else. We're possibly going to blame it on our company. We might even blame it on our boss. We might blame it on our husband or wife. Heck, we may even blame it on our kids. We could blame it on our parents. We could even find ourselves blaming it on the weather.

When we do that blame thing, we don't have to go very far in our own mind, at least through our field of perception. You see, it can be relatively easy to find somebody to pin it all on. But while we're doing so much blaming, it's impossible to take accountability and realize it was us all along, using this Inner Power incorrectly.

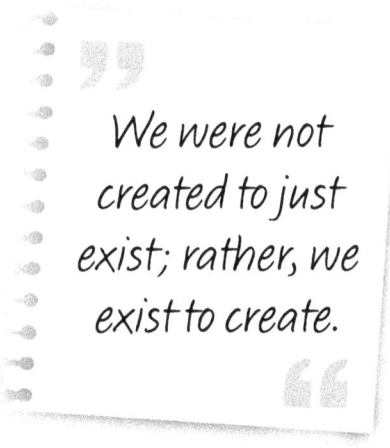

We were not created to just exist; rather, we exist to create.

When we use the Power of Imagination correctly, however, it has the pure potential to change our life—to greatly assist us in creating the life of our dreams.

Remember the Future Self? This is a direct application for this inner power. But we've got to know how to do it correctly.

Unlocking the potential of this Inner Power isn't just about knowing what it is. It's also about learning how to use it in making conscious contact when we're misusing it. If we cannot take responsibility for our choice to misuse it, we're never going to use it correctly. We've got to be able to come face to face with ourselves and confront ourselves when we're using it incorrectly.

You are the creator or at the very least, co-creator of your own reality. You are not the victim of circumstance. You're the creator of circumstance. You are. I am. We all are. That is the truth—like it or not. There are still a lot of people on this planet who believe they're the victim. I would say 90 percent of people fall into this category. What they've been failing to see is that they believe this because they haven't yet transformed the victim archetype (that is still living inside of them in their lower energy centers) into the victor archetype (that is living inside of them in their upper energy centers).

Until we do that transformational work, odds are we'll continue to think like a victim from time to time. And we're more than likely going to be absolutely convinced that we really are a victim. The problem is that when we're convinced that we're a victim, we can't be the victorious creator. And if we can't be the creator or the co-creator of our reality, we can't then consciously create the life of our dreams. We were not created to just exist; rather, we exist to create. Harnessing this Inner Power of Imagination is absolutely fundamental to becoming the creator of our own life—or at the very least the co-creator.

Can you see yourself Manifesting Like a masterMaster? Can you see yourself consciously getting better at Manifesting Like a Master would manifest? Remember you were born with the ability to manifest.

Whether we consciously use this inborn ability of ours or not, things will still manifest in our personal or professional world. No one on

Planet Earth can stop this from happening. Every single one of us is currently in process of manifesting something. Why not get on board and learn how to do this with skill—and then continue to get better and better at it?

> Which part of humanity do you want to be a part of? Do you want to be a part of the 10 percent who use their powerful imaginations masterfully? Or are you okay with possibly continuing to be part of the 90 percent? Do you want to go through an entire lifetime where you never create the life of your dreams? Is that who you've been becoming? Or better yet, is that who you want to become? What do you want? What's your higher goal, or intention?
>
> Check in with your Soul. If there was something your Soul wanted you to have, what would it be? The first thing you would want to do, if you were to consciously *Manifest Like a Master*, would be to get super clear on what it is you really want. Then, create a vivid picture or clear image of you actively imagining yourself in this picture where you already have what it is you most desire.

Whatever you choose... you get to decide what's best or most right for you based on the inner prompting of your Soul.

POWER 2: The Power of Goals

Goals are crucial to everyone's success and overall well-being. Without them it's almost impossible to move our lives forward personally, professionally, and spiritually. If someone is not setting goals for themselves and moving towards accomplishing their goals, whether they are a student, a parent, or an entrepreneur, more than likely they just don't understand the deeper purpose of having goals and why we genuinely need them.

Dr. Michelle Rozen gave a talk at UNLV on how to achieve your goals in business and life which was titled, *The Secrets of the 6%*. She shared her research on a study they did in 2023. They surveyed 1,000 people throughout the United States over a six-month period from January to June. Each participant set goals that they said they wanted to accomplish at that time. These included things like losing weight, getting a promotion, going to the gym, doing better in their career, scaling their business, saving more money, improving their relationships, etcetera. The intention of the study was to see what would happen with all these big goals over time. What she found made her jaw drop. The results were shocking. She found out that of the 1,000 people she surveyed, 94 percent of them dropped whatever they had pledged to do by February—the very next month.

Only 6 percent of the entire group actually stayed with their goals. This produced the most pressing question: what was it that the 6 percenters did differently that got them to the success and happiness of what it was they wanted to achieve compared to the 94 percent?

Here's what she discovered were the three secrets of the 6 percent:

1. Take charge. They took control of their own destinies by setting their minds to do something different. They continued taking charge by following through on what they needed to do to achieve what they said they wanted, which challenged their brains, as this new activity required them to do things they weren't yet used to doing.

2. They engaged the Law of Specification, which means the more specific you are in the way you set your goals, and the way you

follow through with your activities that lead you to your goal, the more successful you are.

For example, let's say the 94 percent said yes to their goal of losing weight and declared that they were going to do this. Whereas the 6 percent broke down how much weight they were going to lose by what time, then by the next incremental time, and so on. They also specified what they were going to do, such as changing their eating habits by dropping the unhealthy fatty foods and having their last meal of the day by 6:00 p.m., and going to the gym Monday, Wednesday, and Friday from 7:00 a.m. to 8:00 a.m. They even decided their specific workout routine in advance and declared, "I'm going to do this specific workout on Monday, this one on Wednesday, and this one on Friday." And if they missed one of their scheduled workouts, they would add an extra 30 minutes to their very next workout as a penalty.

The 6 percenters, by using the Law of Specification, had a 100-percent success rate. This means the more specific we are, the more granular we are, the more we use this law, the more successful we are.

3. The 6 percenters used what Dr. Rozen calls the 0 to 10 Rule. This would entail them rating their tasks on a scale of 0 to 10 in order of importance—the most important task being given a 10 and the least important task being given a 0.

The 94 percent would often talk about how busy they were almost as if this made them feel important. They would say, "I'm so busy running around all day! I didn't even have lunch." As if being busy equals being important or successful.

Now there was something very different that the 6 percenters did. In the course of a day, we all have a lot to do. Perhaps even too much where we simply can't do it all. The mindset of trying to do it all leads to burnout. The 6 percenters, just like the 94 percenters, also had a lot of things to accomplish. The big difference, however, was they would save the things that were lesser than a 9 or 10 for another day or delegate those things to someone else. Their mindset was to focus on the most important tasks that were a 9 or 10. These were the activities that would lead them to the success of their goals and happiness.

> *When we have clear written goals and we're working towards them each day, this will give us more energy and more motivation.*

The 94 percent never even got to their nines or tens, as they were too busy with the zeros, ones, twos, and threes on their lists of priorities. The 6 percent, rather, did their tens first and got very clear on what their tens were for the day. And in some cases, all they did were the tens. They knew it wasn't just the act of doing, doing, doing or running around that got them to their goal, like what was happening for the 94 percent; rather, it was the act of doing their tens that got them there.

Unlike the 94 percent, that 6 percent didn't mistake all the doing or all the running around for what would accomplish their goal. Applying what the great, late Zig Ziglar would often say about the confidence of ignorance: with the confidence that goes with ignorance those less productive people would now call this progress.

Clearly, it was the focusing on the tens each and every day that ultimately moved the 6 percent to the outcome of successfully achieving their goal.

Another one of my earliest and dearest mentors in this life, Brian Tracy, would often ask his audiences as he traveled around the world to do this simple yet powerful exercise: He had them take out a clean sheet of paper and write down a list of ten goals that they would like to accomplish in the foreseeable future. Everyone would write them down in the present tense as though they had already achieved their goals. For example, they would write: "I have growth-oriented relationships that are very meaningful and deeply fulfilling to me"; "I weigh X number of pounds"; "I am a successful consummate sales professional"; "I earn X number of dollars"; "I sleep deeply and peacefully every night"; etcetera.

After they'd completed their list of ten, he would have the audience then go back over the list and ask themselves this question: What one goal on this list, if I were to accomplish it immediately, would have the greatest positive impact on my life?

Now in my classes, I've since expanded upon this by asking the participants to answer this question two more times: What other goal on this list, if I were to accomplish it immediately after the first one, would have the second greatest impact on my life? And then again a third time. It is these three goals that can have the most significant, positive impact on their lives and on the achieving of their other listed goals.

Brian would also say, "Without goals, little can happen. Goals are the key to being self-motivated." You see, when we have clear written goals and we're working towards our most important goals each day, this will give us more energy and more than likely more motivation throughout the day as well. Someone with written goals and plans who intentionally works on them every day will eventually accomplish 10 times as much as someone without goals.

I learned through Brian that Harvard did a detailed study on this some years ago in which they found that 3 percent of their graduates who had clear written goals when they graduated 10 years later were earning 10 times as much as the people who didn't have written goals or had no goals at all.

I always find it interesting when I ask someone, "What are your three most important goals?"

They'll usually look at me like they're stunned, or they'll answer me in a shallow way. Or, in some cases, I'll get some of the most disconnected answers. Some of these answers don't make sense in terms of manifestation. I'll wonder, *"How is the Universe even going to calculate this?"* An example of this might be when someone says, "I want world peace" or "I want more money" or "I want more love."

If this is the answer to your three most important goals, there are no specifics here. You might recall the second secret to the top 6 percent within Dr Rozen's study group on applying The Law of Specification. So, what does it mean to have more money, love, or peace? More money could mean an extra 10 dollars. More love could be somebody saying, "I love you." World peace could be a group of people protesting for world peace.

When we show up in this way, we are basically saying to the Universe, "Universe, you clarify for me what my most important goals really are." In other words, the clearer and more specific we are in answering the question, "What are my three most important goals?", the easier it becomes for the Universe to support us and/or help us in successfully achieving those goals.

Remember, the power lies within the goal itself. In my twenties, when I first got started teaching people how to achieve their goals, I noticed that the majority of people wouldn't go out of their way and really take the time to learn how to set a goal. There was this aversion to it. When my students would go out into the world and talk about my class, some of their friends would say, "You don't need to do that. Save your money. That stuff doesn't work." They had no idea. What they were doing was advertising their own ignorance of, number one, the power of the goal, and number two, how to actually set and then ultimately achieve the goal.

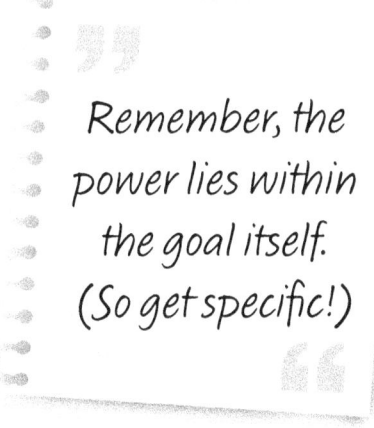

Remember, the power lies within the goal itself. (So get specific!)

If you ask someone what their goals are, and you get shallow answers, they haven't learned how to do this yet. Yet we all have this Inner Power inside of us to do this. We were born with this Inner Power; many of us just aren't accessing this properly yet. By the time you're done with this section, you're going to make your own discovery as to exactly where you are in terms of utilizing this Inner Power.

The Greater Reason for Goals

When you're using the Inner Power of Goals correctly, you have clarity. Clarity is everything, as it gives us clear direction.

Later on, we're going to explore the Law of Consciousness, but for now, we're going to touch on this concept because it relates to clarity.

When it comes to the topic of consciousness, and more specifically, your unconscious mind, you might have an urge to zone out because you have a deep-seated need for protection. Going deeper can be a very scary proposition. Go ask Carl Jung, or Sigmund Freud, or Napoleon Hill. Napoleon alone studied over a thousand successful people in this country many, many years ago. Each of these men became famous in their own right, and all happened to discover the same thing—people are terrified to go deeper into their own consciousness. And they are terrified because in order to do so, they're going to have to confront something; they're going to have to make a change. This idea of confronting something and making changes is going to take multiple touch points—it's going to be an ongoing process.

This is why the first book in this trilogy is titled *Being Called to Change*. At a fundamental level, you've got to develop a conscious relationship to the world of change. And then, you'll ultimately want to turn this into a lifestyle.

When you look around the world, you see people resisting change like the plague. Someone might even come to mind for you right now. Why are they resisting it? Because they're terrified of change. And more specifically they're terrified of the process they're going to have to go through to embrace that change.

Look at what happens when people know they're going to have to move the location of their residence or office. Their stress levels can go through the roof. They often live in anxiety. Why? Because they don't like change. They've been resisting change. They've been fighting change. They've been blocking change. They've been trying to control the process of change. Because deep down inside, there's a fear around losing control. And when it comes to real change at a cellular level, it will mean letting go of our needy energy that wants to control the process.

So, when we go deeper into our consciousness, clearly this is why we can become afraid. Now, if you're one of those people who is completely unconscious—who hasn't journeyed into your unconscious at all—the first step, then, is to be willing to say, "Yes, of course, it's going to be scary as we journey into the world of the unknown—implying we don't know what we're going to have to face or confront within our own consciousness and/or life. And yes, more than likely this is going to be uncomfortable, and even somewhat unpleasant." Discovering the truth is often scary. But we can get a handle on it. Addressing this and wrapping our brain around it will serve us well along our journey in moving onward and upward.

In fact, this is the only way this planet is ever going to change. This is the only way humanity is going to evolve. Enough of us—whether it's 100,000, 1 million, or 10 million—need to turn this into a lifestyle, where there's no more back and forth; there's no more one foot in, one foot out; there's no more running away—even when it is inconvenient.

When we're living our life afraid to look into our own unconscious, it's the kind of thing that can make us sick, whereas when we're living our life with conscious awareness, all of a sudden, things just manifest differently.

I'm making the assumption that you picked up this book because you're ready for something new; you're ready to get something on a much deeper level. You're ready to rise up to a whole new level of being—as in being a new and better version of you.

Clarity has a strong relationship to expanded consciousness. For a moment, I invite you to ask yourself what it would be like to have real clarity of direction—to have that state of consciousness where your direction is crystal clear. What that means is there is nothing that can veer you off your path. Period. You're completely clear with both feet in. And as a result of this, nothing and no one can stop you along your journey in manifesting whatever it is you have now chosen to manifest.

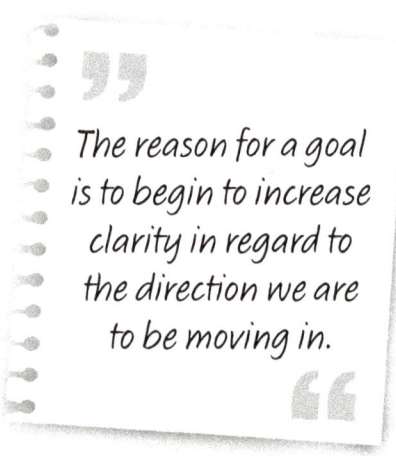

The reason for a goal is to begin to increase clarity in regard to the direction we are to be moving in.

One of the problems in our society is we lack serious clarity. As a whole, we just don't have it. Every now and then, somebody comes along, enters into our world, and they do have it. They're clear on their direction, and you can't sway them. This is part of the reason we like people like this. It's part of the reason why we're inspired by people like this. They're like a rock in our world. They become a profound anchor in our lives. You might even try to sway a person like this, but you can't. They don't waver.

There are others who can be swayed very easily. All that has to happen is they get a bad text or telephone call, and they're all over the place. They're not grounded and therefore lack clarity. Because of this something unexpected can happen in their world to easily knock them off their path. They're just not well grounded in the energy of a real clear direction.

So, the reason for a goal is to begin to increase clarity that is well grounded within our mind and body in regard to the direction we are supposed to be moving in. So, what does that mean, exactly? Well, you could set a goal today, and literally seven days from now, realize that's not your goal.

If you recall, we covered previously that a goal that comes from the ego is different from one that comes from the Soul. Similarly, a goal that comes from the Future Self is very different than a goal that comes from the Past Self. And yet the majority of people on Planet Earth have gotten hoodwinked into creating their goals that were inspired or prompted by their Past Self or their ego. Then, they began creating from those places.

This is like a building-block process. We're building upon this concept of clarity. Long ago, I discovered that when a goal is coming from my Soul, one of the ways in which I could tell is that I would become crystal clear, meaning my path, my direction, became crystal clear.

Now if the goal is coming from the ego, we can go back and forth like a yoyo for the next two years and burn up all kinds of good energy that could have been better utilized elsewhere. We might even drain ourselves, deplete ourselves of energy, going back and forth like this because we don't have the clarity. The ego doesn't operate in the world of clarity. It operates in the world of confusion. The ego does not operate in the world of simplicity. The ego operates in the world of complexity.

So, if I'm in the presence of somebody who has a really complex life, I already know where that has come from—the ego and the Past Self. The Soul and the Future Self, on the other hand, aren't wired like that.

When you're with someone who is always confused, or they talk about how hard things are, that means they're dealing with complexity. Their reality is heavy. It's like a dead weight they're dragging around with them all day, every day. They're experiencing this because they've been creating without clarity; they've been creating from their ego or their Past Self. In all fairness to them, they obviously haven't been aware of it because if they were, they wouldn't choose to live their life this way. But this complexity can be a life sentence. This can keep you stuck in the continuum, which is why the exploration of consciousness, and finding clarity, is so important.

The Deeper Purpose of Goals

The Soul purpose of goals is for personal, professional, and/or spiritual growth. Let's say I'm traveling along my journey, and I've manifested a relationship. And we'll even say this relationship is more on the complicated side. It's not a relationship that's whole or complete. Rather, it's out of balance and disharmonious.

Maybe I've become aware of this, and I think, *I don't know if I want to stay in this relationship, but I've been in this situation for several years.*

When I come back to this place over and over again, it's a continuum experience—repeat, repeat, repeat. And then, at some point, I find myself feeling this inner prompting of my Soul, and I realize I don't want to keep doing this. This is how it starts. Then, maybe I realize it's time to set a new goal. Better yet, maybe I realize it's time to set a clearer, higher-vibe goal.

> *The Soul purpose of goals is for personal, professional, and/or spiritual growth.*

Now, that might look like wanting to exit the current relationship and create a new one. Or maybe I want to transform the one I currently have. In order to do that, I have to get my partner on board. Whatever this looks like in terms of the relationship, the important thing is that I begin to set a new goal. And that goal is there to give me a direction and to help access a part of my creative power to manifest with on a conscious level.

Then, I will begin this process of creating, manifesting, or achieving this goal. But underneath all of that, if I get to this goal's purpose and am aware of it and I choose to align my life with this purpose, that's where the magic starts to happen. This new goal—to create a functional, in-balance, harmonious relationship—has a higher frequency to it.

When you set a higher frequency or a higher vibrational goal for yourself, whether or not it fully manifests is dependent upon its purpose—which you may or may not be aware of. Now, obviously, it would serve you well to become aware of its deeper purpose.

I'm all for prayer, but I've come across so many people who have prayed for the exact same thing over and over again, to the point where now, eight years later, they're still praying, and it still hasn't shown up. What the heck is up with that?

One person might say, "Oh, you just need to have more faith." Well, maybe they do, because faith is a very powerful thing, but most of the time, if it's been eight years, something else is going on here.

Usually, what's going on with this individual is they've never gotten to the deeper purpose of that higher goal. They didn't even know what it was. They're unconscious to it. They went to a goal-setting seminar or read a goal-setting book that was fluff. There was no depth to that goal-setting practice.

Maybe that person watched *The Secret* and thought they got the secret of all secrets, but they didn't get the full picture of the Law of Attraction. It's understandable. When somebody's more inexperienced, they'll always take the shallow route. They'll never take the deeper route. They will resist the deeper route like the plague. And yet the deeper route is what ultimately changes everything for the better.

So, if I'm sincere in my intent in physical form to actually manifest this new goal in my world, I need to deepen my understanding of the actual purpose of the goal. Which is not always what I think it is. And guess what? The purpose of the goal isn't just to simply manifest the goal. That's a shallow interpretation.

Again, the deeper, richer purpose lies in the growth, whether on a personal, professional, or spiritual level. Because in order to manifest a goal, we have to change ourselves; we have to grow. In fact, depending on the size of the goal, and the vibrational frequency of this goal, we might have to change ourselves multiple times before the goal actually manifests. Think back to book one, *Being Called to Change*. The only way we're going to get the growth is through changing ourselves in that ongoing process of moving towards achieving our goal until it manifests.

So, if you want to achieve bigger, deeper life-altering transformations, you're going to have to do some serious changing. This is the way it has been set up by your Divine Soul Essence Self, rooted in Universal Law. These Universal Laws are all networked together, constantly complementing and augmenting each other, supporting each other. It's an electric, living network that cannot be fooled and can't be bargained with. You have to play by the rules or in this case, by the Universal Laws. When you become the real deal—when you experience the growth that you are meant to achieve within your own being—the bigger goal will fully manifest.

Remember from *Being Called to Change* that you are essentially answering the call to change, then answering the next one and the next. Each time you do this, you are growing. This is like a stair-step building process. There is no elevator here.

In our society, we tend to try to go for these shortcuts and bypasses. But they don't work. The results never lie. The results will always show what exactly is going on inside that person and how they're living within their own inner life.

So, you need to become the real deal. Whatever amount of growth is encoded within your new goal is exactly what you need to achieve. And your Future Self knows exactly how much growth that is. The only way you are going to get what you want in your physical reality is to achieve the growth that's already been encoded in the experience—in the heartfelt desire that you would like to see manifest in your physical world.

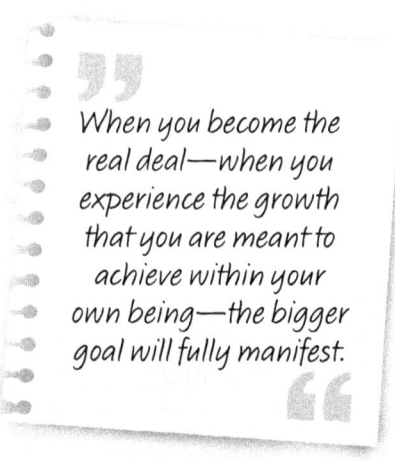

When you become the real deal—when you experience the growth that you are meant to achieve within your own being—the bigger goal will fully manifest.

This is powerful, potent, life-altering stuff that extends far beyond the concept of a goal. We're talking about you as a Soul here—as a spirit that lives on forever. Why would you want to pussy foot around this anymore? Why would you want to waste any more time? Again, we're talking about your magnificent Soul.

In book two, *Transform Your Destiny*, recall when we learned about karma. Resolving our negative karma is key to our growth. And our karma is encoded with a reward once it's resolved—one that is very specific and unique to each of us as a Soul. This karmic reward was set up before we took our first breath in this life. But here's the deal—there's no accessing the reward until we resolve the negative karma. We've got to become the real deal. And when we do, the reward gets released.

Maybe you've been resisting the work it's going to take to resolve your karma because change is an uncomfortable thing. It's inconvenient, it's unpleasant, and sometimes it's downright ugly. It can even be rough. But again, here's the deal—once you achieve the growth that has already been encoded in this goal, which is coming from your Soul, not your ego, you're playing by a completely different set of rules.

A goal that's truly right for you emanates from your Soul Self. Your Soul, your Future Self, one year from now, carries a higher frequency than you currently do. This frequency of your goal also carries a higher frequency than it does now. So, what you are going to have to do is raise your frequency to a level that matches the full-on manifestation of your desired goal. Why? Because that's what your Soul wants from this experience—growth. In other words, higher frequency equals growth... period.

There are a lot of Souls on this planet right now that are tired because they have not been achieving what they've set out to achieve—Soul growth. Now if you want to drain, deplete, and frustrate your Soul then keep it, and you, from growing. Just simply stay in that continuum experience and keep repeating the same thing over and over again. And then try to convince all your friends that you're doing really well—that you're actually advancing—when, in fact, your results are saying something different.

So, the purpose of the Power of Goals is to know and identify what the true purpose of a heartfelt desire that emanates from your Soul is.

Once again, results never lie. This is one of my most basic teachings, and I integrated it into my own life as a young man because it's always served me impeccably well. And perhaps it could serve you really well too.

Goal-Setting Exercise

All right, so now let's move on to the creation of the List of 10 Things You Want to Manifest.

Take out your notebook and write down the numbers 1 through 10. This will be your list of 10 things (or 10 desires or 10 wants) you would like to see manifest within the next year. It's important to keep this process simple for right now, and not think too far into the future.

When you make your list, I suggest you go into complete silence and connect with your Soul. Listen to the voice of your Soul or your Future Self as you create your list of 10. Do this by focusing on the questions from above and reflect back on those answers. This will help you get connected and stay more connected to your Soul during this process.

List up to 10 things that you want or genuinely desire in any area of your life—relationships, career, business, finances, health, recreation, spiritual advancement, and so on. All areas of your life are now on the table.

Just remember, when you're making your list, this is your Future Self speaking to you, saying, "I want this for you." Ultimately, you're becoming that Future Self. You're becoming those wants or genuine desires that your Future Self wants for you.

Again, there's this battle going on within us. The ego might try to get in there and encourage you to go after something that has nothing to do with your Soul whatsoever—that has nothing to do with what your Future Self really wants. So, once you get to the point where you are your Future Self, you're going to say, "What's this? I never really wanted this."

This is why it's key to connect with your Soul on a conscious level during this creative process. Your Future Self not only knows what it wants, but it also knows what it has. It already knows this is what has been scheduled. Your Soul knows which results come from who it is you truly are. This is the big difference when it comes to manifesting at a conscious level.

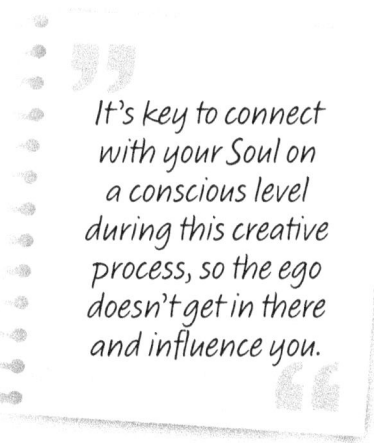

It's key to connect with your Soul on a conscious level during this creative process, so the ego doesn't get in there and influence you.

Remember that your Soul communicates through feelings, images, or impulses. Your Soul will utilize your mind as a creative instrument, but it doesn't live there. Your 10 wants or genuine desires will feel meaningful to you at the level of your heart space—your fourth energy center. That's where your Soul ultimately resides. When you are truly connected with what it is your Soul genuinely desires for you, it will literally fill every cell of your body.

Another way to think of this is that when you're tapping into your Soul's desire, it is one that you're discovering or re-discovering, because it's already there. It's not something that you're coming up with; rather, it's something that you're becoming aware of.

Your ego's desire, on the other hand, will exist exclusively in the mind. It's important to mention here that there's nothing wrong with a desire from the ego. We've all set and achieved goals that were the wants or desires of our ego. It's a good thing to deepen our understanding as we experience the difference between a Soul's desire made manifest versus an ego's desire. Over time as this happens, we start to notice the difference between these two as it begins to create contrast. Without this contrast we would never come to know our Soul and ego in this lifetime.

Our Ego Self has its purpose, just as our Soul Self does. At some point along our journeys, for those of us who are waking up to the greater truth of ourselves, we start to notice that we don't get the same meaning or fulfillment from a goal created by the ego as we do when our manifestations are coming more from the Soul and/or the Divine.

Now our ego might surface when we're writing out our list. It might say, "Who do you think you are? You can't have that." Or "What will others think of you if you go for this? You can't do that." Or "What are others going to think of me if I go for this?" These are small signs that our ego has been activated and is something for us to look out for. The illusion here is it possibly looks like our ego just wants to protect us. But this is not true... What's true is the ego wants to protect itself because it doesn't like forward movement. And until we tame it and train it, it'll continue to say these things as a way to maintain status quo. So, don't let your ego thwart your desires, and don't let your ego steer them either.

The crossover between the ego and the Soul is the biggest battle you're going to face here. And it's all happening within. You'll know when the battle is over because you'll feel inner peace. There's no more anxiety, no more stress, no more trying or pushing, and no more resistance. Everything will calm down. When you get to that place and it's sustained, you'll know the battle is won.

> For each item that you're exploring from soul level on your list of 10, you could also ask yourself, "Is this a genuine desire? Is this something I really want? If my life was ending at the end of the year, would I even care about this thing?"

> This puts each item on your list to the test. All of a sudden, it puts things in perspective. It will help you discover if this desire is really coming from your heart... or if it's merely coming from your mind—meaning your personality that is run by your ego.

Ultimately, everyone has the ability to connect with their Soul, but we've all developed this ability at varying levels. This may be something you need to practice a bit. Maybe you'll discover this is something you want—to have this ability to connect to your Soul with more ease and consistency.

> You might need to return to this list in a few days and see what you feel then. You might come up with an entirely different list that comes from that feeling place. Everyone is different, and this process takes more time for some than others. You might wake up three mornings from now, emerging from sleep, and your cells are flooded with a knowing of exactly what to put on your list—knowing exactly what your

Soul wants for you. You may have had this feeling of knowing before. That's the higher part of you telepathically communicating with you. The truth that you feel when this happens is incredible.

This process of creating from your Future Self is quite different from anything you may have done up until this point. We're used to creating from our past selves and even our present selves. In a sense, you're helping your Future Self by connecting with it. You're helping yourself to become your Future Soul Self.

So, take your time, connect within, and come up with your List of 10. This isn't about driving forward or figuring it out. If you feel pressure, pull back. That's a function of the ego. Make sure every item on your list feels right. Feel into the sensations or impulses from your heart.

Keep your list within reach so you can see what you've achieved in a reasonable amount of time by referring back to this.

Select 3 Goals from Your List of 10

Okay so here's one final exercise as we wrap up this Inner Power...

Take a moment to connect with your Future Self, one year from today. If you're not sure how to do this just yet, you could simply picture the words on the screen of your mind: "Future Self One Year from Today." And as you do, go with whatever comes to you.

From your list of 10, what one goal on your list, if you were to accomplish it immediately or within the next 12 months, would have the greatest positive impact on your life? Make a note of it and take a breath.

Then ask again, what other goal on this list, if you were to accomplish it immediately after the first one, would have the second greatest impact on your life? Make a note of it and breathe. And then one more time...

Your 3 Most Important Goals

The objective here is to narrow our focus down to what we now feel to be our three most important goals to achieve within the next 12 months. It is these three goals that can have the most significant, positive impact on your life starting right away.

As for the other goals on your list, you can bring them into focus after you've achieved your first three goals. And you might find yourself somewhat surprised that one or more of your remaining goals just simply falls into place.

A Final Question to Ponder...

Before we move on to the next Inner Power, I'd like you to think about what it would be like if you were to actually get better at manifesting on a conscious level. Hold that in mind and as you do, go with whatever answer comes to you as you read this final question:

What would it mean to you if you were to get better at manifesting what it is you truly want on a conscious level—personally, professionally, spiritually, financially, and relationally?

This is a spiritually significant question to ponder, as our Divine Soul Essence Self has been prompting us from within to get better at conscious, intentional manifesting. As we contemplate this question and the answers that follow, this also assists in the opening of the doorway to one's Soul—and more importantly to what it is our Soul has wanted for us or wants us to have.

So, what is it that your Soul might want for you to have manifest? Not sure just yet? Then I suggest you read this section on goals again… Take your time. If there are specific parts that you're sensing, it would be beneficial for you to take a pause and let those words simmer within you, and when you're ready, continue on with your reading or listening.

POWER 3: The Power of Thought

Now, if you recall, thoughts create your reality. Recall some of the thoughts that have shown up on the screen of your mind recently. Would you want the reality of those thoughts to manifest in your day-to-day world?

What happens when you start entertaining negative thoughts? What happens when you get hell bent on holding those negative thoughts in place for like three days in a row, where it's a constant repeat of the exact same stream of negative thoughts? What happens then? Will these thoughts possibly manifest somehow some way in your daily life? Possibly so.

Negative thoughts can turn into negative self-talk. And negative self-talk, if not corrected, can have you go down a dark rabbit hole in your mind and can influence you to unconsciously engage in unhealthy choices and negative projections. Whereas positive self-talk can bring a lightness of energy, or an authenticity in the form of healthy expressions that support or empower one's journey.

> *Negative self-talk can take you down a dark rabbit hole in your mind. Positive self-talk can bring a light energy that empowers us.*

Psychologists have told us for some time that the average person will entertain approximately 50,000 thoughts a day. Now, what's even more interesting to look at is how much time a person spends thinking the same thought over and over—versus a truly new and different thought. According to the National Science Foundation, 80 percent of our thoughts are negative and 95 percent of our thoughts are repetitive.

Wow... Can you see that as a possibility or perhaps even a reality in your own life right now? If so, what does that suggest? Most of our thoughts have been trapped inside of us, implying many of us have been basically thinking the same thing over and over again. Therefore, we are getting the same manifested results over and over again. Until, of course, we free ourselves from this.

> Over the last seven days—and be honest—how would you describe the majority of your thoughts? Of those 50,000 thoughts that have run across your mind throughout the course of your waking day, have the majority of them taken you to a positive, beautiful, and more productive place? Have you experienced a preponderance of powerful thoughts, peaceful thoughts, happy thoughts? Are your thoughts filled with prosperity, abundance, or gratitude? Or have the majority leaned towards something else?
>
> Now, if you're not sure, then just look at your results that have manifested in your physical reality. That's all you have to do.

The great and late master martial artist, Bruce Lee, used to teach his students the concept that *thoughts create your reality*. But do they, really? Absolutely. If you get enough intensity, clarity, and focus on that one thought, then you'll pleasantly surprise yourself. You might even shock yourself. But this is not what we've normally done…

Every belief is made up of a thought form or a thought structure. Meaning it's not a word. Rather, it's a body of words that make up a sentence, such as, "I can't have what I want." Whatever the limiting belief is, it can influence us, and we can actually use our Inner Power of Thought in a way that can hurt us.

Now perhaps we're not aware of this. But think about it… That's just one example of a thought form that could be running around in the mix of our 50,000 thoughts in our waking day. We do that over and over again, and presto! Through the Law of Correspondence, we're going to end up with a reality that corresponds directly to the thought structure that makes up that emotionalized belief. And if that thought structure says, "I can't have what I really want," then that's going to be the reality.

What this potentially means is our reality is going to constantly show itself in our results. Here's what can often happen within that 97 percent of people on the planet that have a challenge in manifesting the life of their dreams: they'll set a goal, and they often stay in the trap of just idling in stage one of the process of achieving that goal. This means they'll continue to stay in the "wanting" of the goal; they'll never get to stage two of creating the "having it" within their physical vessel or body consciousness. And never mind stage three.

> *If a thought structure says, "I can't have what I really want," then that's going to be our reality.*

In stage one, they're collecting evidence (without likely knowing that's what they've been doing), which further supports the emotionalized belief, the limiting belief that says, "I can't have what I want." This doesn't happen because we're doing something wrong. It happens because it's Universal Law.

It all comes down to the way we set it up. If we set it up where we lean more towards our limited beliefs—our limited thoughts—this means we lean more towards negative thoughts, angry thoughts, miserable thoughts, toxic thoughts—then, next thing we know, we get a physical manifestation. Perhaps we get really sick; or our body becomes acidic—it becomes toxic. Well, guess what? If someone had enough toxicity running through their mind every day of their waking life (such as the 80 percent of their thoughts being negative), would it really surprise us that their body then would manifest some sickness or illness?

Consider for a moment the number of physicians who are finding that a good percentage of their patients' doctor visits are stress related. That would be bad or negative stress (there's good stress or positive stress as well). So, what do think is happening with someone's thoughts when their bad stress levels are up? At the very least, they haven't been managing their negative stress all that well. Now if by chance your answer to this question was repetitive thoughts or negative thinking, you're right. As in, where are the positive thoughts when we're living in bad or negative stress? Put it to the test.

> Watch your thoughts when in this type of negative stress. This type of negative thinking or stress is 100-percent influenced by fear. The question here then would be: what is it we're possibly so afraid of?

The manifested sickness is nothing more than a corresponding reality to what's been going on inside of them in regard to their thoughts and poorly managed negative stress levels. Now, yes, more than likely they were totally unconscious with just how powerful their negative or positive thoughts could be. But come the end of the day, it doesn't matter.

Ralph Waldo Emerson once said, "Great men are they who see that spiritual is stronger than any material force—that thoughts rule the world." He advocated for only entertaining the highest forms of thought. Those higher-vibration thoughts are what makes great men and women, and those higher thoughts rule the higher realms.

Well, now if you go down into the lower world, what do you suppose rules that place? Negative thoughts, critical thoughts, judgmental thoughts, toxic thoughts, acidic thoughts. And so, if you're in a lower reality, meaning you're manifesting more of what you don't want to have manifest in your life, you just got your answer.

Now will you go to work and really solve this problem? You might; you might not. You might get really focused for 10 days, and then you might fall off the path because all of a sudden, that bottle of vodka or whiskey is looking pretty good to you right now.

"I had no idea it was going to be this inconvenient." "I had no idea it was going to be this tough." "I had no idea it was going to be this unpleasant." That's what the coward within us says and does. It cowers down. Unless, of course, you've already healed this, or this is not an issue for you.

Anyone who has achieved a great level of success will tell you it wasn't easy, it wasn't comfortable, and it didn't come fast. They'll also tell you that they had to delay immediate gratification on a day-to-day basis, over a long period of time. On the other hand, the people who haven't achieved a lot of success in their world have a completely different recipe for life. Of course, most of them don't know that. If they did know there was a different formula, they might change theirs.

When I was a young man, I created a course called Your Formula for Success. At the time, it was my most popular class. It lasted about four weeks, and on average we had about 200 people per class—which was the maximum capacity for the room. Why was it so popular? Because people wanted to know what the formula was.

At the beginning of class, I would ask them to write an essay. The prompt was: "Tell me what you think the formula for success is." You wanna talk about getting some good laughs? That would have been a great premise for a reality TV show.

What came out of most of these people when they were asked to write about success was shallow, weak, not grounded, unclear, fantasy based, or just disconnected. No wonder their lives were so messy and so upside down at the time! But they were wise in that something about the title of the course spoke to them, and they showed up to become the beneficiaries of this knowledge. Which, according to their essays, was exactly what they needed.

> Now let's go back to you and your thoughts. Over the last seven days, you've had approximately 350,000 thoughts. At an average of about 50,000 thoughts per day, if you were to multiply that by seven, you'd get 350,000 thoughts. Think about that for a moment... it's an incredible number.
>
> Now, of those 350,000 thoughts over the last seven days, what's been the percentage of the thoughts where you found yourself thinking about how much you really love and appreciate your life? Answer truthfully.

Most people haven't been trained to think about this properly. I used to be a sales trainer, and I became quite masterful at this skill. I was thriving financially as a sales trainer because you could give me anybody that was towards the bottom of the totem pole within a sales organization, and as long as they had a burning desire to learn how to sell successfully, I could teach them how to do it. I could help them increase their level of sales effectiveness, and often by as much as 200 to 300 percent in a relatively short period of time.

I did this for quite a few years, working with tens of thousands of salespeople. I had success as an external sales trainer because I knew they needed to be taught clearly. If their companies could have done this on their own, they would've done it. But they didn't have the formula. The good news was their sales manager, or the owner of the company was wise enough and practical enough to recognize they needed to bring somebody in that really knew what they were doing.

When I was teaching salespeople how to be better at selling, I knew that it all had to be broken down step by step. There's a recipe here. There's a formula. Although manifestation is much more intricate, it's similar in that there's a formula you must master.

This is what Napoleon Hill did in his wonderful book, *Think and Grow Rich*, which has sold tens of millions of copies since its original publication. This book is nothing more than a compilation of interviews that he did over a period of 20 years with a thousand people. But these people weren't just anybody—they had to qualify to be interviewed. Each person had to prove that they had already achieved a certain level of success. Twenty years, a thousand people... and who knows how many other people he interviewed who never even made it into the book? That was the criteria—one thousand. He was breaking it down. He came up with a formula that was backed up by real success.

Before my mentor Bob passed on, he would speak on the teacher who wasn't the real deal, at least not just yet. He would go on to say, "There are a lot of 'em out there." That they're inexperienced, and more specifically, a lot of these teachers are teaching something that they haven't yet proven even to themselves. In other words, they're not a walking embodiment of what they're currently teaching. They have not yet demonstrated how powerful their teachings are or are not. They have not organized their teachings in a way that's broken down into a formula, a recipe—and yet they're out there teaching. So, let's remember the importance of a formula for your thoughts and your results. How beneficial would it be for you to find mentors who have proven success that backs up their claims?

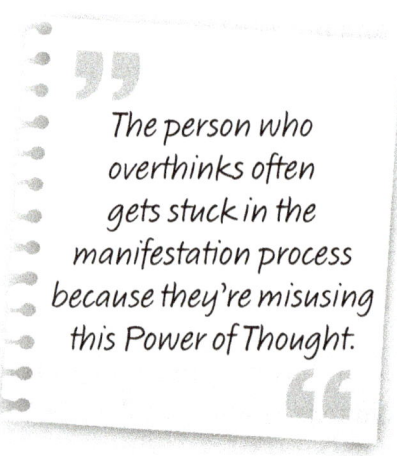

The person who overthinks often gets stuck in the manifestation process because they're misusing this Power of Thought.

When it comes to the Power of Thought, another important factor to note is that if you're one of those people who loves to overthink things, if you're one of those people who will get inspired, but then it will wear off and you'll repeat this process over and over, you're more than likely going to end up with a sore head because those thoughts aren't being released. These types of thoughts are just repeating themselves. The person who overthinks often gets stuck in the manifestation process because they're misusing this Power of Thought. It literally can back up the channels or the neural pathways within their brain. Their brain is not functioning properly. This might even explain why some people get recurring headaches or migraines.

Someone like Bruce Lee, on the other hand, knew how to use his thoughts masterfully. And he had the results to back it up. He didn't have recurring, scattered thoughts; rather, he focused on one thought aimed at something, and his actions were in complete alignment with that structured form of thought. He was laser focused.

Many have not yet mastered this. Until we do, there's a big likelihood that we're not in control of our thoughts yet; rather, they're likely still in control of us.

The truth is, if you go out with a Master in physical form—one of the ways you can spot them is that they have tremendous control over the power of their thoughts. In other words, they only think what they want to think. They only have high-quality thoughts, which, for the most part, become the focal point in how they utilize their minds to manifest what it is they would like to have and/or experience in their world, whether personally, professionally, or spiritually.

Now imagine if you could get 5 percent of your 50,000 thoughts all moving in the same direction at the same time… if you could get that 5 percent focused on one goal, and if what Bruce Lee said was true that thoughts really do create your reality, just imagine what you'd be capable of manifesting in your own personal, professional, or spiritual world.

POWER 4: The Power of Feeling

This Inner Power, when used correctly, has not only an empowering effect when manifesting with intention, but it can also have a transformational effect when communicating with others in our lives. When we communicate with feeling, it causes a better, richer response from those we're connecting with.

Take, for example, Celine Dion, with her beautiful crystalline singing voice that deeply moves everyone in her audiences around the world, or one of the most authentic, famous actors in Hollywood, Matthew McConaughey, or a performer/athlete like Sami Zayn in the WWE, or a masterful sales trainer like Andy Elliott (who, like me, began his career as a trainer with a stuttering challenge), or the legendary motivational speaker, Zig Ziglar, or Tony Robbins. These people all have something in common. Can you guess what it is?

They all use the Power of Feeling when communicating or performing. And it works incredibly well, as they move people emotionally—partly due to their conscious ability of skillfully using this Inner Power.

What about on an individual level? What's it like when you're in conversation with someone where the words they use lack feeling? Where there's little or no feeling behind their words? Where you're only *hearing* the words of the other person... you're just not *being moved* by them?

An old friend of mine from years back, Roberto Monaco, who masterfully specializes in working with communicators, says, "In the world of professional speaking, the average presenter communicates or presents without feeling. They use only words."

Now this is interesting, as speaking or performing at its truest essence is greatly influenced by the correct use of this Inner Power of Feeling, which is connected to one's Soul.

The Power of Feeling is also directly connected to the Power of Thought. Our feelings influence the quality of our thoughts and can deeply influence what it is we manifest, be it positive or negative. Our life can change in one direction or the other simply by the way we feel inside. This implies that if you don't like the way your life is going, change the way you feel inside.

This is another master key—as in, if you don't like the way your life is going, you can change it. And the most crucial part of changing it is to change the way you're feeling on the inside. So, if one has a lot of negative feelings or emotions that they haven't consciously dealt with, this is a clear signal it's time to do some transformational inner work. Good transformational work is what helps one to properly heal, resolve, and ultimately release these old buried negative feelings or emotions that have been inside of us within the underbelly of our consciousness for who knows how long.

> Another master key is that if you don't like the way your life is going, you can change it... by changing the way you're feeling on the inside.

I might have a painful, dysfunctional past that has produced these types of feelings and thoughts or the mental images that would result from those past experiences. Now, I can't change the past (none of us can), but it could be highly beneficial here for me to recognize that these old, buried feelings, mental images, or thoughts are of my past as well.

Which means they have been influencing and even recreating their like in my now reality—as well as on my future timeline.

> So, if I truly want to change this, I totally can (we all can). Even though I can't actually change the past, what I can do is completely change the way I've been feeling and thinking about the past. One of the most important things we can do in the name of our own transformation is to change the way we think and feel about something, for when we do, this is what changes the way we've been perceiving that something. In other words, as Wayne Dyer would often say, "When you change the way you look at things, the things you look at change."

Our feelings are the language of our body and Divine Soul Essence, whereas our thoughts and mental images are the language of our brain. Do you know anyone who is temporarily disconnected from their feelings and/or Soul? You know, those types that for the most part only try to stay focused on their thoughts? Meaning they don't have emotional depth—they just continue to overthink. Or do you know anyone who is emotionally hung up on their negative feelings, and as a result couldn't entertain a positive thought or hold that thought for a period of three minutes in a concentrated way—even if their life depended upon it? There's a disconnect in both of these cases between the mind, the body, and possibly the Soul.

Let's go back to the concept of beliefs. What makes a belief? A belief is when a thought structure has taken root in an emotion, at which time, the belief becomes an emotionalized thought form. Beliefs run our life, and beliefs, by law, must produce a corresponding reality in our life. Whether it's an unlimited belief or a limited belief, it doesn't matter. The Law of Belief could care less. It's completely impersonal.

So, our feelings drive our thoughts. Ultimately, what this translates to is that they influence our vibrational state. Now, this vibrational state is another master key when it comes to achieving our most important goals.

You might recall from Chapter 6: The Creative State that how we think and feel creates our vibrational state. So, if how we think is negative, judgmental, or overly critical, our emotions are going to be on the negative side—as in they might be anger, hatred, shame, guilt, jealousy, resentment, etcetera. Meaning we've got negative emotions that are driving the quality of those critical, judgmental, and negative thoughts.

It's this vibrational place of being that dictates our creative state. So, if the majority of our thoughts are leaning more towards the negative, this means the majority of our feelings must by law also be leaning more towards the negative. If we put those two together, it produces a low vibrational state, which then becomes the state of being in which we are now creating from (also known as our Past Self).

Now if I go out in the world and create my goals from this state, what do you suppose will happen next? What would I then be manifesting? Exactly! Things I don't want to manifest! I could manifest the weakest and most dysfunctional of relationships. I will possibly manifest debt. Heck, I might sabotage a career that I really value. I might even manifest illness and a lack of energy in that of my own body and become unmotivated.

There's really no mystery to this when you understand how it truly works.

You might also recall those four areas and reflective questions from Chapter 6. There was one in particular that really applies here: How often do you naturally feel good?

When you're naturally feeling good, what then does that do to your vibrational state? When you're feeling bad, when you're feeling miserable, when you're feeling lazy or unmotivated, when you're feeling moody, when you're feeling all that icky stuff, what does that do to your vibrational state? Does it raise it, increase it, brighten it, or does it possibly do the opposite? Pretty obvious, right?

> *Our feelings are the language of our body and Divine Soul Essence, whereas our thoughts and mental images are the language of our brain.*

You see, we're manifesting 24/7—even when our vibrational state is low. None of us can stop this from happening. The best we can do is to reroute this to where we rise back up to a higher vibrational state. Remember the 97 percent of our populus who haven't been able to live the life of their dreams (at least just yet)? This is the reason why most people have been manifesting what it is they don't want. And then they often just repeat it like a continuum—like a Groundhog-Day experience, over and over again.

No wonder we have people who want to commit suicide. No wonder we have people who actually do commit suicide. I don't know how long I could even go for if I didn't tap into this, if I didn't uncover this, if I didn't discover this and choose to rise up to a new and greater way of working with my state of feeling and eventually mastering the art of conscious, intentional manifesting.

I don't know how long I could survive, constantly living in a lower-vibrational feeling state—not even knowing that I'm manifesting from that state, meaning I'm personally manifesting most of the things that I clearly don't want to have in my life.

At some point, I would begin to think or start to believe, *I'm never gonna manifest what I really want to manifest. I'm never gonna achieve the goals I really want to achieve. So, what's the point? What's the use? This isn't working. Gosh this life sucks.* When we have thoughts like these running through our mind, this is when we can entertain thoughts of giving up and possibly even thoughts of ending it all.

Now when somebody's on the verge of getting really sick, you can be assured they've been in a low-vibrational state for a sustained period of time. I used to move in and out of a higher vibrational state when I was younger—but I would drop back into a low-vibrational state for periods of time. And when I was in those lower vibrational states, I would sometimes manifest major illnesses—because that's where I was creating from. Now, I didn't recognize that during those times as I was more unconscious than conscious back then.

So that idea of feeling good ought to become a transformational intention of ours. When we are able to vibe in that good-feeling state, magic starts to release organically. Our personal and professional productivity increases. I teach this in my Productivity Powerhouse course as well. And yet I've had people who have gone through this course, and six months later, it's like they forgot they even took the class. They've defaulted back to their old ways—feeling miserable, feeling negative, feeling critical, feeling judgmental, feeling spiteful, feeling vengeful, and feeling unmotivated. They're doing the complete opposite of what they were taught in the course. Talk about unconscious resistance towards something that could actually help them!

> That's why we often have to go back to the same course, the same book—sometimes over and over again, and many times over a sustained period of time. Those of us who are Soul wise and disciplined enough to actually do so become the lucky ones. No question about it. This feeling good state plays an important role here in terms of manifesting our goals. And we're going to need constant reminders or healthy mood elevators—such as listening to a great audio program in our car while driving around town, or having it play in the background while we're washing the dishes as a way to get us back into this higher-vibrational state of feeling.
>
> You need to feel good about what's going on in your world, where you're going, and what you've already been given. Can you identify some things to feel good about right now? You might take a moment to jot these things down on your notepad that you feel good about right now. And are you willing to get into that state of feeling good about these things? Because if you are willing to do that right now, and acknowledge these things to yourself, then you are correctly exercising this Power of Feeling.

Here's another aspect of this Inner Power: if you're going to manifest a goal, you need to feel it before it actually manifests. And more specifically, you need to feel it exactly the way your Future Self feels it; your Future Self who already has it. Most people are completely backwards when it comes to this. They think when they get it, that's when they'll feel good about getting it.

This is how some people have been dealing with their weight issues. They decide they'll accept their weight once they lose the weight. And these are the people who struggle their whole lives to lose the weight. All because they have it backwards.

People think, *When I get this brand-new car, I'll feel so good.* Again, they've got it backwards. Even if someone comes along and buys them the brand-new car, they didn't achieve the state of feeling good naturally from the material possession. Because they didn't learn anything. They didn't tap into the formula. They still can't manifest what they want in their world. That formula—getting $50,000 from someone else—has no legs. It has no roots. It has no anchor.

I've had both friends and clients who have inherited or won a lot of money. And they went out and spent it like crazy. They thought they had tapped into the success money formula—the goldmine. Hogwash. It was nothing more than an illusion. Now I'm not saying it's a bad thing to inherit or win a bunch of money. That's not the message here. The message here is that it's not the formula to positive manifestation. This recipe you're learning about is serious business—it's what the Masters have learned to do. We're talking about deliberate manifesting with precision on a conscious level and without issue.

The masters who can do this will just go out and manifest $5,000 when they need it. There's no drama. It's no big deal. They can go to bed and sleep like a baby because they know that come the next morning, they can get up and manifest $5,000 by the end of the week. It's so simple. They've got the formula. Which is a very different experience than the person who got a bunch of money but didn't get the formula.

Who do you want to become—the person who's relying on getting a bunch of money from somebody, or the person who actually masters the formula? Of those two options, who would you rather become?

The Power of Feeling is inside of you. And when you're exercising that power in relation to the manifestation of a goal, quite frankly, what you want to do is emotionally fall in love with the goal that you're in process of manifesting, as if it's already manifested.

This might be a stretch for you because you've possibly never done things this way or you downright don't know how to do things this way. You've done it the other way. You'll think to yourself, *I'll feel it when I get it*. But that's not going to work if you're going to become a deliberate, intentional manifestor.

If you're going to manifest a goal, you need to feel it before it actually manifests.

You've got to learn about the Power of Feeling and the Power of Thought and then learn to connect them. You have to learn how they connect with each other and work together to create that higher vibrational state. You've got to utilize these powers properly and correctly on a regular basis—as in make them a lifestyle—so that when you identify a goal to achieve or manifest in your world, you stay connected to that goal from its inception to its complete materialization.

POWER 5: The Power of Aligned Action

If you were to reflect on the word "attraction," what other word do you see in this profound word? That's right, it's "action." So, to attract what it is we genuinely want or desire will require us, by the Law of Attraction, to actually step into a certain amount of consistent, aligned or imperfect action—where we are deliberately disciplining ourselves into the embodiment of that higher-energy pattern of consistency, with our action steps.

Without action, and more **specifically** the right kind of action, **it would be almost impossible to successfully manifest our deepest heartfelt desires.** We are human beings that are destined to be actually doing something, implying that a large part of our focus genuinely needs to be on taking meaningful, consistent action. Someone who simply avoids action is only **holding themselves back** from their own unique expression of Soul greatness.

You see, when it comes to action, or more **importantly**, divine action—or action that is aligned with one's Soul or Higher Self, this seems to be something that has challenged **many** of us. This is probably why some think way too much about their goals and desires, and not enough time is spent acting on them. Perhaps this is what Goethe meant when he once said, "Thinking is easy, acting is difficult, and to put one's thoughts into action is the most difficult thing to do in the world."

Now, when consciously manifesting, the actions that we're most often engaged in will reveal in advance what it is we're in process of manifesting. In other words, whatever it is that my heart genuinely desires to have manifest, there will be a specific aligned action or **steps of action (one at a time)** that I will need to take. If my heart is desiring to have more love in my life, in the form of a new friend, business associate, a romantic partner, or a family member, there will be a specific action that I will be prompted to step into or take by that of my Higher Self or my Soul. This is also known as inspired action, as in, our Soul or Higher Self is inspiring us from within to move in a direction that's in alignment with itself or what it is that you've been inspired to achieve or have manifest in your world.

Now the cool thing is, you don't have to figure out exactly what the action is; whatever this action is, it becomes inspired by your Higher Self. You see, once I get really clear on what it is that I want and begin to feel into that want or genuine desire, then shortly thereafter, the aligned action step that I need to take becomes revealed to me. Then, all of a sudden, I'll find myself thinking about this action step that I not only know I am to be taking but am now inspired to **fully step into** or **engage in**. And if there's more than one action step for me to take here, then whatever the next step is, it will be revealed or will come to me and be really obvious.

The idea here is to simply trust in this process that my Divine Soul, or Highest Self, already knows what the next step of action will be in moving me towards the manifestation of my goal or my heart's desire. So as long as I'm not only willing to trust in this process but am also willing to follow through in this process of manifesting my goal, then I will always be inspired to take the very next action step that would be most right for me. In other words, whatever we're in process of consciously manifesting, there will be something for us to actually do, knowing that's the very next aligned action step for us to **engage** in.

So, whether it's love, money, success, or health, if and when we want something better, it will require us to actually do something. Maybe it's time for us to change our career. Or maybe it's time to level up with the career we already have. Or maybe it's time to check out a new approach to healing. Or maybe it's about accepting the invite to the social gathering or networking event that's coming. Perhaps there's someone that you're to be meeting there that potentially becomes the realization of one of your goals or desires. Or someone is there that ends up introducing you to the person that brings you to the realization or manifestation of your goals or desires.

> Trust that your Divine Soul already knows what the next step of action will be in moving you towards your heart's desire.

The key here is to identify the right action—the aligned action. And often we need to experience a few action steps that are not in alignment with our Soul or Higher Self to come to know the ones that are. This is known as imperfect action. Imperfect action is where we no longer have to know if this is the best action for us to take. Sometimes we're not sure of the action to take. And this is where this idea or this form of action can be very beneficial in our own conscious path of creating whatever it is we are intending to create. This is where we would just simply step into imperfect action as a significant way to advance ourselves in moving towards the best and most aligned action. This is a much better proactive strategy than the strategy that says, "I'll wait until it comes to me."

Action in itself is one of the highest active forms of prayer, as the action (imperfect or already aligned) when taken, becomes a way in which we express to the Universe or the Divine just how serious we are about having our heartfelt desires **actually** manifest. To echo the famous words of Emerson, "Your actions speak so loudly, I cannot hear what you are saying." Just as our actions speak louder than our words when it comes to others, our actions have a fair amount of volume when speaking out loud to the Universe what it is we genuinely desire to have manifest. They also give valuable feedback so we can adjust the next action step accordingly.

The courageous act of taking conscious action can also give us a new level of clarity around what it is we really want to create. It's also interesting to note that if we were to go for days on end without stepping into the action (imperfect or already aligned), our energy overall will begin to stagnate. You see, our body, thoughts, feelings, and even our being are all made up of energy, which means if the body is not allowed to physically move the energy that makes up our body, **our** thoughts and feelings within our body will start to move slower and grow denser. If this is our lifestyle, then eventually we will start feeling like we're stuck.

The only way out of this stickiness that was created by too much non-action is to consciously choose to take action. It is the higher act of proactively taking action (imperfect or aligned) that can literally change the energy around you for the better. This can ultimately be incredibly beneficial, **very empowering**, meaningful, and deeply transformational.

Action (not knowledge) is the fuel that powers the Law of Attraction and the Law of Manifestation; it is the energy behind your intention. To put it another way, just concentrating on your desire or goal is not enough. By taking aligned action or imperfect action, rather than accumulating more knowledge, you will be able to manifest all that you genuinely desire and often in a more expedient way. To quote the late, great Jim Rohn, "Don't let your learning lead to knowledge. Let your learning lead to action. And then you can create a life beyond anything you've ever dreamt about." And again, a general good rule here would be that it's always more powerful to get started with action than it is to wait for what it is we're to be doing in the form of an action step. Within the Soul's DNA we are encoded to be doing something, which will mean taking deliberate, intentional action steps that move our lives toward that something.

Aligned Action Step

Before every action you can ask yourself: Will this bring a distraction energy that moves me away from my greater goal? Or will this action bring me closer to my goal? Will the result of this action be a blessing or possibly a distraction? Will this action step be a positive progression, or possibly a heavy burden? If it becomes nothing more than a distraction that's keeping us from moving forward in our personal or professional world, it's more than likely a heavy burden. If a heavy burden, this is where we can possibly run the risk of it creating a negative consequence as well.

Now if it brings you closer to your goal, it's aligned with your Divine Soul. If it's a blessing, it's aligned as well. So do ask the question, as you will get the answer.

Here's a little hint: notice that when you're engaged in right, aligned action, there's a more relaxed energy behind the action—with the exception of perhaps the beginning phase of actually stepping into the action when we've been resisting or avoiding it. When it's aligned however, there's a somewhat effortless energy you notice once fully engaged in the action—often this can be a joyous energy as well.

On the other hand, when the action is more contrived, there's a tight or more pushing-oriented energy behind the action. Another way of saying this would be that you're trying too hard to make the action happen.

This is why intentionally embracing imperfect action as the way to get the energy moving in the right direction can be so empowering; it will lead us to aligned action. Then, as we practice a higher energy pattern of consistency to this action, over time it will have a compounding effect on the overall process in whatever it is we're manifesting on a conscious level.

POWER 6: The Power of the Spoken Word

We speak into existence that of what we wish on both a conscious and unconscious level. Jesus was a living, breathing example of this power. Often, he spoke something into existence with the power of his words. We can do the same. Now to get good at this we also need to realize that some of the words that come out of our mouths can be from our unconscious or subconscious. Sigmund Freud referred to these types of happenings as Freudian slips. This is where something just rolls off your tongue unexpectedly or without any advance notice. These Freudian slips can have a negative tone, a positive tone, an interesting tone, or a profoundly fascinating tone—all of which can reveal something of even greater significance.

> Vocalizing, where you're speaking into existence what you want to create and declaring what you want to have happen, would be using this power on a conscious level. Now if you were to connect these words to the feeling or emotion, into what you want to create or declare,

this would take your conscious manifesting ability to another level. In other words, when speaking a desire into existence, get connected to the feeling that'll lend even more power to your words.

You could use your words to make a commitment to someone else, affirming what it is you're going to do. Let's say, you give them your word. Which begs the question: on a scale of 1 to 10, 10 being really good, 1 being not so good, how good are you at honoring your word? How good are you at honoring your word with other people? How good are you at honoring your word to yourself?

A 9 or 10 answer would imply that you are connected to this power. Now if your numbers are lower than 9, this suggests you are disconnected or are becoming more disconnected from this Inner Power. This all comes down to: how good are you with your word? Or better yet, how impeccable are you with your word? The more impeccable, the more connected you are with our word, which means you have greater access to this Inner Power when consciously speaking one of your deepest desires into existence.

We can also use our words in the formation of powerful affirmations as a way to program our subconscious to get it to do what we need it to do. This would be us programming it to get fully on board with what it is we want to have manifest in our world. That said, there is an effective way of working with affirmations and there is also an ineffective way of working with them. More on that a little later in the pages that follow.

Our words, when connected to this Inner Power, can have a magical and life-changing effect on whatever it is we're in the process of manifesting. Some say that the spoken word is far more powerful than our thoughts. Words are thoughts that when expressed out loud can speak something (positive or negative) into existence. The Law of Expression says that when something is expressed, it is then pushed out into the Universe. And once pushed out into the Universe, it creates, or physically manifests, into more of its like.

Remember that Law of Energy, which also says that everything in the Universe, both collectively and in our personal worlds is made up of energy. How we choose to use our words is up to us. We could use our words to build someone up or to tear or wear someone down.

> How much honor do we place on our words? Once again, do we honor our word with others? Do we honor our word with ourselves? Do we follow through on what we say we're going to do? And have we made it so others can trust in our word?

Now let's this put this together with a couple of other Universal Laws. You might recall from earlier, the Law of Vibration and the Law of Attraction. Our words not only carry our energy but our vibration as well. You see, when we speak we're not just making sounds. We're literally sending out energy waves that affect everything and everyone around us. So, if the energy influencing our words is one of a lower vibrational frequency—as in fear, anger, blame, guilt, jealousy or judgement, it will then attract more of its like to itself. The Law of Attraction states that whatever the energy, it will always seek more of its own. In other words, if the energy that's driving our spoken word slants towards the negative, we will, by these laws, get more negative experiences or people of this like in our lives. If, on the other hand, the energy behind our words is truly more positive, we will attract more positive.

As it turns out, what we say and where we really are coming from (as in positive or negative) matters... because what we speak about most, eventually becomes matter. What we speak about comes about. What we talk about most will manifest. And here's the cool thing. It's a much greater challenge to control our thoughts than to consciously take control of our words. As Florence Scovel Shinn said, "Change your words and you change your world, for your word is your world."

Our words carry enough power to change our lives for the better. Our words can and will influence the spin of our magnetic force field–whether it's an upward or downward spin. Just as our thoughts create our reality, our words shape our reality. This is especially true of the words we use most that carry their own frequency in not only speaking with others but to ourselves as well.

> To use this Inner Power correctly however, we want to be paying more attention to how we speak about ourselves and others. How do you use your words when speaking of others? How do you use your words when speaking about yourself? Do your words slant more towards the positive or the negative? How much of your day do speak positively about yourself and/or others (when they are not around)?

Some can really talk badly about others behind their backs—is this a repetitive habit for you? If so, be mindful that this habit disconnects you from your own word and hinders your ability to manifest on a conscious level.

Ideally, we would want more of our spoken word to be in alignment with our divine essence or Soul. We would be using our words more consciously, more integrously, and more responsibly. We would be using our words in a way that is aligned with what it is we genuinely would like to see manifest in our personal and professional worlds.

The Universe, the cells in your body, your subconscious, and your inner child all respond to the vibration of your words. Whatever you follow with the two most powerful words in the Universe comes to be. I AM... I AM healthy, wealthy and wise. I AM Manifesting Like a Master. I AM able to manifest anything. I AM so happy and grateful that I live in a rich and loving Universe. I AM open to receiving far beyond my current dreams, goals, and intentions.

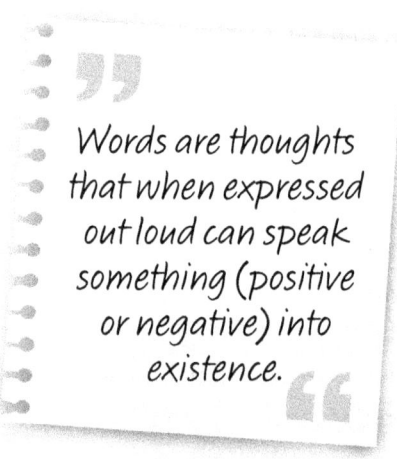

Words are thoughts that when expressed out loud can speak something (positive or negative) into existence.

Or, it could have a negative slant, which will manifest as well: I AM a loser. I AM fat. I AM negative. I AM miserable. I AM poor. Whether positive or negative, this is what will more than likely come to be. One of the master keys here is to become more aware and present with what follows these two words as they roll off the tip of our tongues—because whatever that is, it's likely we will get more of exactly that.

When you say, "I AM," you are calling forth the presence of God or your Higher Self. Instead of using our words in a way where we repetitively talk about what we don't want, we could (should we choose to) develop the habit of talking more often about what we do want. What might happen in our lives if we were to talk more about what we love, or what it is that makes us happy instead of what we hate or don't like? It would be good to remind ourselves over and over again that what we talk about most often comes about in our own personal Universe.

In the bible it says, God created the Universe and everything in it with words. This implies that our words do carry incredible power—as in, our power. The words we use and how we use them in communicating with others, whether our colleagues, our employees, our kids, our partner, or friends, can affect them. They can be empowering or disempowering. They can be constructive and beneficial or destructive and non-beneficial. What we choose to do with our own Inner Power of the spoken word is *up to us*. It's us choosing to use this power (whether consciously or unconsciously) as we wish.

POWER 7: The Power of Discipline

This Inner Power of Discipline is also a life-changing principle, as there is nothing that'll help you move the needle forward in your life more than self-discipline. To Manifest Like a Master, you will need to become conscious of bringing this rich and dynamic power into your day-to-day life. Should you choose to do this... should you choose to stick with this... this alone will level up your personal and professional life when it comes to consciously manifesting what it is you would love to see literally materialize in your physical reality.

To quote the famous Dr. Maxwell Maltz, "Self-Discipline is the golden key; without, you cannot be happy." Anyone who has achieved a greater level of sustainable success has been disciplined in the fine art of the right daily routine, whether it's a phenomenal athlete like the great one, Wayne Gretsky, or an iconic superstar, like Celine Dion, one of the most amazing singing artists in the world today (I mention her yet again because of how she has disciplined herself over time, especially in the earliest years of her extremely successful career). Both Wayne and Celine demonstrated the real power of this principle in their daily routines. This is where success is usually found...in one's daily routine. Celine trained with her vocals every day for 18 years. She also disciplined herself to cut out dairy from her day-to-day life, as she didn't want anything to affect her throat. Wayne began his most successful hockey career at the age of two. His father noticed he had a talent for skating. So, they got him in a daily routine as well.

Discipline is what differentiates someone mediocre or even ordinary from someone extraordinary. It is the super ability one can possess that will take them further than others. It is that powerful.

The great secret of success, as the prolific author Brian Tracy says, is there are no secrets to success. There are only timeless principles that have proven effective throughout the centuries. And this one principle (or Inner Power) of discipline will do more to assure that you accomplish wonderful things with your life than anything else.

Now if you don't integrate this principle into your daily life where you're using this Inner Power correctly, and you haven't ultimately turned it into a daily practice yet, it'll more than likely be impossible for you to ever achieve what you are truly capable of achieving. This super ability of self-discipline also comes along with real good self-control, and these two are always interchanging. It'll always take a certain amount of self-control when it comes to disciplining ourselves to follow through on the very thing we know in our bones we are to be doing.

Jordan Peterson says, "The most successful among us sacrifice; the successful among us delay gratification." In other words, you could say, discipline means you›re capable of making sacrifices... you›re capable of being able to delay self-gratification, which also takes a good amount of healthy self-control.

> *Success is usually found in one's daily routine... Self-disciple is the ability to make ourselves do the thing we may not feel like doing.*

Self-discipline is the ability to make ourselves do the thing, even when we don't feel like doing that thing. It's one of the most important qualities in life to develop and choose to express every day.

One of America's best sales trainers during the seventies through the nineties, Tom Hopkins, would teach during his sales seminars that the pain of discipline weighs ounces, whereas the pain of regret weighs pounds or even tons.

The opposite of discipline is procrastination. The age-old question: why do today what you can put off till tomorrow? The higher voice within us says *get it done*. It goes on to say, *do it now and continue doing it until you achieve your desired result*. The lower voice within says, Don't worry. You can always do it tomorrow. Or, Do what you can but not what you must. As one of my earlier mentors Jim Rohn would often say, "Discipline is the bridge between goals and accomplishment." Discipline is more important than motivation... motivation can get us going, whereas discipline keeps us growing.

In life we're constantly presented with two choices: Do it now or do it later. Jim would go on and say, "The rewards of a disciplined life are great, but they're often delayed to sometime in the future. The rewards for the lack of discipline are immediate, but they are minor in comparison to the immeasurable rewards of consistent self-discipline. An immediate reward for the lack of discipline is a fun day at the beach. A future reward of discipline is owning the beach. For most choose pleasure rather than tomorrow's fortune."

It's not success that makes us strong. It's the pain from where we are in the early stages of the conscious practice of disciplining ourselves, that makes us strong. You might think of what it was like when you were younger, and your body was still growing. Did you ever experience growing pains? Of course you did. We all did. This kind of pain is a very real part of growing. If we're on a higher energy pattern of progressive evolution and growth, it's going to hurt from time to time. It just is. It's like those pains in our body we experienced when we were younger. As our body was going through its growth spurts, it could or would hurt. That was the growing pain. And just like in life, if we want our career, our relationship, our finances, or our business to expand and grow, we're going to experience the pain of that new expansion and growth from time to time.

In life, we all suffer one of two things: the pain of discipline, or the pain of regret and disappointment, which comes in the lack of results we knew we could have achieved.

In order to be successful in whatever area of your life, you'll need to practice the right amount of discipline each day in a consistent way. In order to consciously *Manifest Like a Master* and perhaps with great precision, you're going to need to build a strong, powerful discipline muscle. The rewards that can result in the building of that inner muscle could be a happy relationship; a super healthy body; a rewarding, fulfilling career; a wonderful family; a productive, thriving business; a well-managed and fruitful bank account; financial freedom; and the list goes on.

> So how can we make the more powerful choice of discipline over procrastination? In Transform Your Destiny, one of the lessons that's highlighted in the book is learning how to better discern between temptations and opportunities. Temptations are usually disguised as what appears to be a good opportunity. However, should we choose to go for the temptation thinking it's a good opportunity, then the temptation will become a distraction. "A distraction from what?" you might ask. From moving your life forward.

The ego, your ego, can get very attached to maintaining the status quo, only because forward movement is often scary, as it poses an element of uncertainty or the fear of the unknown. As soon as you decide to move some aspect of you and your life forward, it often shakes something up in your external world and/or jars something loose that you had been hanging onto that was suppressed within you.

As soon as you decide to go to work on getting better at self-discipline on a consistent basis, everything will begin to change for the better. I'm not saying this will be easy. True discipline is not the easy option here; rather, procrastination is. It's easier to do just enough than do it all. It's easier to surf the internet for hours on end than to read a book. It's much easier to not do the thing you know is best for you to do when you say, "I don't feel like doing this right now," than it is to actually do it. It's easier to give in to your fears or even worship them than it is to face them. It's easier to keep doing it the way we've been doing it for years than hiring a real good coach—or attending a great seminar and learning a newer, richer, better approach. It's easier to continue to avoid the tough conversation with someone that's dear to you than it is to get on the phone or a Zoom call and courageously embrace the conversation. It's easier to stay in one's comfort zone than it is to courageously step into what's uncomfortable. Someone once said, "A comfort zone is a beautiful place, but nothing ever grows there."

Disciplined Action Step

Start with one disciplined action every day, and then, at some point, increase it to two disciplined aligned actions every day. It could have something to do with your eating habits, as in letting something go or adding something into your diet. Or it could be with your work habits, as in getting something done (hint: it's the thing you've been avoiding doing.). Or it could be a new business practice, such as making five calls a day... or a daily practice such as making your bed every day. Or spending a few minutes each day visualizing the achievement of your goals, or on the focusing of creating and installing new thought structures into your mind.

Remember, the right amount of discipline performed in a consistent way equals freedom. So, whatever the activity or project you're committed to doing, the more you stay engaged with the aligned, consistent, disciplined activity, the sooner you begin to feel and experience the freedom in your life personally, professionally, and even spiritually.

To maximize the transformational magic of these Inner Powers, we want to utilize these powers properly and correctly on a regular basis—as in make them a lifestyle—so that when we identify a goal to achieve or manifest in our own world, we stay connected to that goal from its beginning of inception to its complete end of materialization.

CHAPTER 8

PRINCIPLES OF MANIFESTATION

When we look at the Laws of Manifestation, many of them are governed by certain principles, so, in order to manifest consciously, we want to be aware of these principles.

The Principle of Suggestion

The first principle I want to highlight is the Principle of Suggestion. Suggestion is a very powerful thing, especially when it's done correctly. However, most people don't know anything about this principle, let alone know anything about how to actually work it in a way that's positive, healthy, and empowering.

There is a concept which I refer to as an old memory buried alive. This means all of the emotional charge around a past memory is still active inside of our cells. We could think of this like a repressed memory. It's typically a painful, traumatic, wounded memory that's been buried deep within the underbelly of our consciousness. It's still alive, however—and it will stay alive as long as that emotional energy is charging it. This is governed by Universal Law.

The Principle of Suggestion is completely dependent upon you being open enough to be suggested upon. You could be completely unconscious of this memory, but it still has energy—there is electrical, thought-based energy built into this memory, which means it's running the show in the background.

Somewhere along the line, you made a decision to disconnect from this memory—to bury it deep within your psyche. The Principle of Suggestion means that something was suggested upon your psyche, and your psyche took it on, hook, line, and sinker. In other words, there was no filtering. The suggestion part of this equation happened through whatever it was that we were experiencing—such as being abused by someone or some shocking event, like maybe we walked into a room to find our partner having sex with someone else. Or we received a call from someone letting us know we just lost a lot of money. Or we were notified that someone dear to us passed during the night, etcetera... It shocked us—as in, we didn't see it coming. Because it came from the experience that shocked us and it created the memory that has the emotional energy attached to it, the mind tucked it away because the experience was so shocking to our system. This is how it becomes a repressed or buried memory.

> If we're going to get good at manifesting on a conscious level, we've got to know how to use this and work with this, and there are very specific ways to utilize this principle with consciousness.
>
> One of them is referred to as an affirmative command. This is an affirmation said with conviction. It needs to be specific, clear, and should

directly speak to the part of you that takes on this command. Say, for example, we would like to become a more productive person, but we have a lazy part of us that gets in the way of us being more productive. So here would be a good affirmative command: *I love getting things done in a timely manner. It feels really good when I get things done. Every day in every way it's easier for me to step into action around the things I really need to get done.* (This might even be a good time to exercise your Inner Power of Imagination. To do this simply get a clear picture of yourself on the other side of you completing whatever it is you want to get done. This is where you would see yourself and what it would actually feel like on the other side of this activity.)

We developed a tool called the *Deca Tuner*, which is based on the Principle of Suggestion. When I designed the commands for this tool, we recorded my voice in the studio. My team and I got my voice exactly where it needed to be in order to record the specific affirmative commands. Now, if you play this tuner at the right time, in the right way, you're going to get tremendous benefit from it.

When you understand how to work this principle, it's so powerful, and it starts with these affirmative commands. Creating these affirmative commands is similar to dream interpretation. The more care and thoughtfulness that you put into this, the more richness you will get from the experience.

The Deca Tuner is a sophisticated tool. Hey, carpenters have 50 different tools, but what good is a carpenter if he doesn't know what each tool is for? What good is he if he can't utilize each of these tools correctly? It's the same concept when it comes to these principles. These principles are there all the time, 24/7.

So, you have to design the right affirmative command and do it properly. It's got to be done with conviction. And then, you've got to create an opening for the suggestion to be taken.

The Principle of Association

The second principle I want to highlight is the Principle of Association. This is a principle that is commonly misused all over the planet.

If we wanted to mess you up, if we wanted to pull you down to the lowest vibrational state, all we would have to do is bring in a couple of people and plant them in your day-to-day life that are already at that lower vibrational state and then find a way to get them to hang out with you on a rather regular basis. That's it. A year from today, the job will have been complete.

You see, if we're associating with thugs and we continue to associate with them, it might take a while, but at some point, we will become a thug. Now we can fight it all we want, but chances are we will become a thug too.

If we were to make a decision today that we're not going to smoke marijuana for whatever reason, and next thing we know, we end up with three friends that we spend a lot of time with who are always smoking marijuana, it might take a year, but somehow, some way, those three friends will most likely get to us.

This principle is so powerful. Talk about suggestion. This one is closely related to the Principle of Suggestion, as it is 100 percent suggestive to your psyche.

If you're going to get better at manifesting consciously, quite frankly, your absolute best strategy here would be to find a couple of people who are already really good at manifesting consciously and purposely associate yourself with those people on a regular basis for at least a year. Somehow those people are going to penetrate your psyche, just through this Principle of Association.

Charlie "Tremendous" Jones, a previous teacher of mine, used to say, "You will become like the three to five people that you spend the most time with."

> *We sometimes don't realize the consequences that are being created as a result of the choices that we make or continue to make.*

Relationships can be utterly detrimental to your being. When you decide to stay in an abusive relationship, a toxic relationship, or an expired relationship, it affects your psyche. If you could see the result that this is bringing about, you would get outta Dodge so fast it would make everybody's head spin around you.

But that's not the case, right? We sometimes don't realize the consequences that are being created as a result of the choices that we make or continue to make. The person stays in a toxic situation for five more years. They stay in an abusive situation for five more years. They stay in an acidic situation for five more years—and the situation will always have something to do with another person, another person that they're associating with.

I've watched entrepreneurs brought to their knees because they decided to remain associated with who they considered their top salesperson, who just happened to be the most negative person in their entire organization. They would not let him or her go. They were not willing to make that tough decision at the time. And when you have a top salesperson, that top salesperson always gets to spend more time with the sales manager (or the owner of the company).

The sales manager or the entrepreneur has no clue about the risk that he or she is putting himself or herself and their entire organization into because of these two principles—the Principle of Association coupled with the Principle of Suggestion.

I discovered these principles a long time ago, and I also decided a long time ago that they were going to be my guidelines to live by. Yet I'll watch people around me stay in nasty situations for years. Or they wonder why they get sick and have to be hospitalized. Then they wonder why they've lost all their money. They wonder why they have all this stress, all this anxiety that they've been living in 24/7. Now, all of a sudden, they have a heart condition, or they have a respiratory condition, or possibly have a hip condition. Whatever it is, there's a real good likelihood they did that to themselves. Why? Cause there's probably a lesson or two that they're to be learning about this particular situation in that of their own life, or in that of their own being.

This principle is similar to the laws in that you can't stop it from working, whether you like it or not. That's why I often say it'll serve you really well to learn how to like these principles. And what better way to learn how to like them than to understand them—to do exactly what you're doing right now?

An Exercise Around the Person You Spend the Most Time With

Here's a little exercise for you if you are a parent, or if you have a child in your life you mentor such as a niece, nephew, grandchild or godchild...

> Think about the person you spend the most time with—the person you associate with most. Would you want this person to associate with your son, daughter or the child you mentor? This person could be an aunt or an uncle, friend of the family, a grandparent, spouse, stepparent, next-door neighbor, babysitter, etcetera.
>
> If you were to know, beyond a shadow of a doubt, that if this person associated frequently with your son or daughter over the next year or so, then your son or daughter was going to become like that person, how would you feel about it? There's no right or wrong answer here, but it does put it ingive a whole new perspective on things now, doesn't it?
>
> The person, and your response, could be negative or positive. The outcome could be constructive or destructive. If the person you associate with the most in your life is a person you would love your son or daughter to be like, consider yourself blessed because of this principle.

I'm a big cheerleader of this principle, and I'm a walking example of this idea that many of us need an adoptive parent or family member because some of our birth family members, for whatever the reason, just didn't cut the mustard. And that's not to blame the biological family member because at one point, they were a child and had a parent, and so on.

> This example illustrates the choice you have—the choice to wake up and ask for someone to show up in your life.
>
> If you don't have kids, apply this example to someone else in your life whom you care dearly for.

I'm sure some of you have said this before: "I'm never going to become like my mom" or "I'm never going to become like my dad." Or maybe you've had a friend you heard say this. And then, 10 years later, what happens? They become the very thing they said they would never become. How the heck did this happen?

It's the Principle of Association at play.

Is the person who becomes their parent aware of this principle? Of course not. Had they been aware of it, what might have happened then? Well, it's still unclear because the person has to make the choice and they still have to do the work, but the reality is, should you choose accordingly and constantly renew that choice and go to work, you can change the outcome for the better.

Later on in a subsequent chapter we'll be learning about the Power of Control. Which means, according to epigenetics, we can actually change our genetics. We can change the behavioral patterns we picked up from our family members. Science has now confirmed what the true spiritualists knew long ago—that this change is actually possible.

Now I'd like you to do another exercise in your head, one that I've done so many times myself...

Ask yourself: Who are the three people that I spend the most time with? Who are the three people that I associate with most? Then ask yourself: "Do I want to be like them?"

Maybe you think, *No, one of these people is downright nasty. I don't want to be like them. They're way too negative and self-absorbed.* Or perhaps you have a really awesome person in your life that you can honestly, genuinely say you'd be honored to become like. If this is the case, maybe you can come to the realization that you've been blessed. This might just be the grace you've been asking for for years, and it's right in front of you.

In accordance with this principle, you need to start becoming aware of these things and doing some self-examination in your day-to-day world. Hopefully, once you start to apply purpose and consciousness to your life when it comes to these principles, you'll reexamine how you've been utilizing them in your world.

This is where I'm going to gently challenge you. I've broken down these principles so that you can increase your awareness and deepen your understanding, but now you need to examine your life—your precious life, which is a sacred gift that you were given by the heavens or the Universe. You don't want to abuse this gift anymore. You don't want to take advantage of this anymore. This is something we all ought to get right.

I look forward to the day when we have a university teaching our younger people to get this right. Until that day comes, our humanity is going to stay in this lower-energy type of patterning, where it's simply going to repeat like Groundhog Day, over and over.

We've had so many people who have taken their own lives and so many who have contemplated it. *This place kind of sucks*, they think to themselves. But, in all fairness, what kind of education did they receive? What kind of organized structure have they been living in? What have they learned about thus far in their own lives, prior to considering suicide?

> You could spend the next four months on any one of these principles in order to get them right, and that's assuming you're doing the right things each and every day to bring yourself into alignment where you're utilizing these principles effectively.
>
> It's like when you're doing a physical exercise, your physical form or your breathing could be off if you haven't taken the time to learn to do it correctly. Think about a sophisticated calisthenics pose. You have to make these little tweaks and adjustments, or else you're going to hurt yourself. It could take months to familiarize yourself with the specific exercise and get yourself into position. But once you're doing it properly, you've got magic happening.
>
> Once you've got these principles down correctly, magic will happen. You'll get better at manifesting those types of experiences that you genuinely would like to manifest in your day-to-day world, personally and professionally.

On a conscious level, once you get to this point, it gets very exciting.

At the beginning, when you're doing a new exercise, sometimes it's not very exciting because you're sore, and you don't see results right away. Maybe you've got a pattern of slouching over, and you've had this pattern for the last 20 years. This postural deviation might affect what you're trying to do, and it won't be easy to correct. You might need someone like a personal trainer to help you because it'll be so easy for you to slip back to your default. Your whole system has been rewired to accommodate this posture.

And yet all of that, just like your internal state, can be rewired. It really can. But this is where the work comes into play. This is where consistency comes into play. This is where the adjustments, the ongoing adjustments, or the ongoing tweaking, comes into play.

So, with this Principle of Association in mind, knowing what you do now—do you have somebody in your world right now that you can honestly and genuinely say, "I would love, or I would be honored, to become more like him or her?" If you do, you'll want to acknowledge that. You might even want to celebrate that. And you most certainly are going to want to cherish that because it's a pretty awesome thing!

If all the kids who were born on this planet had at least one person like this, that in itself would make a huge difference. All because of this beautiful and dynamic Principle of Association.

So, choose to be selective. Choose to be discerning. Your psyche is at stake here, and this part of you, deep within the underbelly of your consciousness, is part of your Soul.

The Principle of Gain

The Principle of Gain is an important one because if you aren't gaining anything on the inside, you're not going to build up your inner confidence—your self-esteem. In fact, it's more than likely going to move in the opposite direction.

> Life, believe it or not, is about achieving gains. We are divinely meant to have victories. In order to capture these gains or victories, however, we're going to need to slow everything down a tad. The very act of slowing everything down can challenge some people a lot. They're not used to slowing down and focusing on one of their gains for even five minutes. Though this is a short period of time, it challenges people because they just aren't used to it.
>
> However, if they don't focus on the gain or celebrate the victory, they don't reap the benefits that the gain offers. The biggest benefit being the increase in self-esteem and inner confidence.
>
> Now sometimes the celebration of the victory could be something as simple as taking a couple of minutes to acknowledge what it is you've just accomplished, either privately or with others. Other times the celebration of the gain could be a little more elaborate—as in treating yourself to a nice meal or to a fun outing. The point here is to help increase our confidence and self-esteem, we want to be sure to acknowledge our gain, even if it's brief.
>
> You're going to want to live by this principle, and by that I don't mean that you have to go to a five-star restaurant and blow $200. You could, if that's what you want to do, but that's not the message here. The point is that if you're going to get better at manifesting at a conscious level,

with precision, you're going to need a stronger level of self-esteem and a higher level of inner confidence.

We all know the value of having or building a winning mindset in life. It's equivalent to having a great attitude. How important is it for a great athlete to have the right mindset? How important is it for anyone that succeeds in life to have a winning mindset? The profession or area of life doesn't matter... this is one of the master keys.

Having the right, or a healthy, mindset steers everything down a better path. In sports, in business, in sales, or with one's personal or spiritual transformation, there's what's referred to as the winning effect. It's something we can create. When the winning effect is at play, everyone does better. So, the question might be, how does one go about building a winning mindset? Having a winning mindset comes down to this: How many wins have you had? When was the last time you had a win in your career, or your relationship, or in your finances?

Perhaps you just broke through a self-imposed ceiling you had been dealing with for years and as a result you're now experiencing a new level of success. Maybe you recently faced and ultimately healed one of your fears, such as the fear of rejection, failing, getting hurt, making the wrong decision, etcetera. Maybe it was the healing of an old safety issue, and you're now feeling and experiencing a whole new level of inner security and no longer have that controlling pattern. Maybe you've healed a karmic pattern... which is one of the most challenging patterns to completely transform... (For more information on karmic patterns, check out book two, *Transform Your Destiny*.)

Now considering your wins, how many of those did you take the time to actually acknowledge and celebrate? This is such an important step, as this is one of the keys to building real confidence in oneself. It also raises the odds of a person feeling better about themselves and their world. As you're getting better at consciously manifesting, you're doing so partly because of the way you're feeling about yourself. When you're feeling more confident about yourself, and that inner confidence is real, everything in life will become better, brighter, and richer.

What produces a winning or healthier mindset is having and building upon the wins and victories. This is how we create that winning effect that the team, the family, the soul group, or the individual can so greatly benefit from. It's healthy, it's fun, and it's intrinsically rewarding, as it fosters personal and professional growth. It helps to upgrade our frequency too. In other words, we're literally rising up to a new version of ourselves.

When we're upgrading our frequency and learning to manifest with precision, sometimes there are moments that are really exciting. They could be simple things. One example comes to mind with one of my students who excitedly told me that after she began this process, she saw a large bump in her credit score without any clear cause.

Something gets rewired within our nervous system at a cellular level, and moments later, there's a noticeable change that takes place in our external world. It happens naturally and organically. And we didn't even do anything (so to speak) to make it happen. Wow… how bout that?

More often than not, when I do a custom manifestation class for a company or an organization, by the time we're through the curriculum, the CEO has already given the command to get me on their schedule again. Why is that? It's because they now know, beyond a shadow of a doubt, that one of the problems they've been experiencing is that their people lack confidence in themselves; they lack self-esteem. And they know if that could be increased, so could productivity—and fast. Once the CEO sees that this is the issue, and they know what's at stake, they rush to guarantee that I'll come back. They've seen the magic that's happened, and it's now a no brainer to immerse all of their producers into the teachings on how to get better at this.

A Simple Exercise for Building Inner Confidence

> Find something that's going to lift your inner confidence, your self-esteem, by at least 10 percent in the next 12 months. Why? For a couple reasons... Number one, you'll become a better person because of it. Number two, you'll actually get better at manifesting what it is you genuinely wish to see manifest.

If we don't do this lift our inner confidence, then we're just going to get more of whatever it is we've already gotten. If you're okay with what you've already been getting, then you're already onto something. But if you're not okay with what you've been getting, and you want to have a richer existence, a more expanded life experience, then it would behoove you to do this. If you do, you'll become more effective and powerful. You'll become a better career professional, leader, entrepreneur, or coach. You'll become a better husband, wife, mother, father, teacher, healer, or student.

> Where do you want to take this? What do you want to accomplish? Because you can, most certainly, accomplish it. Remember, keep checking in on your results. Make sure you're getting new results because if

you aren't, something is off, especially if you're already a few months into the routine or program you've created for yourself to manifest. Then, celebrate those new results.

When designing your program, you need to have a specific focus to intentionally and deliberately look for gains. Hey, if all you did was take the time at the end of each day, where you write down your one to three wins from the day, and you were to do this for 30 consecutive days, you'd be amazed at the new way in which you start feeling about yourself and your life on all levels; personally, professionally and spiritually.

This aligned action step done at the end of each day becomes a simplified approach to capturing those victories or gains. It's a guaranteed way to assure they are being acknowledged on a regular consistent basis. With time, or over time, wins or gains that are celebrated in this way will naturally increase one's self-esteem and inner confidence while producing a winning mindset as well.

The Principle of Detachment

The Principle of Detachment is really one of "neutrality." This is one of the keys to manifesting our heartfelt desires faster. If I become too attached or stay attached to the achieved outcome of my goal, I will energetically jam up the manifestation process of achieving that goal. This is one of the reasons why affirmations, no matter how much or often you write them out or vocalize them, seldom work. They can put us into a state of attachment to the desired outcome.

Once we become attached to the outcome, we lose our ability to remain flexible to whatever adjustments need to be made along the journey in the manifesting of our desire. We also lose the ability to correctly see things as they truly are in reality. Therefore, we can miss out on those subtle signs or signals that are letting us know to slow down, back off, proceed forward, go left, go right, and so on... The detached state is the neutral state. The neutral state (aka, the flow state) is what we want to achieve, as this is where we get the greatest and most consistent access to our creative power.

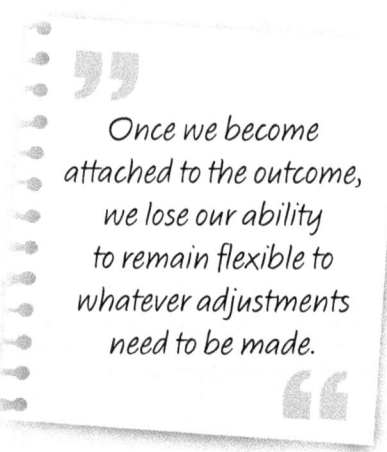

Once we become attached to the outcome, we lose our ability to remain flexible to whatever adjustments need to be made.

An example of this would be you're on your way out the door and you remember your car keys, as you don't have them on your person. You proceed to look for them and yet you can't find them. You frantically begin looking for them and you still can't find them. Then you finally let go of the want (or your attachment to the outcome of finding them). Shortly thereafter, you're prompted from within to go to your table or the countertop to move some things around, and there they are... your keys! The key here (no pun intended) was we actually let go of our intense attachment to the act of finding our keys.

So what happened? Can you see it? You temporarily misplaced your car keys. For the life of you, you couldn't remember where they were. You quickly became attached to the outcome of finding them, at which time the craziness ensued. It only began to resolve itself when you chose to resign to the idea that they were nowhere to be found. Which now meant resolving inside of yourself that'll you'd be late for your meeting, or you'd have someone else in the family go pick up your kids. And shortly thereafter, you were prompted to do something like move something around in your house or office, at which time your car keys materialized once again. Why? You got yourself back in flow. You were then in that flow state. All of a sudden, you were no longer trying to force anything.

To live in this healthier state, we must learn how to let things happen. This is one of the most profound teachings of Taoism known as *the art of not trying.*

Trying to make something happen is another form of needy energy. If we become needy for whatever it is we desire, we then weaken the magnetic pull for us manifesting that desire. Non-neediness is another one of the keys to increasing our magnetic energy field. The magnetic energy of someone automatically strengthens when they become non-needy. This is where they no longer need anyone or anything to be a certain way for them to feel safe or secure in their own world. When we detach our energy, and we don't care about the outcome, or we're not attached to a desired outcome, we are back in the flow state, simply being more of our Divine Soul Essence. This is where our most meaningful goals, deepest desires, and real opportunities reveal themselves to us.

In this state of neutrality of flow, we are deeply anchored in the *now*. In this state, we aren't distracted by past regrets or future anxieties. Every ounce of our attention is riveted on the present task. In our current time of today's culture of psychology, the flow state has been linked to heightened creativity, increased productivity, and enhanced well-being.

Choosing to create or manifest that of which we truly desire is best done by living in this flow state or this state of neutrality or detachment. This is equivalent to living our life in a state of letting go—letting go of any attached needy energy to a desired outcome, for as we do, the Universe or the Divine, as my Higher Self, can now assist me in manifesting whatever it is I wish to see manifest in my world. There's another principle at play here as well. "What it is that you seek is seeking you." In other words, whatever we genuinely desire is also desiring us. And we can literally jam up or downright block the manifestation process when we become attached to the outcome we're so desperately trying to accomplish or manifest.

So, as we let go of our attachments and choose to trust that it's coming, we can gently remind ourselves that it too is seeking us. In fact, it might already be here. Similar to the car keys. They were already there, even though back in that moment we thought they weren't.

The Principle of Active Visualization

This principle is like a potent tool that can transform one's inner landscape. And according to the Law of Correspondence, as our inner landscape changes, so does our outer landscape. As within, so without.

This is the principle we use that activates the Power of our Imagination. We use it all the time in a multitude of ways. We use it every time we get a picture in our mind. We use it when we are engaged in self-talk. You know, whatever it is (positive or negative) we tell ourselves over and over again. This produces images that we then visualize or imagine on the screen of our mind. The funny thing is, we've been active with it, whether we are aware of it or not. Recall one of Einstein's discoveries touched on earlier in this book: what we imagine mostly is a preview of life's coming attractions. You see, imagination (along with your mind) is the most powerful creative instrument you possess when it comes to manifesting your deepest, most genuine desires. As the late, great Neville Goddard would teach, "In reality, the imagination is the bridge between the invisible and the visible."

> *Imagination is the most powerful creative instrument you possess when it comes to manifesting your deepest, most genuine desires.*

Now as we become aware of this dynamic Principle of Visualization, we could use it actively for accomplishing our most meaningful goals, strategic objectives, and higher intentions. Athletes, entertainers, professional salespeople, businesspeople, and leaders of organizations consciously and regularly use this principle prior to their performances, presentations, and meetings. The practice here is where the professional will always take the time to mentally rehearse the desired result they wish to achieve from that of their performance, prior to doing whatever it is that they do. This is where the body will follow the mind. And when the mind has been prepared properly prior to showtime, the body then will follow that which has already been mentally rehearsed well. And sometimes the body will recreate it precisely how it was rehearsed in the professional's mind prior to the actual performance.

As we deepen our understanding of how this principle really works and we are truly working with it as an active daily practice, we will get better at consciously using this Principle of Visualization. The new and improved results that manifest in our life will serve as our gauge letting us know just how good we're becoming in masterfully using this powerful principle.

Again, as mentioned above, everyone has already been using this principle towards the positive or the negative—whether they've been aware of it or not. That is a fact. Put it to the test. Hey, see if you can catch yourself using it. How are you using it? Towards what means? Were you using it towards the good, or the not-so-good? The English poet and civil servant John Milton wrote, "The mind is its own place, and in itself can make a heaven of hell, or a hell of heaven."

> Active visualization is about learning how to build clear, vivid images or pictures in our mind. We also want to infuse the right emotion into these images. This would be us consciously engaging in our Inner Power of Feeling—to fully feel what it would feel like, as if we are already in possession of it, on a consistent and regular basis. Just be sure to place yourself in the scene of your visualization. Imagine you already have it. What does that feel like? What are the emotions you're experiencing now that you're in possession of your wish.
>
> Emotion is what gives your visualization life when it comes to conscious manifesting, we want to shift our focus from how we're going to manifest our desire onto what it will feel like when we actually have it. This is a very crucial point, or a most powerful dynamic for

> manifesting—which is emotion. You see, it's the feelings you experience while imagining or visualizing your heart's desire that's key. It's the master key in programming your subconscious. And when you fully feel the feelings, the Universe then responds. In addition you can pull on other senses and details, as in shapes, colors, taste, and hearing others who are dear to you congratulating you; telling you how proud they are of your incredible accomplishment and/or how happy they are for you.

This is where our brain starts to think this is real. This is where your subconscious starts to believe this is real. And this is where the magic of manifestation truly begins. I believe this is what William James meant when he wrote, "The greatest discovery of my generation is that human beings can alter their lives by altering their attitudes of mind." Attitudes of mind are the same as beliefs that empower us to alter our lives in the best of ways. You see, your positive thoughts and mental images that you focus on most have the transformative power to reshape your personal universe and to manifest your dreams and goals into reality.

> Whenever visualizing, always do so with intent and follow with aligned action. Decide on what it is you want. Pick an outcome you specifically want to accomplish. This could be in the area of your spirituality, your relationships, your career, your health, your parenting, or your finances. Then, create a vivid picture of it in your mind. One that's clear and detailed, where you can touch it, sense it, feel it—really feel it. And believe that you deserve it; assume you already have it. And from this place of assumption, how does it feel now that you've achieved your desired outcome in the construct of your own mind?

EXERCISE: 6 Steps of Active Visualization

Here are 6 steps to actively work with this Principle of Active Visualization:

1. Pick a career outcome, relationship outcome, health outcome, financial outcome, etcetera—whatever is up for you at this time—and write it down.

2. Once you have visualized this and its outcome, specify on paper what you want to have manifest regarding this visualization.

3. Imagine the end of what it is you genuinely want here.

4. Repeat this visualization before bedtime, as your subconscious is more receptive at this time of day.

5. During your visualizing time at the end of your day, be sure to feel it "as real." Meaning, feel it like it is yours already—it has already been achieved. See yourself on the other side of having already accomplished this. Remember whatever it is you're seeking is also seeking you.

6. Aligned action: taking action is what changes the energy around you. What's the one action, if you were to do it first thing tomorrow morning, that would move the needle forward faster than any other action for the day, towards the achievement of your desired outcome? Write this down before you go to bed, as this will help your subconscious to better engage this action step the following day.

Lastly, the active daily practice of visualizing becomes much easier to do each day when we're enjoying what it is we do. When we enjoy what we do and who we hang out with most, it keeps the channel within us open to greater creativity, aligned soul action, more aliveness, and that higher-frequency feeling of freedom.

This is when our real self effortlessly shines through. Being happy with who we are now along with the conscious pursuit towards the life of our dreams is a powerful recipe for manifesting synchronistic events. We are magnetic. When we feel so at one with ourselves where we are no longer worried about the outcome, things start appearing right in front of us.

The regular practice of active positive visualization is not only an effective tool to use but it's a superpower as well. Hey, if we were to get good at using this Inner Power correctly, it could literally transform our reality in the biggest and best of ways—in any area of our life, whether that be personally, professionally, financially and/or spiritually.

> With each specific outcome or desire, identify an action step. Once you've executed on a specific action step, and as you're coming to the completion of that step, you can ask yourself what it is that you'll need to do next. As in, what would be the next beneficial thing for you to step into? For most of us, this particular part is usually more important than the visualization itself, as it sends a clear, powerful message directly to your subconscious. This action, when fully engaged in, is how your subconscious ultimately takes in the message that you really believe you deserve this, as you're willing to stand up for it by doing the right thing—the right thing being the aligned action step. It's the right action step taken that liberates you from whatever energetic shackles that have been holding you back.

Prolific author Joe Vitale says, "Liberating yourself is the missing secret in all self-help programs. Often, we contradict ourselves in declaring a desire or a want to manifest a specific outcome, while our actions speak otherwise." When we show up this way, we are programming our subconscious with the message that says we don't want to manifest that specific desire or outcome. And it (being our subconscious) will steer us away from our dreams and goals when we contradict ourselves in this way.

So, if we're in that heart place of genuinely wanting something to successfully manifest in our world, we then want to make sure that our actions are also lined up with our visualizations. Actions that are truly aligned with what it is we are visualizing as a consistent intentional practice are how we send a powerful message to our subconscious and the Universe about what it is we truly want to see manifest in our own personal and professional universe.

CHAPTER 9

THE THREE PILLARS FOR MANIFESTING

The triangle on this page represents the creative process, the next step to manifesting what you want.

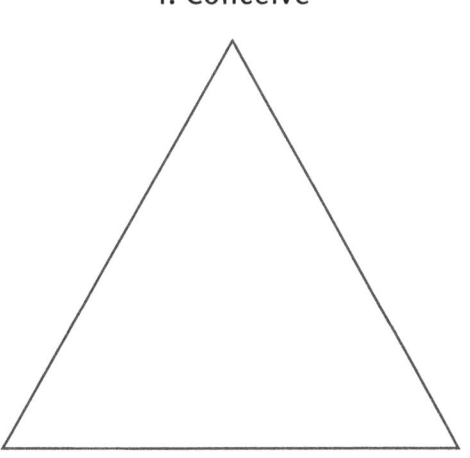

1. Conceive

2. Believe
State of Being

3. Receive
State of Doing

In order to manifest your desires, you must touch each of these points, or the three pillars, on the triangle. Each point on a triangle is connected, and you can't have one point without the other two. This triangle represents a field of energy to support the creation of whatever it is you're in the process of manifesting.

Pillar 1: Conceive

The first pillar, which is at the apex of the triangle, is to conceive. Once again, we are going to want to conceive what it is we wish to manifest from the place of our Soul. Like mentioned before, we can also manifest, and often do, from our ego—or the lower realms. To be clear, it's not that manifesting from the ego is a bad idea. It's all part of everyone's journey in learning how to manifest from the Soul.

We spend a portion of our life manifesting from the ego. This is all being done on purpose. We do this until such time where we get better at manifesting from our Soul, or our Divine Soul Essence Self. Another reason why it is a good idea to get better at connecting with our Soul is to discover the wants and desires of our Future Self.

So, what does conceive mean in this context? You're likely thinking of the birth of a child. Well, in order to give birth to a child, there needs to be a conception. An idea, a goal, or a dream, quite frankly, is no different. You first conceive the dream; you conceive the goal.

Now, the birthing process coming from the Soul will be very different than the birthing process of what's being conceived in the lower realm—which is the ego, shadow, or inner child.

For example, the inner child might conceive a mommy in the form of an adult relationship. It sounds strange, but if your inner child wants a mother, and you are unconscious of this wanting energy, then you might manifest a relationship that is a result of that want. So, if the inner child conceives this relationship where the other person is going to be the mommy, then it's going to seem like a love relationship. But after the honeymoon phase, reality is going to set in. You might find your behaviors are like that of a child around this person, as they are becoming the mommy in the relationship.

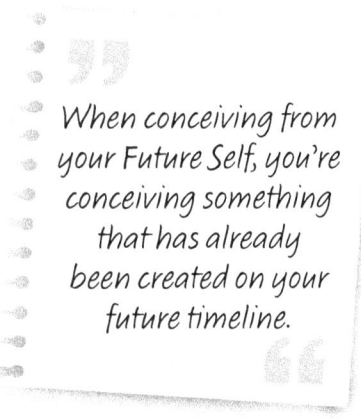

When conceiving from your Future Self, you're conceiving something that has already been created on your future timeline.

Now the reverse can happen, as well. You might have an inner parent who conceives a child in the form of a relationship. Once the inner parent conceives this relationship, then you start putting out the signal—a broadcast—and then this whole experience begins where you will manifest the one that is operating from the wants of the inner child.

If you're more unconscious than you are conscious, this is the type of manifesting you probably will do. Your Higher Self will take a back seat, willingly, until you do the work to become conscious. The Soul is patient, and it will allow this process to take as long as it takes. If that's the case, you're going to experience more pain. That's why it's important to consciously connect with your Soul—your Future Self—when you are conceiving your goals, your aspirations or your dreams.

Essentially, when you're conceiving from your Future Self, you're conceiving something that has already been created somewhere on your future timeline. Your Future Self already has it. I know that's a mind twister. It's a big idea to wrap your brain around. But if you can get your mind to work through this concept, it's a very powerful teaching.

If you're conceiving from your Future Self, the birthing process is still going to happen. It always does. The difference is now what you're conceiving is already in consciousness, which is very different than attempting to create something outside of consciousness (this is where the ego creates from—unless, of course, the ego has been trained to approach this differently).

Pillar 2: Believe

> The second pillar is to believe in the conception—to believe in this process. Now, to do this, you're going to have to activate an inner muscle and strengthen it. It's not a muscle you can see, but it does exist, and the more you work it, the stronger it gets. The belief is what begins to pull that which has already been achieved by your Future Self towards you like a tractor beam.
>
> The active part of this pillar is installing that belief into your consciousness. That's where you apply this muscle. Once it's installed, you don't need to actively do anything. It's like a program on your computer. This program once installed—this belief once strengthened—is now running in the background at all times.

Beliefs can be tricky as well. How much time do you normally put into believing what's being birthed or manifested into your life? Or do you not give this much thought? Many people bypass this pillar, and that's just denying this part of the creative process. But by becoming conscious of it, we can utilize it to *Manifest Like a Master*.

> There is so much creative power to manifest with that naturally releases when you totally believe at a subconscious level that you truly deserve this and actually believe you already have it within you. The ongoing master key here is in becoming the very thing you genuinely desire to see materialize in your physical reality. To this however, *we continue to believe it until we become it.*
>
> We often have beliefs that don't serve us—as in beliefs that limit us, sabotage us, or hold us back from achieving a higher and greater good. So, how do we change those beliefs? Well, the first step is to recognize that they're not serving us—which also means becoming conscious of them.

So, what about creating a belief?

I was born and raised in Canada and lived there for the first 30 years of my life. There was a show called *That's Incredible*, which created an immediate following. The series lasted a few seasons and did really well. The reason why it did so well is because the whole show was based on incredible stories, the type of stories that would leave you wowed—chin-hanging-on-the floor wowed—and they were all true.

One of the stories that impacted me most had to do with this lady who was driving northbound from Calgary, which was my home city. She was making her way northbound and was coming through a little town called Red Deer, Alberta. There were maybe 40,000 to 50,000 people living there at the time.

Just as she was approaching Red Deer, she noticed this car off from the side of the highway that looked abandoned, but she had this sense—this gut feeling—that told her to pull over.

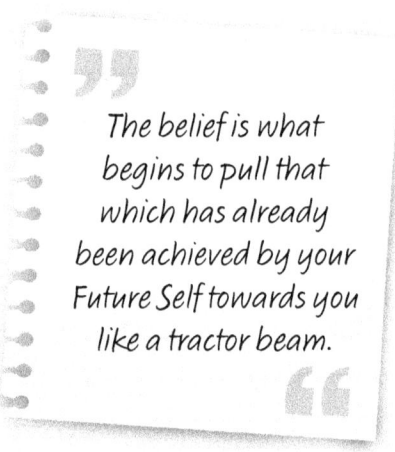

The belief is what begins to pull that which has already been achieved by your Future Self towards you like a tractor beam.

She pulled over and got out of her car to look inside the vehicle to see if there was anyone in there. There was nobody inside the car. Suddenly, she heard this noise that seemed to be coming from the front end of the car. She made her way over and saw feet hanging out from underneath the car. Right away, she knelt down, and she realized that it was a man gasping for air.

Something had happened to the hub of his wheel, so he had pulled off to the side of the road and taken out his pump-up jack to remove his wheel. He had taken the wheel off and gotten under the car, and the jack had slipped. This was a common occurrence back then with those types of jacks. The hub of the wheel had come crashing down onto his chest.

And there he was, hanging on by a thread. He could barely breathe and was gasping for air.

Yet in a split second, this woman grabbed the bumper of the car with both hands and lifted the front end of the car off the ground. Then, in the next second, she released one hand from the bumper, knelt down, and grabbed the man's leg, dragging him out from underneath the car. She saved his life.

Now, you might be thinking, *Well, that's no big deal. I've heard stories like that before.*

But this lady had a petite frame. She was no more than five foot two, maybe 105 pounds. And she was 84 years old.

This was an incredible story, a real story, a story that literally happened only miles up the highway from where I lived.

And this woman saved that man's life because she believed in a possibility. She believed in a possibility that she was going to turn into a reality, and she only had seconds to do it in, or the man would have died.

I had a life-changing experience the night I heard that story. I discovered something very important, which was that this power wasn't just inside of me; it was also inside of the hundreds of people that I was leading—that I cared for at the time. That day I decided that I would dedicate my life to helping people believe in a higher and greater possibility. Helping people believe in that of their true self. Helping people believe that they can conceive, that they can go through this birthing process, that they can create the life of their dreams, that they can achieve their goals.

This tiny little woman had a remarkable power inside of her. I know 285-pound men who couldn't do what she did if their lives depended on it, because they don't believe. They haven't turned on that muscle yet. And because they haven't been building that muscle, they have no idea what they're really capable of doing.

So, when you conceive something, guided by your Future Self, it goes into this creative birthing process. And once you begin to believe in this higher and greater possibility, magic happens. That magic comes upon you and enters into your field of consciousness. That magic of belief empowers this sacred creative process when you're manifesting something that's of value, that's of significance to you at soul level.

Pillar 3: Receive

The third pillar, or point of the triangle, is receiving. To receive means that you do nothing, and some of us aren't very good at this. To some people, this is the trick of all tricks. This third step challenges them to the very core of their being.

I want you to reflect on this concept of receiving when it comes to your life in general — and you need to be brutally honest with yourself here. On a scale of one to ten, 10 being you are really good at receiving, 1 being you suck, how would you rate your ability to receive? Do you block what's coming your way? Or do you welcome it with wide-open arms?

If you're having trouble with this, here's an example: For me, this receiving issue is very easy to spot. There are some people where if they drop something, say from their pocket or their purse, and when I reach down to pick it up from the floor, they won't let me. Even though I'm already there. They have a receiving issue.

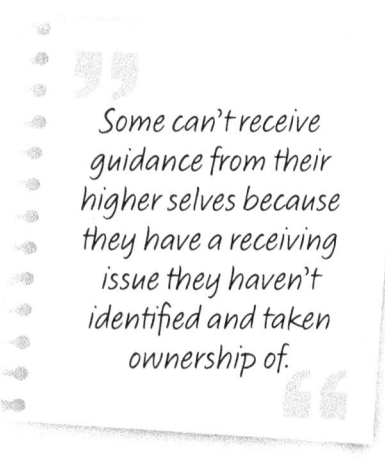

Some can't receive guidance from their higher selves because they have a receiving issue they haven't identified and taken ownership of.

If you can identify with this—if you have an issue receiving from a friendly person picking something up off the floor, or opening a door for you, or any other small form of assistance—then you can be assured you're gonna have an even more challenging time receiving from your Future Self. For those of us that are so accustomed to reacting this way, this will more than likely be a big-time struggle for us. We've got this hardened belief system that we're so driven by. In other words, everything's gotta be so freaking hard.

I have watched people die working themselves to the bone. I've seen people live in front of their computers. I'll try to give these people guidance, and they can't receive it. And it's not just from me. They can't receive guidance from their higher selves because they have a receiving issue that they haven't identified yet and taken ownership of.

> So, I invite you to spend some time reflecting on these questions: When you're manifesting what you want, once it starts to show up, can you just receive it? Can you simply allow it in? Or are you still going to struggle for it? Or do you still have to work hard for it?

When somebody has a receiving issue, what's really going on is they have a self-worth issue. This is highlighted in *Being Called to Change*, book number one in the trilogy. If you really strip down this receiving issue, you'll see that the person who has trouble receiving doesn't feel worthy of something that might be healthier, or more vibrant, or more loving, real, sacred, or special.

Now if we have a difficult time receiving, the only way to fix this is to just sit there and receive. That's it. It's so simple. When our Soul is trying to communicate with us, just receive what our Soul is telling us. When our mentor is saying something to us, just receive what our mentor is saying to us.

So, as simple as this is, what's worthy to note is when we choose to sit there and receive, this is where we want to pay attention to what comes up for us. How do we show up around this simple exercise of just sitting there and allowing ourselves to receive? Will we notice what it is we do next, either in thought or deed? Can we continue to sit there and simply receive? Or do we find ourselves having to do something else as a way to cover up whatever it is that's coming up for us around the act of receiving?

We might have a tendency to pretend like we're listening when someone is trying to help us, to give us guidance—when really, we're already thinking of our defense. We're already thinking of what we're gonna say next, and we get stuck in our mind. As soon as he or she takes a breath, our mind is diving into all the possible responses, because when we have a receiving issue, we also have a listening issue. One of the ways this deep-seated receiving or self-worth issue shows up is when we are not listening.

When we're speaking to someone with this issue, we always have to repeat ourselves, who knows how many times. And then when they finally listen, they're hearing it for the first time, even if we've said it five times before. And then, they want to defend. They're too much in their head. Somebody who lives in their head a lot is not a good receiver. They're not a good listener.

So, coming back to the triangle—the creative process—let's say you're able to conceive from your Future Self. You're now in the birthing process of creating whatever it is you want to manifest. You believe in whatever it is you're in the process of manifesting, but... you're unable to receive. You've got a serious self-worth issue that you're not on top of yet. In other words, you haven't been doing the work to heal this, so it continues to show up as a receiving issue.

What does that mean? The triangle gets broken. It gets broken at this receiving point, and you know what happens when one of the points breaks? You guessed it. The triangle doesn't work. The field of power is rapidly weakened, despite two of the points being strong.

In this case, you obviously have at least a couple of limiting beliefs in your overall system of beliefs. They're living somewhere in the underbelly of your consciousness saying life has to be hard, life has to be a struggle that never ends, life has to be hellish even.

As long as we maintain these limiting beliefs (whether we are aware of them or not), we'll maintain this receiving issue. But once we start going after the receiving issue—once we heal the self-worth issue—it's just a question of time. That limiting belief is going to surface so that we can address it and ultimately clear it.

When we have a receiving issue, we also have a listening issue.

So, in this process of creating whatever it is we're going to create, if at any point this triangle gets broken, the birthing will not happen. There will be no conscious manifestation. This is where we would continue to manifest what it is we don't want, for the most part. We will manifest from the lower realms instead of from our Future Self or our magnanimous Soul. Eventually where we all want to ultimately be manifesting from is from the Soul Self.

State of Being

On the triangle, within the Pillar of Believing is the State of Being. The State of Being is foundational to belief. It would be really beneficial to take a look at this aspect of your life. Do you enjoy doing what you do? Do you enjoy hanging out with whomever it is you hang out with?

So many times, I've heard people talk about how they don't even like their own family or a certain family member. They get all stressed out when they're getting together for a social gathering. Maybe there are people that have you feeling anxious when you're around them. Maybe you have to watch everything that comes out of your mouth, and you feel like you can't be yourself. What does that do to your state of being? What does that do to your creative process?

"We'll see" they say... Is there anyone in your life who, when sharing the new direction that you're now moving in, when you're expressing what it is you believe that you're in process of manifesting, they reply, "We'll see"?

For some, that might motivate or spur them on even more, as they have something to prove. With others, they could walk away with the thought, *Wow they don't believe in me.*

To this, it might be helpful to know, the one who typically uses that reply, "We'll see," is the one who only believes it when they see it—not only with you but with themselves as well.

You'll want to safeguard, or cherish, your state of being because when you're creating, you want to come from the highest place. In order to do this, on a practical level, you must genuinely enjoy what you're doing and who you're around. This is going to directly impact your ability to believe in yourself and that higher, greater process of manifesting whatever it is you wish to see manifest in your day-to-day life—it's going to strengthen it. You want to be mindful in who it is you choose to share one of your most important goals with, as they might only be able to believe you when they first see it manifest on a physical level. Some have made the mistake of sharing their goals with someone they care about, thinking that the person will be excited for them, only to be crushed minutes thereafter, mainly because the other person is still wired or programmed to think that way. They'll only believe in a higher or greater possibility in anyone, including themselves, when they first can see it physically manifest with their own eyes.

On the other hand, those people you also care about and genuinely enjoy hanging out with or being associated with are going to affect your state of being in the best of ways. It's super important to understand this. As your state of being rises, this ability or muscle inside you will strengthen, as it's now being empowered. You'll be able to believe in this birthing process in a deeper, greater, and more powerful way.

State of Doing

On the triangle, within the Pillar of Receiving is the State of Doing. Your state of doing will be directly correlated to your self-worth and receiving ability.

If your state of doing and/or action is in alignment, you really are good at receiving—and you're in touch with your worth. You've healed any worth issues you may have had. You know that you are worthy—not cocky, not arrogant, not entitled.

This worth begins to pervade every cell of your physical body. It's a state of knowing. You know that you're worthy of whatever it is you're manifesting. This all gets reflected in your doing. How so? Well, you'll end up doing the right thing the first time around!

You'll end up marrying the right person the first time around.

You'll end up befriending the right person the first time around.

> *If your state of doing and/or action is in alignment, you really are good at receiving—and you're in touch with your worth.*

You'll end up taking on the right project—the one that's most right for you to take on at soul level—the first time around.

You find the right investment at the right time.

That's how you'll know you've really got it. Everything about you from the inside out is functioning on a healthier, higher level. That then becomes reflected by you.

If, on the other hand, your self-worth, your listening, your receiving, is off, you're going to be knocked off course. You'll go and decide on something to invest in, and then, eight months later, you'll realize that the timing was off—or it wasn't the right decision for you to be investing your money in the first place. Maybe there was something else you were meant to do with your money, but you never discovered it because your receiving ability was off.

You'll know it when you're there, because there's also a feeling that comes with this. There's an energy that comes with this. It's a pure energy. It's a smooth energy. It's a graceful energy. It's an energy of alignment with your Divine Soul Essence Self. There's serendipity and synchronicity, and it's magical. It's divine. And it's all due to you being lined up properly with your ability to receive. Your receiving is embodied because you feel worthy. Your worth has permeated your cells—your real worth.

As a result, it's easy. It's natural for you to receive whatever it is that you're receiving, whether it's a smile from somebody, or a compliment from somebody, an act of kindness from somebody, or an act of generosity from somebody.

In the context of your creative process, you're able to receive the full-on manifestation of your greatest goal, which is emanating out and from your Future Self—the part of your Future Self that already has the goal. It already has the dream. It already has the desire.

Whatever the desire is, you are making contact with it, you're actually touching it, and then you're bringing it into this creative process where you conceive it and begin to believe in it. As it comes in, you're already in a fully receptive state. You are just naturally able to receive it. There's no more fight. There's no more struggle. There's no more of the hard stuff. There's no more unconscious resistance.

Using these three pillars is going to activate any limiting beliefs you hold. But in this case, you want to activate them so you can chip away at them with the intent to dismantle them once and for all, from the underbelly of your consciousness. Once every point is connected, this triangle is extremely powerful. It's a force field that you create as a way to turbo charge or even go quantum within this process of manifesting whatever it is that you really are divinely meant to be manifesting—as in your most genuine, heartfelt desires.

CHAPTER 10

BECOME WHAT YOU DESIRE

Does the athlete achieve greater levels of stardom and success when they're an intermediate athlete or when they become a great athlete? Does the university student achieve a high GPA when they're an average student, or when they have become a great A+ student? Does a parent raise a mature responsible son or daughter when they're an inconsistent and sometimes overly critical parent or when they become a great parent? Does a sales manager produce super star salespeople when they're a low-performing sales manager or when they become a great, high-performing sales manager?

> Reflect on something significant in your life... where you had a specific area of desire to manifest something specific in your personal, financial, or professional success that you had a genuine desire to manifest.world. And then it manifested. You achieved it. Did you become someone different from who you were before achieving something meaningful—such as the student who became a great student prior to manifesting a 4.0 GPA? Or did you roll out of bed one morning and

your genuine desire just manifested without you having to become something new and better? Likely not, at least with most of us. We had to become something that we hadn't yet become.

As we look at those who have truly accomplished something great or manifested something beautiful in their day-to-day lives, we'll see that they all became someone or something new. So, the question here could be: what came first... their manifested desire or becoming something/someone new?

This chapter is all about becoming and the transmuting of lower-frequency energies along our way in doing so. We'll also explore our next Universal Law, the Law of Perpetual Transmutation of Energy, and a few more principles for powerful manifesting, beginning with our first principle.

The Principle of Becoming

The Principle of Becoming is a higher-ground principle. This principle is always running in the background but needs to be activated in order for you to benefit from it.

In book one of the trilogy, *Being Called to Change*, the reader was introduced to the idea of who it is they are becoming. More specifically, I implored the reader to ask themselves: "Who do I want to become?" In book two, *Transform Your Destiny*, we approached this concept from a different angle. And in this, the third book, we're again coming at this question from yet another point of view.

This concept, this question, falls under the Principle of Becoming. Even if we don't activate it consciously, it is still in effect. We are always becoming something—whether we become the bank robber or the law enforcement officer; the victim or the victor; a pessimist or the optimist; the unavailable, checked out, immature parent or the available, responsible, mature parent; a wonderful, honoring, respectful partner or a disrespectful partner that possibly becomes abusive; an ineffective, weaker salesperson or the more effective, consummate sales professional; an empowering, authentic leader that is totally in service to the people or an inauthentic, controlling leader that is mostly in service to themselves, etcetera. The truth is, whether it's positive or negative, we are always becoming someone or something.

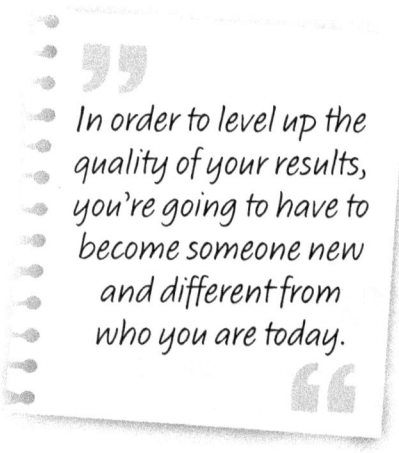

In order to level up the quality of your results, you're going to have to become someone new and different from who you are today.

If we're conscious of this principle, then we can work with it, not under it. And ultimately when we come to the end of our life experience, we'll be happy and content—but more specifically, we'll be at peace with who and what it is we've actually become.

We can become toxic not only in our bodies but also in our personal and/or professional lives (and not even know it). Or we can become healthy, vibrant, and radiant and actually be fully aware of it. See the difference? Someone who's becoming toxic very seldom knows they're becoming toxic. They usually need the loud wake up call. They usually need the Mack truck experience. That's this principle at play.

When we look at the 97 percent of the people on the planet who still have not yet created the life of their dreams versus the 3 percent of the planet who has, the differentiator is found, first and foremost, in the quality of their real-life results. The top 3 percent have a much higher quality of results than the bottom 97 percent.

In order to level up the quality of your results, you're going to have to become someone else. You're going to have to become someone new and different from who you are today. There is no way around this. And to become someone else, who is new and different, it's going to take some work. But it's worthy work. It's high-level work. It's the type of work that will get amazing results for you.

As you already know, one of my earlier teachers and beloved mentors, Jim Rohn, who is no longer with us, would often say, "Instead of chasing after it, just become it." In addition to being one of Jim's students for some time, I also worked as a salesperson for him. For a time, I was his top salesperson in Western Canada. I was in my early twenties at the time. I loved selling for him. I loved it partly because I loved him and what he was teaching. I loved the way he was teaching. I was fortunate enough to have a fairly close relationship with him, and we'd go out to dinner and have those sorts of personal experiences. Real success that truly fulfills us is what we become, not what we pursue. Jim taught me to be the kind of person that would naturally magnetize to me the kind of success that I genuinely desired.

Becoming conscious of this principle, which is a step-by-step process, enables you to literally get in touch with that Future Self of yours "one year from today" and enables you to become conscious of whatever and whoever it is you're truly to BE becoming.

Let's look at another example… As you know, many people on the planet are poor. Most people are struggling—living in abject poverty or from paycheck to paycheck. If those people living from paycheck to paycheck were to go into their job tomorrow and find out that they'd been fired, they'd be in deep trouble—deep, deep trouble. And the truth is they know it. They have very little in savings. They're one level away from financial ruin.

Now nothing happens by accident in the Universe. That's an impossibility. In fact, there's another Universal Law that governs this. It's the Law of Cause and Effect. But, in accordance with this Principle of Becoming, we don't just become poor. First, we somehow, some way, start believing we're poor. Once we start the process of believing this, at some point in our past timeline we begin to look for and gather evidence that says we're poor. Then, over time, we actually become poor. This is where our thoughts and feelings and even certain words that come out of our mouth further support this overall process in having become poor.

So, if I've had three lifetimes prior to this, and in these previous lifetimes I became poor and never course corrected or transmuted this old energy of "poor," this could then mean that I will be poor in this life, and perhaps in subsequent lives. Until, of course, I wake up to this and I ultimately realize what's really been going on here.

The tricky thing about this principle is that the person who is becoming less than, who is becoming sicker, who is becoming poorer, never knows about it. It's only the person who is healing, who is becoming better than they were, that actually becomes aware of this principle.

Long before the movie, *The Secret* came out, I had been attending Jim's seminars. It was in the seventies and early eighties when he was giving a series of seminars on the principles of success. In one of his classes, he really impressed upon me and the other students that "Success is not something we pursue; rather, it's something we attract by the person we become." Jim exemplified how the Law of Attraction at the higher levels really works, as he was the embodiment of this powerful teaching and principle. It was why this teaching impressed upon all of us at the time. We were so blessed by just being in his presence.

> *Real success that truly fulfills us is what we become, not what we pursue.*

Now living by this principle runs contrary to the business of always chasing after success. One of the reasons I had my first burnout experience when I was a young man was that I was chasing after success exclusively. If you chase after success with the amount of fervor that I had during that time, you're bound to collapse. You might even crash and burn because your system can only handle so much when you're living that way. My system could handle a lot, but eventually, I crashed, and there was not a darn thing I could do about it. I've seen so many people crash like I did. That was their consequence for the choices they'd been making to lead up to that crash. My crash-and-burn experience was my consequence.

Then, I became more conscious of this principle than I had ever been before. I started to become a little more aware of who I actually wanted to become. I decided to evaluate what kind of success I most desired to attract into my world. I started believing that I could become who I desired to become. I started believing that I could have what I most desired to have. I was now better understanding on a much deeper level how the laws I had been studying for some time truly worked.

I was literally experiencing the Law of Attraction in a whole new way, at a completely different level. I was becoming aware of some of my own points of attraction. I would ask back in those days, *How is it I can attract something in business that is incredibly positive, and yet, at the same time, attract in its complete opposite in another area of life?* It was two different points of attraction coming from within my energetic field. Wow... I remember thinking and feeling at the time that I had the formula, or at least a real part of the formula for a successful life, both personally and professionally.

Think of someone who, over time, became more of their true self, like American activist Rosa Parks, who the United States Congress called "the first lady of civil rights" and "the mother of the freedom movement." She was best known for her key role in the Montgomery bus boycott. Or the fearless boxing legend who went on in becoming widely known as "the greatest" heavyweight boxer of all time, Muhammad Ali. Or the American entrepreneur, lifestyle innovator, and self-made billionaire, Martha Stewart. Or one of the most legendary presidents of the United States, Abraham Lincoln. Or Cher, who came seemingly out of nowhere and struggled greatly just to be seen, only to become one of the biggest superstars to ever grace the stage. Or the American actor and professional wrestler Dwayne Johnson (also known by his ring name The

Rock). He has become one of the highest-paid and highest-grossing actors of all time. Or the British nurse, social reformer, and statistician Florence Nightingale, who became known as "The Lady with the Lamp" because she would walk among the beds at night, checking on the wounded men while holding a light in her hand.

Or how about that timid insecure little boy that couldn't speak or stand up for himself all that well but then eventually became a great man of immense unwavering resolve? With this resolve he became the catalyst in the tearing down of the Berlin wall... It was when he spoke those clear and concise words, "Mr. Gorbachev, tear down this wall," he chose for the entire world to witness them on live TV. That's right, if you haven't guessed it by now, it was the 40th President of the United States of America... Mr. Ronald Reagan.

It doesn't matter whether we believe in what these people do or did professionally or not; just look at who they were before they evolved into who they became, and you'll see how these powerful dynamics in "becoming" have played themselves out in the best of ways.

How about the actors who portray someone who became great on the large screen? Such as Sir William Wallace in the movie *Braveheart*, played by Mel Gibson; or General Nanisca, leader of an all-female regiment of warriors, in the movie *The Woman King* played by Viola Davis; or the role of Nelson Mandela in the movie *Mandela: Long Walk to Freedom* played by Idris Elba. What do these people all have in common? Somehow, in some way, they became something more than what or who they were. And we become inspired by these types of people who rise up to a greater version of themselves. When actively working with this principle, we're also working with the Law of Growth mentioned earlier in this book.

I love what Paul Levesque, Chief Content Officer of one of the most thriving, expanding, growth-oriented organizations in the world today, the WWE, said in a recent press conference, "If you're still the same person you were five years ago, you just wasted five years of your life." Wow, think about that. Do you know of anyone who has possibly just wasted the last five years of their life? If so, this would be someone that more than likely is not even aware of the Law of Growth and/or this higher ground Principle of Becoming, let alone how to align their lives and themselves with this law and principle.

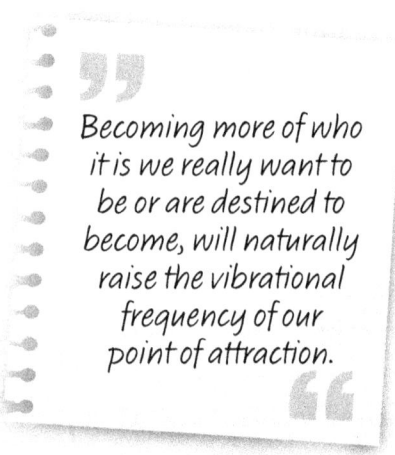

Becoming more of who it is we really want to be or are destined to become, will naturally raise the vibrational frequency of our point of attraction.

As we become more of who it is we really want to become or are destined to become, this is what will naturally raise the vibrational frequency of our point of attraction. This is the real secret hidden within the Law of Attraction. This is when we begin to feel like we are in a new world. We actually experience the sensation of moving forward in our life personally and/or professionally with our new elevated "points of attraction."

We'll know when these new inner points of attraction have actually manifested, for the new and truly different change that has taken place within will become obvious, as the change from within will physically project itself out into our external world. Let's remember, this is governed by the Law of Correspondence: as within, so without. Another way to state this law would be: Go within... Go without. At this stage there can be no denying, doubting, or discounting. It's that powerful. It's that real and more importantly, completely transformational at a cellular level.

The greater power in achieving the goal does not come from the achievement of the goal; rather, it comes from the deeper purpose of the goal, which is... who it is you'll need to become. In order for you to achieve the goal—to manifest it and sustain it—you're going to have to become something that you haven't yet become.

It's been perfectly designed that way (by your Divine Soul Essence Self) to ensure that you evolve and grow—even if it takes some time in this life for you to do so, or possibly a couple more lifetimes. That part will have more to do with how you're exercising one of your divine birthrights... the freedom to choose, aka freewill.

One of the highest points of attraction is found in who it is you really are to become or to be, in order to attract what it is you genuinely want to see manifest in your own personal universe. When you get a high-vibratory point of attraction, and it becomes well planted in your subconscious along with the lower aspects of your energetic field, it then naturally magnetizes to itself more of its like. This is where it consumes the entirety of the field, and your heartfelt desire that already exists within the field will then simply manifest. Remember this is all governed by Universal Law and higher ground principles.

Without understanding and utilizing this principle correctly, along with the Law of Attraction, we're not going to be able to manifest in an unlimited way—meaning there will be limitations on our ability to manifest our best life. We will get blocked. We will be held back, or at least it will feel like we're being held back. It will be really tough for us to achieve whatever larger goal we've set for ourselves.

One of the ways in which we can recognize this would be that we'll notice we're going for the same goal, month after month, year after year. Eventually, we'll either do something in a new and truly different way and actually start to achieve this goal, or we'll throw the goal out the window and possibly give up on our dreams or goals altogether.

A lot of people have given up on their dreams and aspirations because they lacked the understanding of how this has been set up. They don't understand what it takes to come into alignment with their greater selves and just how powerful and life-altering this truly is. To note here, there's a real difference between the energy of the *"wanting for"* and the *"becoming of."*

Even though the conscious manifestation process begins with identifying what it is you want, it is important to remember there's a big difference between wanting it and becoming it. These are two different things. To ultimately have what we truly want we must first become it. This is one of the most significant parts of a highly effective success formula when it comes to manifesting our best self and creating the life of our dreams.

> Imagine a world, imagine a community, where everybody is creating the life of their dreams. What's now happening in your community? Think about it. What about your family? What would happen if everybody in your family were manifesting the life of their dreams? How would your experience of your family now be? What happens if you're running a company and you've got a hundred people in your company, and everybody in the company is now manifesting the life of their dreams?

This is one of those incredible higher-vibe principles that the whole world ought to know about. And as they do, we'll rise up to a new and brighter way of inhabiting our planet.

When you know how to do this, what you can accomplish is beyond comprehension. In my view, it's all about becoming. If a person were to ask, "How did you heal yourself and change yourself?" The shortest, simplest answer I could give is that I literally became a new person. I became someone completely different from the person I was when I was struggling, when I was in crisis, when I had (on an unconscious level) manifested serious health issues. And that's why, decades later, these illnesses never came back. I became someone else, and I kept becoming someone else who was new and different from that of the person I used to be.

The truth is: we don't get what we want; rather, we get who we are—or who it is we've become in our present reality. My strongest point of attraction is who I am. So, if who I've become is a negative, lazy, undisciplined, critical, judgmental, miserable, angry, resentful, or bitter human being, then guess what? That's what I'm going to get more of. I could set goals all day long, all month long; but come the end of the month, come the end of the year, I'll be no closer to the manifestation of these goals than I was when I originally set them.

"Why?" you might ask. It's because I'm working with something that's far more powerful than simple, straightforward goal setting and pushing towards the goal. I've already become that angry, bitter, resentful, lazy, undisciplined, judgmental, critical human being. And when I become that, once it consumes the entirety of my electromagnetic field, it then becomes my major driving point of attraction. I just get more and more of that. Experiencing my life in this way will put me in the biggest fight ever with manifesting what I say I really consciously desire to have manifest in my life. You see, when I show up this way, my experience in setting and achieving a goal just becomes weaker and weaker.

> If you study people like I have, you'll see this in full living color. There's constant conflict between who they are and the goals they're aspiring towards. Whomever it is they are or have become will always win out. Do you know of anyone who approaches their life this way? If so, who? Now simply observe without judging them. What do you see? Is there a disconnect between what they say they want and who it is they currently are?
>
> I encourage you to go back through my first two books; more specifically, go back to the last couple of chapters in *Being Called to Change*. You're going to see this concept with a fresh perspective. This is important. Why? Well, you've got to get this down because you don't want to manifest more of what you don't want.
>
> In real terms this principle says: If we don't like what's manifesting in our world, then we need to change where the manifestation is coming from. This would be us—whoever it is we've become up to that moment. To get something that's truly new we first have to become someone new. And when we're lined up with the higher divine energies at play, that someone new is already going to be connected to our Future Self "one year from today."

If I were working with a group of kids, teaching them how to manifest, this is the point where I would start. It would be so much easier. Whereas when I'm working with adults, they've already been becoming someone for decades. Somehow, some way, we have to get them on board with their own personal and/or professional transformation.

Somehow, we have to get them to become someone else–even though they've spent their life becoming whoever it is they are today.

Often, even though they usually don't know it, they are their own worst enemy. I'm sure you've heard that phrase a time or two before. When you're becoming a negative beam of energy, that negative beam of energy is out to destroy you. It is out to block you and hold you back from manifesting your highest and best self... from achieving your most heartfelt desires, from creating the life of your dreams. The enemy is on the inside.

> By choosing to change, by choosing to transmute or transform yourself, you are choosing to love thine own enemy; you are choosing to love yourself, to learn how to love yourself unconditionally. This is one of the most worthwhile acts we could possibly engage in during the course of our lifetime.

The Principle of Acting As If

> This is one of the more significant keys to creating the life of our dreams: *act as if* we're already living our greatest life. When we embody the energy of our dream life, it sends a powerful signal to the Universe that we're ready to receive what our heart truly desires.

As a young man, at around 19 years old, I had the opportunity to work for the Dale Carnegie Institute and study the teachings that Dale Carnegie brought forth after his long personal journey. The institute wanted me to work for them and were grooming me to become one of their head trainers. They spotted something in me right away that they really took a liking to. They literally moved me to the top of the class in a matter of weeks.

Next thing you know, I was in the private office of one of the high-level managers where I was being presented with this opportunity. At this point, I had already identified my passion and what it was I wanted to be doing, so I graciously declined.

However, I did work for them for about the next year and a half on a part-time basis. I contributed my time for free, and I loved every moment of it. If I hadn't already identified my calling at the time, I definitely would have gone onto their payroll. There was something about Dale Carnegie, (beyond our shared first name) that I greatly admired and respected. I just immediately had this affinity for his spirit. I still do to this day, partially because I know the backstory to his life, what he ultimately went through, and how long it took him to do it.

Dale blessed us with a lot of principles, including the one I'm about to share with you…

> If you're going to get better at manifesting whatever it is you desire at a conscious level, you need to know how to work this Principle of Acting As If. You need to know how to integrate it. You need to know how to embody it.
>
> You need a certain level of awareness to really work well with this principle. To act as if you're already the person you need to become. To act as if you're already in possession of your goal or desire. This can be a tricky one, because at first when you're using this principle consciously, it's going to feel like you're possibly being inauthentic or phony.

You're going to need to find a way to come up with the behavior that matches the very thing that you want to manifest in your day-to-day world. Then, you're going to have to emulate that, not just for days or weeks but likely months. And you're going to have to do it every single day. But while you're doing it, it's not going to feel authentic for the most part.

Back when I was offering my goal-achieving class, this was one of the principles that I taught a lot on. There would be 400 people in the room, and about 50 of them would be so challenged by this principle, partly because they felt like I was teaching them how to be phony. It was the same thing when I taught this at the Dale Carnegie Institute, and the same again when I taught this to companies. Almost every single time, 10 to 20 percent of the participants would be challenged by this principle.

Of course, I'd welcome the challenge because when people start throwing questions my way, that's where the greater learning can occur. That's where I can really help to adjust people's thinking and present them with another way of viewing this.

It's important to understand the why behind this principle. We need to operate in this way in order to get the result we're after. Our normal, natural behavioral patterns haven't been manifesting this result.

Once you know what you want and who it is you need to become, you'll need to identify the behavioral patterns that go with who it is and what it is you desire. You have to ask yourself: *If I actually had what I want, how would I now be acting? How would I now behave? What would the habit or habits be that I'm now acting on? How would I now be speaking? How would I now be thinking? And how would I now be feeling?*

You have to identify all levels if you're going to do this properly and powerfully. And once you've identified the answers, that's when the work begins. But more than likely you're gonna get challenged.

So, to *act as if*, to help us get through this awkwardness, we must bring in that Power of Feeling. Once we identify what the action is, what the behavioral pattern is, then in order to convince this part of us that we are the real deal (even though it feels like we're possibly being phony) we must come up with a feeling that further supports the new pattern.

To come up with the right feeling let's explore the Law of Assumption. Neville Goddard spoke of this law in many of his lectures back in the sixties. In which he would state, that it's to live in the assumption of the goal or wish fulfilled. Neville would go on to teach that we are to start assuming that we already have this. This is where we would *act as if* we've already got it.

If we were to infuse our aligned actions with the complete assumption that the wish or desire we're carrying inside of us has already been fulfilled, and then to this we were to *act as if this was true*, we would be manifesting whatever it is we most desire.

Here are a few practical applications where we can use this principle:

ACT AS IF... you have everything you need.
ACT AS IF... you're already living your dream life.
ACT AS IF... everything always works out for you.
ACT AS IF... you're the person you wish to become.
ACT AS IF... you already have the success you desire.

This would be a powerful way of consciously working with the Law of Assumption, as by doing so we're simply acknowledging that whatever it is we seek already exists within us. And every time we choose to act *as if*, it sends a message to that of what we desire or want to become, by assuming the truth of its existence within us.

The Principle of Aliveness

The magic of manifestation accelerates into a higher gear when we're naturally feeling more alive in our own skin. This propels us towards manifesting whatever it is we want to have manifest in our world. When we *feel alive*, it naturally lifts us to a higher frequency. When we're at this higher frequency, we feel good about who it is we are or have become.

> What makes you feel more alive? How alive do you feel right now in your own body? Why are these questions so important? Well, this is how we set ourselves up for attracting more of what it is we really want in our personal and professional lives.
>
> You see, to set ourselves up to manifest more effectively, we must understand the significance of the "feeling state" when it comes to what it is we want to have manifest in our world. This is referring to that Inner Power of Feeling we learned about earlier in this book.

We don't experience aliveness just because we're physically alive. We all have met someone who is alive but doesn't experience much aliveness in the way they live their life. Some complain a lot, speak negatively of others, and often have some kind of upset going on in their lives. What do you suppose this way of living does to our electromagnetic field? Exactly… It weakens it.

> Another way to consider this principle would be in answering the questions we started this section off with… On a scale of 1 to 10, 1 being a little and 10 being a lot, how much aliveness do you have in your life right now? What is it that makes you feel alive?
>
> At the present time, how good do you naturally feel about yourself and your own personal universe? What could you do to feel better about yourself? How accomplished do you feel? How much fun is it for you to accomplish things?
>
> What brings you joy? What ignites your Soul? What lightens you up? Is there an area of your life that is especially lit up right now? If so, is it your health and well-being, your finances, your love life, your alone time, your relationships, your career path, your recreational activities, or your business? How many friends, birth family members, extended family members, or business associates do you currently have in your life that you really look forward to hanging out with?
>
> The experiences we have with others serve as the currency of our aliveness, fun and joy. They are also the necessary components for forward movement in our personal and professional lives, as well as in our Soul's evolution and expansion. Our lives are a series of relational integrations that help us to grow, progress, heal and evolve.
>
> How much pleasure or play time do you have in your life? How much fun do you have? When was the last time you had a lot of fun? Fun, aliveness and happiness all go hand in hand. When we're having fun and feeling alive because of what we do, or who we're with, this alone

increases the vibrational frequency of our magnetic energy. As our energy raises in frequency, we naturally become more attractive to the good things and the wonderful opportunities that life and the Divine have in store for us.

When we're feeling alive, we become fully present in our body and more open to receiving the gifts and blessings that life and the Divine have to bestow upon us. Think about it. When are you most attractive? Is it when you're in love with someone or something? Or is it when you're hanging out with someone you don't even get along with? Or when you are doing things you don't even like to do with someone?

You see, when we're in love with what it is we do and/or who it is we work with, hang out with, or live with, we simply become more present. This is because the emotion of love running through our veins makes us feel more alive. This is the first and most important purpose of our life... it's to feel alive.

Let's remember from earlier in the book that our real manifesting power to create with is found in the now. It's not when we're vested in our past or we're too far out in the future. It's when we are fully present—when we're engaged in the moment, when we're not even thinking of the past or the future. Rather, we're totally here in this present moment. And it's fun when we're completely engaged in whatever it is we're doing, as it just enlivens us.

When do you suppose you're most present in your body and in your day-to-day life? Is it when you're feeling alive, open, and fully engaged in whatever it is you're doing? Is it when you're having fun with whoever it is you're with or whatever it is you're doing?

Or is it when you're avoiding someone or something because you don't want to be bothered by them? Or you don't want to deal with whatever it is you've been avoiding? Or is it when you become bored with someone, or something that you're doing—like your job?

When you're bored, have you noticed what happens to your relationship with time? Exactly... it drags on seemingly forever. Whereas, when you're having fun and feeling alive with what you're doing, or who it is you're with... it speeds up.

When I'm engaged in something that naturally makes me feel alive, it automatically makes it easy for me to be present—to be living my life in the here and now. This is where I'm at my best. This is where time just flies by. This is where my energy is more magnetic in attracting to me everything I need in order to accomplish my goals and manifest my most heartfelt desires.

On the other hand, if I'm involved in something like a dead-end job, or an outdated or even toxic relationship, or in an ongoing conflicted partnership, not only is this weakening my magnetic field... it's now increasing the likelihood of more pain, stress, anxiety, negativity, and suffering. These would be some of the consequential effects of living my life from this place of being non-present.

I recall from some time ago the executive vice president of a company that I worked with who would take a four-day trip to one of his favorite resorts every 120 days without fail. At some point in our working together, I asked, "Why do you do this?" He said this was his secret sauce for staying the course of being present and fully engaged in his higher-level responsibilities as the second in command of a $30-million-a-year company.

He would often say, doing that getaway every four months was his assurance policy for him enjoying his life and his work on a more regular basis. And taking that time off would help him get back in touch with just how much he appreciated the role as EVP of his company and all that he had to be so grateful for in his life. He was born into financial hard times and yet, he became wealthy. He was someone who over a long period of time did the work and rose to a wealthy status.

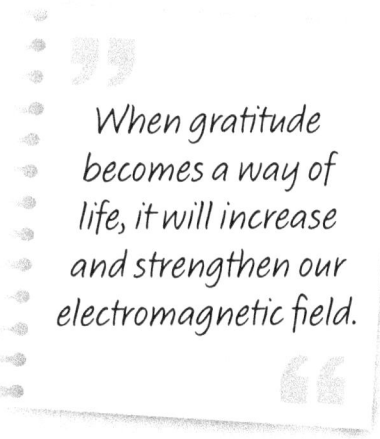

When gratitude becomes a way of life, it will increase and strengthen our electromagnetic field.

Of all the leaders that would come across my path throughout the years, I found him to be one the most effective, productive, and successful leaders I had the honor of working with. His ability to stay focused and get things done was like no other. Even though he's no longer with us, in his day he was the real deal. You would never hear him complain. Rather, he was always focused on what they accomplished, or on what they were in the process of accomplishing and what it was they needed to do in moving their company onward and upward.

You might recall from Chapter 6: The Creative State, we learned about the importance of gratitude for our life, just like the EVP who found a strategy that helped him to stay in gratitude for what it was he already had in his life (both the positive and negative).

It's helpful to know that one of the master keys to a richer and more meaningful life is living in and with gratitude. When gratitude becomes a way of life, it will increase and strengthen our electromagnetic field, which will naturally attract more blessings and miracles into our personal and professional lives.

Further, it's much easier to enjoy what it is you're doing when you're in the energy of gratitude, which naturally elevates your mood. This is where you just feel better about you and your world. Being in joy, living in joy is such a beautiful energy. Why? Because life becomes easier, better, and smoother. Whatever it is that life is challenging you with... when you're coming from this place of lightheartedness, appreciation for what is, and happiness or joy, everything (regardless of what you find yourself going through from time to time) no longer has to be so jagged or abrupt. Rather, things can be a little easier and possibly somewhat smoother.

Another way to consider this is that there's always a solution to whatever the challenge or problem is. However, to gain better access to the part of you where the solution resides, check to see where it is you're currently coming from in solving the problem or rising up to whatever it is that's been challenging you. If and when you're truly coming from a more joyous, grateful place, the most perfect solution will simply flow into your brain/body consciousness—and more than likely when you least expect it.

In other words, it'll be like an a-ha moment of realization. You'll know it when it happens, as this higher idea will flood your cells like a wave of clearer energy coming upon you. It is this greater or higher idea that will be the answer to solving the problem, or whatever it is that's been challenging you.

What makes this principle so dynamic is that whenever we choose to mindfully operate from this sweet, divine place of gratitude for *everything in our lives*... the easier and more powerful it'll be for us to consciously manifest that which we would really like to see materialize in our lives.

Exercise...

> Let's revisit some of the questions we started this section with. If you haven't answered these on paper yet, now might be a good time to do so...
>
> What can you do to lighten up? How good do you naturally feel about you and your own personal universe? What can you do to feel better about you? Come the end of your day, how accomplished do you feel? How much fun is it for you to accomplish things?
>
> What makes you come alive? Is it your work (as in the entrepreneur or career professional who considers their work fun, for it brings them much joy and deeper fulfillment)? Is it caring for your kids or grandkids (as in being a great parent or grandparent)? Is it some creative project that you love doing (like becoming a master gardener)? Is it being in a beautiful partnership or a very successful relationship of some kind? Is it taking a trip to an exotic place? Is it playing a fun game where you become so involved in the best of ways that time doesn't even exist? Or is it possibly completing something of spiritual significance?
>
> Whatever it is, this is what engages the generating of a higher-energy positive feeling. It's this higher, more positive, powerful feeling state

that you want. As in, when you're feeling really good about something you just did (like spending time with someone really dear to you), or completing something (such as a daily task or major project), or experiencing a meaningful breakthrough in what was a very challenging conversation or having accomplished something significant with your day. Maybe you followed through on something you said you were going to do or gave your word to someone or to the Divine that you would do this, and now you've actually done it.

This is one of the most practical and yet super effective ways of setting ourselves up for attracting more of what we really want to have manifest in our lives. When we naturally feel good about ourselves and our lives, it causes our magnetic field to increase in vibrational frequency, making our broadcast to the Universe far more powerful, dynamic, and effective.

The Law of Perpetual Transmutation of Energy

The Law of Perpetual Transmutation of Energy relates to most of the Inner Powers, principles, and laws that have been highlighted in this book thus far. If we are going to get better at manifesting on a conscious level, one of the things we need to learn how to do is transmute energy. It's the alchemist who transmutes the energy of lead to gold that many of us have heard about. At the heart of the alchemy process is this law. To succeed at this, we need to create a newer, higher, better, faster-moving vibrational state of being.

Transmutation is a derivative of transformation. Transformation means to change the form of something, and transmutation means to take that energy and convert it to its higher octave.

Transformation occurs everywhere in our lives. We can transform our behavioral patterns; we can transform how we've been showing up, at work, in life, and in our relationships. We might transform our appearance through a makeover—like when we get ready to attend a special date or work event—or we might transform our home through a remodel. Transformation plays out in so many levels of our experience of life. As we become a new and better version of ourselves, we will have transformed from how we used to be… to how we are in our now reality.

Transmutation is an ascension process where we are literally shaping upwards towards its pinnacle. When we expand into a new level of consciousness, we're expanding because we're transmuting the energy at the level that we've been in, up to a higher state.

We do this with the ego. There are parts of the ego that are acidic, but there are also parts that are good. As we transmute the energy of the ego, we can go all the way up to the Soul.

Everything's connected. So, if this is level one, level one is directly connected to level two. If this is level two, level two is directly connected to level three. Level two is nothing more than a higher octave of the energy of level one. It's just richer. It moves faster. It's a little lighter and more expansive in terms of how we experience that level.

With every lower energy pattern, there are corresponding higher energy patterns. If you rise up high enough, for every lower energy pattern, you will find its highest octave. You can think of transmutation in terms of Western astrology. For every one of the 12 zodiac signs, there is a positive and a negative. There's a dark and a light. There's the ego and there's the Soul. Period. All of our lower energy patterns have corresponding higher energy patterns in our consciousness; those lower energy patterns are just waiting to be transmuted to that of their higher octave.

Let's take a look at the Law of Perpetual Transmutation of Energy as it relates to points of attraction. If there are ten points of attraction in your energetic field, and seven of them are of a lower nature, that means that the higher octaves of these seven lower points already exist within that field. The reason we cannot access them is that they're already in existence—they've already been installed within the higher aspects of one's field—but they have yet to be transmuted. These lower points don't get destroyed when we address them; they get transmuted. Energy in of itself does not die; it simply changes form. Once these points are transmuted, they receive all of the energy that the lower points once received.

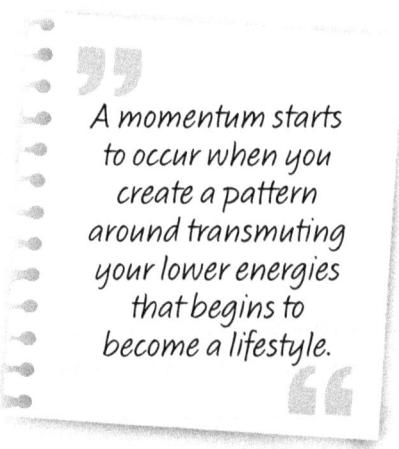

A momentum starts to occur when you create a pattern around transmuting your lower energies that begins to become a lifestyle.

I've already mentioned that at any point when we drop to a lower vibrational state, we run the risk of creating something that we don't want to have manifest in our world. We've also learned that whether it's a limiting belief or a lower energy pattern, if we get stuck or trapped in there, our energetic state is going to be impacted. Points of attraction are key elements here, because if it turns out we have an overwhelming number of lower vibrational points of attraction that are part of our electromagnetic field, then that's what's going to manifest in our physical world.

No matter how hard we try, how many great books we read, we will only create whatever life our vibrational field dictates. If the field is at a steady, higher-vibrational place, then we will create the types of experiences that are in harmony with that higher state. If, on the other hand, our field is operating in a lower-vibrational place, or even if a part of the field is still in a lower-vibrational dynamic that we haven't yet cleared or transmuted, this too remains a point of attraction. If we're still very afraid of something, or we have a lot of guilt, bitterness, regret, shame, insecurity, resentment, or aggression, once again, it will by law accumulate more of its like to itself.

Remember, everything is energy. Everything is governed under the Law of Energy. Emotions are energy in motion. Emotional energy (whether it's buried deep within our subconscious or we're consciously aware of it), if it's allowed or encouraged to grow in strength, over time, will become like a powerful magnet. This applies to both negative and positive emotions. Energy is always attracting more of its like to itself.

Both restrictive limiting beliefs and non-restrictive un-limiting beliefs are composed of energy as well. Therefore, if we want to get really good at manifesting with precision, we're going to need to know about this law. And it would also behoove us to learn how to work with this energy.

There is a momentum that starts to occur when you create a pattern for yourself around transmuting your lower energies. It begins to become a lifestyle.

Transmuting energy can also be done within your dream space—whether you are taking a power nap or having a deep, restful sleep. Now this does take a little skill to do. The most important piece, however, is how aware you are of this actually occurring on the dreamscape of your own inner reality while you are sleeping. Transmuting during this time helps regulate a consistency and creates even more momentum.

Once you get into this momentum, that energy is not just transmuting little by little on a regular basis, but it actually becomes a perpetual dynamic that comes into play, which is governed by this Law of Perpetual Transmutation of Energy. Up until now, it's been in the background. You perhaps didn't even know all of this was happening. And it's really tough to see until you familiarize yourself with all of the other laws, Inner Powers, and principles that are at play.

This is what our Higher Self wants us to have—the ability to transmute energy at a conscious level—though sometimes it takes a while before we can get to the point where we can do this. But once we begin to do this, we build momentum, and we get more grace.

We'll be able to transmute more and more of those lower energies, be it our negative emotions, karmic patterns, limiting beliefs, addictions and/or deep-seated fears. This is all such an important and even critical part of our own journey in the becoming of who it is we truly need to become in order for our most heartfelt desires to materialize in our physical world of reality. For once we fully become it, we will have it.

It's through the transmuting of our lower energy patterns we become a healthier, more vibrant, more alive, happier, newer version of ourselves, as we have now transformed ourselves from how we used to be. And that is the whole point in our overall creative manifestation process. That we become someone or something new. Which then empowers us to live our greatest life, our dream life, or perhaps the life we were divinely meant to live from the very beginning.

CHAPTER 11

CHANGING YOUR REALITY

For most of my life I've lived as if I am the creator or co-creator of my own reality. I've known of my Divine Birthright, the freedom to choose, during this time as well. Even though I know fate can and has interjected itself into my life from time to time along my path, and will continue to do so, I recognize the spiritual significance of free will. I've come to appreciate the unifying energies of these two dynamics where I am choosing my reality along with choosing how it is I will show up during the times where fate interjects itself into my reality.

I've also come to know that our day-to-day life, aka our external world, is very much like a dream we're having while we lay asleep through the night, which means it all can be changed. A skilled lucid dreamer knows in their nighttime dreams that the dream reality can be re-scripted, as it is known that a dream is like a simulation—one can consciously change the direction they want the dream to go in within the context of the simulated reality that's playing itself out in the dreamscape.

As A Course in Miracles says, "Know this is a dream, and once we know that reality is a dream, we can choose to make it a heavenly dream." It's somewhat like Neo in the movie *The Matrix* when he learns that the matrix is not real. The idea being, that once we understand that reality is a simulation in the matrix... we can change our reality and create a new dream. This is where we would begin to use our God-given Inner Powers in a way that empowers us to manifest a happy dream.

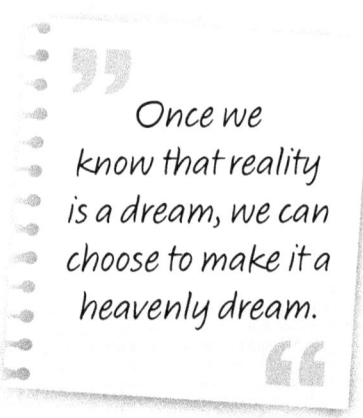

Once we know that reality is a dream, we can choose to make it a heavenly dream.

Some time ago I began to ponder, *If one can do this in their nighttime simulated dream space, could we do this in our daytime dream space? What if we could change our day-to-day reality where we are moving closer and closer to literally creating the life of our dreams? What if we could create a healthy, happy, heavenly waking-dream?*

As we come to know of this birthright, we can choose to live our highest and best life and create the life of our dreams. It's a choice or a series of making good choices in our own day-to-day world. It can be beneficial to further recognize that this whole thing is an on-going creation—whether it's fate, or it's us choosing to create the life of our happiest dreams, or in how we actually show up to what's been destined or chosen by us for us to experience.

This book has been designed to support those desiring to change their reality in that of their life's journey into a richer, better happier dream. And why not? As Audrey Hepburn some time ago said, "Nothing is impossible. The word itself says 'I'm possible!'"

In this chapter we're going to explore a few more Inner Powers: the Power of Responsibility, the Power of Control, and the Power of Intention. We could say these three are like superpowers. Now they're not super abilities, as highlighted in book two; rather, these powers, once we truly understand them, where we are correctly utilizing them, can help anyone that possesses *the true desire to change their reality* actually change their reality whenever they wish to do so. That said, let's now move on to the first of the three powers…

The Power of Responsibility

To the degree that we assume personal responsibility for ourselves and our personal and professional lives, this Inner Power activates and awakens. We've all heard the expression "With great power comes great responsibility," so if we want to get better at manifesting and ultimately become a master of manifesting with precision in our own personal universe, we will need full access to this power on a conscious level.

> There are two key areas within this power for us to explore. The first one has to do with what it is specifically we are to be responsible for. The second key is that one of our higher abilities is within this power, which is the ability to respond.
>
> So, we might ask: *What are we to be responding to?* And the answer is found in what it is we are to accept responsibility for.

What we are responsible for is our thoughts, our feelings, our words, and our actions. There is another Universal Law, the Law of Divine Memory. It states that all thoughts, feelings, and acts are recorded within the body of the Universe. Now we perhaps haven't been aware up till now that all of our acts are recorded and that there will be an effect with each act, which according to the Law of Cause and Effect (aka the Law of Karmic Return), must one day return back to its original sending point.

> It comes down to this question... How much personal responsibility can we take for our own feelings, beliefs, words, and actions? How much responsibility can we take for the words that come out of our mouth? Let's remember the Inner Power of the Spoken Word that we learned about earlier in Chapter 7.
>
> The truth is, according to these higher-ground principles for manifesting, we are to be responsible for the words that come out of our mouth. Which means our words and how we choose to use them could produce something beautiful or something painful and possibly even destructive. How much responsibility can we take for our actions and habits (aka behavioral patterns)?

An example here would be: If we have a habit or pattern of blaming, judging, shaming, projecting, or victimizing but we're not willing to assume responsibility for that pattern, then we will spin around this habit or pattern without forward movement. Because whatever this pattern or habit produces, as in its result and/or the consequential effect, gets recorded.

This means it will invoke the Law of Karmic Return, which says what we send out or broadcast will return back to us at some later point. In this pattern of blaming, judging, shaming, projecting or victimizing, it not only blocks us from having a richer, happier, better life but also ends up creating more of its like. And more of its like could be what produces messy situations, aka messy manifestations.

So, when someone creates a messy manifestation, chances are they had no conscious intention of bringing that upon themselves. And yet this is exactly what they manifested—this is something that they most likely never wanted to have manifest in the first place.

Recall earlier when we were learning about the significance of one's *feeling state*. What feeling state are we creating from when manifesting a messy situation in our own life? It doesn't matter if we're aware of how some lower aspect within our subconscious can manifest something of its like or not, even if we simply remain unconscious towards it. We are responsible for the whole enchilada when it comes to our own individual being.

If we choose to avoid personal responsibility for the effects of positive or negative karma in our life, whatever it is that we've been avoiding responsibility for, and have been unwilling to see correctly, will simply return to us and repeat all over again.

The first area of responsibility... is found in our ability to respond. Heck, it's even in the word itself. If we break the word down into two words as in: respons/ibility. Then, simply reverse the order of them and we get the *ability to respond*.

> When something happens, as in something of an uglier more painful, negative, or messier nature in your own personal universe, how do you typically respond? Whatever your answer, it will show you where you're currently at in skillfully utilizing this Inner Power of Responsibility.

The second area of responsibility... Let's say I've got a lot of anger inside of me, and I project it onto someone else because I'm thinking or believing in that moment that it is them making me feel that way.

> Might it be that the truth is they're making me feel what it is I was already feeling inside of me? Perhaps it was their words or actions that triggered what it was that had already been living inside of me. Maybe I start to victimize that person in my life that I believe is making me so angry. Or I victimize something in my home or my office, or in their home or office. Maybe I damage their property or mine. Maybe I punch the wall or throw a glass across the room, and it shatters all over the floor.
>
> Might there be a consequence for this outburst or type of action? And what happens if an eight-year-old child was to witness this outburst? If you were to look at my ability to respond, within this scenario I just painted, how would you now say I'm doing? Am I exercising this ability really well, or am I exercising it not so well? Am I even responding, or might it be that I'm downright reacting from this place of anger that's inside of me?

You see, if I'm not willing to take responsibility for my feeling of anger, rage, resentment, or guilt, shame, or fear, and I act it out... it will cause more pain and suffering, Not only for the other person I just acted it out on but for myself as well, and maybe that eight-year-old child too. This acting out only furthers the problem and potentially creates a negative consequence and an even messier situation. My action here would then demonstrate that I'm still not willing to take responsibility for my feelings.

Therefore, I'm at the very least misusing this Power of Responsibility, which means I don't get to use this power in a way that empowers me to get better at consciously manifesting my heartfelt desires. If I were to continue with the repressing of my feelings instead of releasing those feelings through consciously embracing them, it would lead to more pain and messier manifestations in my life.

To responsibly embrace our feelings would be to allow ourselves to simply feel them. And if we were to fully feel them, we would now be learning from them—which is the whole point here. Because once we're learning from them, this is us operating from a deeper level of understanding of the Law of Perpetual Transmutation of Energy, as we're now transmuting those feelings to their higher octave of passion, joy, or love.

However, in acting those feelings out or reacting to whatever this is, it not only suppresses these feelings, but it is also one of the ways in which we could create a messy manifestation. You see, by showing up this way, we're coming now from the victim consciousness (where we are possibly victimizing someone or something else) instead of the victor consciousness. It's the victimizing of ourselves, someone, or something else that increases the odds of creating negative karma for ourselves.

When we act in this manner, we're not only in avoidance of accepting responsibility for our own manifestations, and the feelings that are at the root of those manifestations, but we're lacking in self-discipline as well. Wherever there is an avoidance of personal responsibility, there will always be a lacking in healthy self-discipline too. These two Inner Powers go hand in hand.

> To get better at responding to anything in our life both inside and out, it will require discipline to not only get better at it, but, should we choose to... eventually *master it*.

In *Transform Your Destiny* we learned about Soul Themes. Of the many themes our Soul can choose for us, there are two of them that are more than likely playing out in the background of this scenario above (the Soul Theme of the Saboteur and the Soul Theme of the Victor). If the victor is one of our soul themes in this life, it also carries its lower archetype, which is the victim. Even though we really are not victims, the victim consciousness lives in the lower end of the spectrum of our feelings—such as apathy, anger, shame, hatred, judgment, guilt, and fear.

> If we want to free ourselves from the victim and become the true victor, we will need to take full responsibility for our thoughts, feelings, words, beliefs, and actions. We do this by learning how to correctly work with them. Then we can put an eventual end to the projecting or blaming of them onto ourselves, others, or onto something else.

This is where, yet again, the Law of Perpetual Transmutation of Energy comes into play. Remember, *energy doesn't die; it just changes form.* This means at any time that we wish to change the form of our victim consciousness to victor consciousness, we can do so. This is what this law says. Will it be easy to do? Perhaps for some yes, and for others no. This largely depends on how much responsibility we are willing to accept for ourselves or have already accepted for ourselves.

When it comes to our feelings, thoughts, words, and actions, we all get to be responsible for them. Will we choose to get better at responding to life, or might we continue to react (or even overreact) to life? We get to choose.

Now if we choose to avoid the responsibility of "OUR" feelings, beliefs, actions, words, or decisions that we've made, this is where and how negative karma can get created. If this happens, it is then stored in our subconscious until we're ready and willing to resolve, heal and transmute it.

The hard truth is this: we will be held accountable especially for our words, decisions and actions whether we like it or not. Because it's easier for us to actually spot our words, decisions and actions with them being expressed in our external world, than that of our thoughts, feelings and beliefs (which are parts of our internal world). You see, karma ultimately is not good or bad, rather it's here to be corrective. It is corrective in nature.

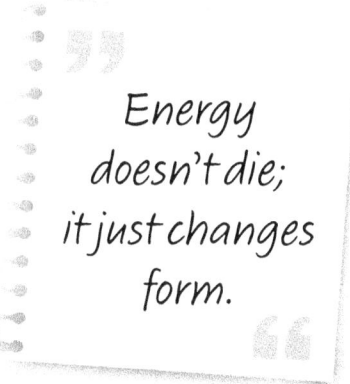

Energy doesn't die; it just changes form.

When we're blessed with good or positive karma, it's simply letting us know that we've been living our life in alignment with our Higher Soul Self and the Divine. On the other hand, when we find ourselves experiencing bad or negative karma, it is course correcting us... letting us know that our choices, words, and deeds have not been in alignment with our Soul and the Divine. And now we're simply getting the result or the karmic effect of those choices, words, and/or actions.

Remember, according to the Law of Divine Memory... every act, or more specifically in this case, every negative act, is recorded for future processing. This would be where and when we actually take personal responsibility for that negative action or karma and then transmute it. This is where we consciously choose to change its form. We ultimately clear our past negative karma by truly feeling into it and really learning from it. These lessons, whatever they are, our Soul has already chosen them for us. These are the Soul Lessons we are to be learning and ultimately mastering.

Karma, in and of itself, does not have to be a series of negative experiences. The consequences of our actions are only as negative or as positive as the actions themselves. It's the spirit in which we do things that creates karma.

It's a powerful dynamic when we consciously choose to correctly use the Power of Responsibility, which is to accept full responsibility for whatever manifests in our own personal universe—whether it's the good, the bad, or the ugly.

Whatever it is... when we assume full responsibility for our own manifestations, more of our own personal power releases. This is where we feel more authentically empowered to do what it is that truly needs to be done or better embraced in our own lives. Think of all there is in your life associated with responsibility. As in, what happens if we are a responsible parent versus an irresponsible parent? What happens if we are a responsible person in a relationship versus irresponsible? What happens if we're responsible with our finances (paying our bills on time) versus irresponsible? One results in higher credit scores and the other in lower scores. As a student, what happens if we're applying for a job or career opportunity, and we have a higher GPA vs a lower one? One increases the odds of being accepted and the other... well, you get the idea.

4 Steps for Embracing Our Inner Power of Responsibility

1. Choose to BECOME the Victor.

This conscious choice alone to become the Victor will help to empower you in becoming better at responding to life masterfully. Learning how to respond to life with its twists and turns is one of the master keys to not only becoming free from our past programming but in rising up to consciously *Manifest like a Master*.

One of the essential keys to manifesting anything we want in our lives is to become fully responsible for everything that already has manifested and is manifesting in our own lives. The key here is to be responsible for what it is we want to have manifest, as well as that of what we don't want to have manifest. This is where we assume self-responsibility without the making of ourselves, anyone, or anything else wrong. This accepting of 100 percent personal responsibility for what manifests in our own world is what gives us access to more of our manifesting power that we can use to consciously create the life of our dreams with, both personally and professionally—and even spiritually.

When we can say, "I am responsible" and actually mean it, this is where we become authentically empowered to trace back the result that has manifested in our lives. This may be a result that we don't yet understand—from where or when in our past that manifestation came from, or from the part of us that we are currently unaware of that is manifesting it's like in some area of our lives. Again, believe it or not, we are responsible when it comes to whatever it is that's manifested in our personal world.

When we truly come to know this truth within our physical cells, this is what changes everything big time when it comes to creating whatever it is we consciously would like to see manifest in our own personal universe. In other words, we'll have the manifesting power to do so.

Now the matrix would prefer we don't become responsible for ourselves. It is known that the complete acceptance of self-responsibility is directly connected to our spiritual power, which is emanating from a higher level within us than that of our personal power residing in the area of our solar plexus.

> *If we want to become a powerful person, we can do so by assuming 100 percent responsibility for all aspects of ourselves.*

This power within, however, is first and foremost about getting back into our personal power and using it wisely. For as we assume complete responsibility for our personal universe, we become more powerful in our own universe. This is our personal and spiritual power that we can learn how to use, whenever we choose to, in becoming more skilled at consciously manifesting.

Again, with each greater level of power comes the next level of greater responsibility. If we want to become a powerful person, we can do so by assuming 100 percent responsibility for *all aspects* of ourselves. On a more day-to-day basis, this also breaks down to… how will we choose to respond in our personal, financial, professional, and sovereign lives?

I began teaching on responsibility without really knowing what I was getting myself into at the tiime. It was early in my career when certain phrases (that had never come out of my mouth before) would roll off the tip of my tongue. I would say things when teaching that would have some participants at the time react negatively, such as: "Nobody can do anything to us that we haven't already done to ourselves." "We are not victims; rather, we are victors." "Nothing is being done to us—it's all being done for us, or it's being done from us." "Everything that happens in our lives is coming from inside of us."

Now at the time I clearly didn't realize what it was I was saying. None of this was written down anywhere. These types of phrases would literally flow out of me spontaneously. I would do my best in responding to the negative and sometimes the very intense reactions this would just simply bring out of some of the members in the audience.

Where this became powerful and life-changing for me was when, a little later on my path, I would begin to have these deeper transformational and even mystical experiences regarding self-responsibility. With each experience, this sometimes painful and yet profound realization would follow. I would come to know of those phrases as true statements—aka truths. Over time this changed everything for me. My healing, my awakening, my ability to consciously manifest accelerated and heightened.

I became more acutely aware, as I was now accepting the full responsibility of not only my choices and actions but for every part of my experience, both positive and negative (that I now knew was all coming from within me). None of it was being done to me. I really wasn't the victim in any of my earlier experiences—even though I often thought and sometimes acted out like I was. I now knew that I had become the victor.

To recall what we learned earlier in this book... we were all born into this life with that natural ability to manifest. How we choose to use this ability is up to us. And to speak of the matrix again, if it was to continue to have its way with us, we would never use this ability on a conscious level, nor even wake up to the truth that we are to become fully responsible for ourselves. For this is where our authentic creative power is truly found.

Do keep in mind, this inborn ability to manifest is in the on-position 24/7—whether we like it or not, or whether we even know about it or not.

To become self-responsible, you could declare for however many times it takes and for however long it takes, "I AM RESPONSIBLE," until you totally come to know that you know this truth at a physical cellular level within your own being.

2. Become conscious of the judgment you have others and yourself in.

> Notice when you're blaming or shaming someone or even yourself for something in your life. Blame or shame can be a sticky energy, as it's rooted in judgment. And once we move into judgment, we lock whatever it is in place (at a conscious or unconscious level) that we've chosen to hold in judgment.
>
> As we get better at catching ourselves spewing out the blame or shame energy, we likely still don't know at this point where those energies

are coming from. Nor have we likely connected to what it is we are to be responsible for.

Now if blaming, shaming, or judging has been our way, this will lead to manifesting or repeating the same experience all over again.

If within our self-perception we still see the world as what it's been doing to us, rather than what it's been doing for us, or even through us, this is what determines what happens next depending on how we view the outside world.

An example of this would be someone, at some point along their journey, realizing that everyone and everything they've been judging in their life, they've also been attracting. This realization alone would have a powerful impact in the way they've been viewing their own personal world. Once we begin to actually see that the world is not happening to us, rather it's happening for us, or even through us, this is where we can transmute the lower energy of judgment to that of its higher octave... love and acceptance.

If I want to get better at consciously manifesting, then I also want to get better at checking myself for being judgmental. There are a handful of energetic blocks we can place in the way of our manifesting ability, such as lower energy patterns like avoiding, procrastinating, getting stuck in fear, or doubting ourselves or the Universe, or being judgy of ourselves and others.

> Take a look at these blocks and ask yourself, if there was one block here that I was to be giving some attention to, which one would it be? Say your answer was judgment. Then pose the question: on a scale

of 1 to 10, 1 being a little and 10 being a lot, how judgmental can you be of others? How judgmental can you be of yourself? How judgy can your words be of others? How judgy can your words be of yourself? How afraid are you of being judged by others? How quick or easy is it for you to move into judgment?

Not sure? We could conduct a self-test. If it turns out we do have a judgmental issue going on, we would more than likely see the truth of this issue as it plays itself out over time, that *whatever we judge we attract to ourselves*. In other words, *if I'm being judgmental or some part of me is, I will attract more of its like to myself and into my life.*

Whatever it is we don't like about ourselves, we judge in others for the same thing. And possibly project our judgement onto another in attempting to get them to feel wrong about what it is we're still holding ourselves in judgement for. It's this judgement we hold in ourselves that becomes a point of attraction, which then simply magnetizes more of it's like to itself. Again, this is where that of what or who we've been judging in our life is the energetic dynamic we've been attracting in our life.

The way in which we could transmute this energy is when we release ourselves from this judgement and learn how to love, forgive, and accept everything just as it is. When we love this part of ourselves without condition or judgement, this is when this restrictive energy of judgment transmutes to its higher octave. Again, energy doesn't die; it just changes form.

The manifestation magic is in letting go of the needy energy, or the lower energy pattern of blaming, shaming, or judging, and then consciously choosing to accept personal responsibility for whatever it is that has manifested in our life from when we were previously judging, blaming, or shaming someone else.

Some time ago, I was asked to coach this woman who had manifested the same kind of romantic relationship with three different partners in a row. Each time, after a certain number of months into each relationship, it would drop into an abusive, lower-energy pattern that would manifest into a love-hate dynamic within the relationship. The partner was the abusive one, which gave her the green light to place the blame.

> Whatever it is we don't like about ourselves, we judge in others. This judgement we hold becomes a point of attraction.

Over time in our coaching sessions, she would come to realize her part in these experiences where the relationship became abusive. In the sessions she began to remember the beginning phase of the coming together with her so-called new partner at the time, and her realization that he was not "the one." But back then she chose to continue with the relationship anyway.

She would temporarily forget that she had been made aware (by the inner guidance from her own super intuition, aka her amazing Higher

Self) that he clearly was not who she hoped he would be. In actuality she was constantly convincing herself that he was who she wanted him to be. But come the end of the day, he never really could be that (for whatever his reasons).

It wasn't until she could accept responsibility for the choice she made to override her own higher intuition around these types of relationships, and that if she chose to continue showing up this way, then those abusive romantic relationships would just repeat. And it was only when she courageously accepted 100 percent personal responsibility for the entirety of her part in this that she started to learn the lessons and to eventually master them. This would set her free from these types of relationship experiences once and for all.

3. Forgive courageously and completely.

> Have you forgiven others in your life for their wrongdoings? Have you forgiven yourself for your wrongdoings? If we're still blaming, shaming, judging, victimizing, or projecting onto others or onto ourselves, then we haven't yet risen yet to a state of forgiveness. This means we're still in the tormenting phase with ourselves and everyone else involved—as a result of not yet getting to the place along our journey in resolving this once and for all and bringing this to a peaceful end within ourselves. Resolving this means courageously engaging in the higher act of forgiving.

You see, when we've completely forgiven ourselves, and whatever it is that we believe or perceive we have done and/or this other person has done to us, this is what truly sets us free from this torment of long-term unconscious pain and suffering.

The story of this woman with her relationship experiences played out over and over again, as she was not getting to what it was she was truly to be truly responsible for. This was causing a repeat of the same old patterns that were manifesting into the same type of romantic relationship that simply followed the first one.

Beyond her just accepting responsibility for her part in this ongoing pattern, it became equally significant to her overall process of healing this relationship dynamic to courageously forgive those men for what she at the time believed they were doing to wrong her.

On a much deeper level within her, she came face to face with the hard reality that she had not only been holding these men in judgment, but she had been holding herself in judgment as well for that first choice in the beginning of those relationships to override her own higher intuition.

4. Embrace inner responsibility.

> If there was a higher transformational goal or objective here, what would it be? Well, how about this? To rise or mature to a point along our own transformational journey where we could respond to anything in life coming from a higher-feeling state such as calm, peace, joy, or love. To quote the sage and prolific author, Deepak Chopra, "The healthiest response to life is joy."
>
> Can you live in this higher state of joy, peace, or calm? If so, for how long? For how long at any given time can you live in this state? A week, a month, or as a lifestyle?

If and when we can live in this higher state... there is no more lower energy pattern of taking things personally, or having to be defensive, or having to be aggressive, or having to hurt others as a way to protect ourselves. There is no more right or wrong... rather, everything *just is*.

There is no more reactionary charge coming from within us when life happens. Instead, there's an acceptance of "what is" when life happens—whether it's negative or positive. It just doesn't matter anymore. It's all a part of the spiritual experience of life's journey. There's now an honoring, a trusting, a respecting of one's greater destiny to just be allowed, where it can simply unfold in a way that's either been chosen in the moment or has already been destined to do so.

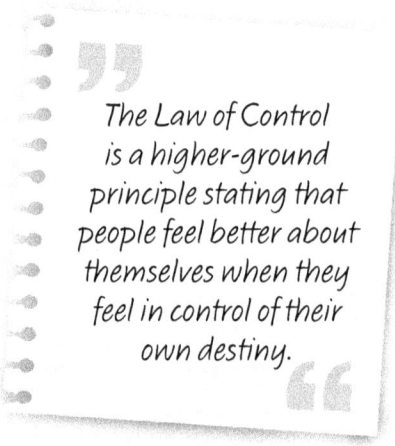

The Law of Control is a higher-ground principle stating that people feel better about themselves when they feel in control of their own destiny.

There's a powerful story that another one of our great sages and teachers, Eckhart Tolle, tells in one of his best-selling books. It's about a master living in the courtyard of the village of those he was in service to. There was a 12-year-old girl within that village who shared with her parents one day that she had been molested by the master. When the parents first learned of such a thing from their daughter, they immediately acted out in a reactionary way, confronting their master.

The master only responded with one word, "Interesting." And then he gently walked away. It was in that moment the parents took on the mission of destroying the master's credibility and his impeccable reputation within the community that he had faithfully and lovingly served for quite a long time.

Twenty years had passed when the girl, who was now a young woman, decided to come clean with her story and shared with her parents that she was never molested. She made up the whole story. Right away, her parents went to look for the master. When they found him, they shared the ugly uncomfortable truth of what they had just learned from their daughter. To which he calmly responded, "Interesting." And, again, he simply walked away.

The moral of this story shows us, in the most profound of ways, what it's like to rise to a level of responding masterfully to life no matter what it presents to us.

The Power of Control

Inside of you, you have an Inner Power of Control. There's also a law that says you have total control of your own personal corner in the Universe. The Law of Control states that we feel good about ourselves to the degree in which we feel that we are in control of ourselves and/or in charge of our own lives. This applies to each and every one of us. The Law of Control is also a higher-ground principle stating that people feel better about themselves when they feel in control of their own destiny.

The opposite of this law is that people feel worse about themselves when they feel they are not in control of their destiny. This is why we took a deeper dive into the previous Inner Power, the Power of Responsibility, which works in tandem with this Inner Power of Control. We need to feel in control or in charge of our own life to the degree in which we have accepted complete responsibility for ourselves, our lives, and our destiny.

It's important to know that we are all required, at some point on our journey, to learn how to actually use this Inner Power of Control, along with the Power of Responsibility. And to this point of my journey, I've never met someone, including myself, who knew how to use these powers when they first came into awareness of them. For everyone I've known who has learned how to use these powers correctly, it's usually taken some major schooling. In other words, there is no quick fix here.

The most obvious way in which we can recognize how well we're doing along our journey in mastering these Inner Powers is demonstrated by how good or skilled we've become when it comes to us Manifesting Like a masterMaster in our own personal and professional worlds.

Now, this Power of Control is also different from *being controlling*. If I'm using the Power of Control correctly, one way I'll know this is that *I am no longer being controlling*. In working with people and helping them along in their journeys, there's a night-and-day difference between an individual who has control versus *one who is controlling*.

Questions for Further Reflection

In order to really understand the difference, reflect on the following questions:

1. Have you been in the presence of a controlling person where you were on the receiving end of their controlling ways?

2. Have you been in the presence of someone where it became really obvious to you that they were clearly in control of a situation in the best of ways?

These two questions are key when it comes to understanding the Power of Control. One is a proper use of this power, and the other is a misuse of this power.

You might have people in your life who have been misusing this Inner Power through controlling dynamics and/or lower energy behavioral patterns. Maybe from time to time YOU have had a tendency to misuse this power. Do you know what happens when you're misusing this power? Do you have any idea what might happen consequentially in your own personal universe if you were to misuse this power?

If you're not sure, then go back to the contrast that we just created with the two reflection questions above—the contrast between someone who's pushy and controlling and the person who actually has control and therefore is in charge of a situation; the person who has been misusing their power that they were endowed with versus the person who is using that same power properly.

The controlling person often tends to push themselves onto others or push their way onto things that they are trying to have manifest in their world. On the other hand, the person who is truly in control doesn't have to push on anything or anyone because now that they have control and are in charge, they simply respond to others and events that happen in their personal and/or professional lives. This always brings them to a more positive outcome, as a direct result of them consciously and responsibly exercising this Power of Control or the Law of Control in the healthiest of ways.

Using This Power Correctly

This is another key point, as we are all *endowed* with this power—among a number of others. Here's the deal... if we were to misuse these powers, there's going to be a consequence. And it's not going to be positive. It's possibly going to sting. Something negative potentially gets created in our lives. Now that's not God doing anything to us. That's not the Universe doing anything to us. That's not Spirit doing anything to us. That's not even life doing anything to us. And that's not anybody in our world doing something to us. Rather it's all coming from some aspect within us.

The question here is: Are you aware that it's been you, or possibly some part of you, that's been influencing you to misuse this Inner Power of Control? Probably not. I couldn't imagine somebody being fully aware that they're misusing this power and then continuing to misuse it. In fact, once I help somebody become aware of this power, I mean really aware, then they want to work with me, or someone like me. They don't want to continue misusing this power—because it can seriously hurt or cause havoc in some aspect of their life when they do.

If I've been misusing this Inner Power of Control in my personal, professional, or spiritual life, it means I've been lacking in discipline as well, which also implies I have little self-control. Some time ago, I was working with another business owner. At the time, he practiced a lot more self-control in his business than he did with his romantic love interests. He would be ending a relationship where he just couldn't wait for something better to manifest…so he would move back into the relationship rather quickly that he was in and stay there discontented. He would do this as a way to fill up the void he was feeling of not having, or being, in a relationship.

> *If I've been misusing this Inner Power of Control it means I've been lacking in discipline, which also implies I have little self-control.*

He asked me, "Is this an opportunity to return back into the relationship, or might this be a temptation?" The real opportunity, even though something was blocking him from being able to see it, was to say no to this old relationship. But at that time, he just wasn't willing to do so. He couldn't or wouldn't exercise any self-control in the decision of just saying "no more" and sticking with his decision. He wasn't self-disciplined in this area of his life yet.

This caused all kinds of problems that would eventually spill over into his business. He had little self-control over his thoughts and emotions. He hadn't yet learned how to turn this around where he would be in control of his thoughts and feelings, instead of being controlled by them. Therefore, he couldn't apply much self-discipline at a time when that's what he truly needed to do. And as a result, his ability to perform and produce in his business would begin to fade away.

So instead of getting better at disciplining himself through exercising good self-control, he would convince himself that this was the relationship he needed to return back to. Somehow, he thought this would make everything better, even though it never did. He just couldn't consider the idea that it wouldn't. As a result, he would let his mind and emotions take control of the situation. A few years later, this relationship expanded into having kids, purchasing real estate, and so on. The whole plot thickened. Now the relationship was even more complex.

What was interesting with this manifestation was that the problem or challenge was the actual relationship itself. You see, it wasn't working and pretty much hadn't been working from its beginning. This, of course, would eventually grow into the two of them destroying of each other by constantly putting each other down. This was perfect from his perspective, as the unhealed issue he came into the relationship with was unworthiness. To this, his fear was he'd end up alone because deep within his subconscious he was afraid that he wouldn't be man enough for the woman he truly desired to be with.

These lower-energy patterns or shadow dynamics that were always running in the background, at a subconscious level, attracted a relationship with a partner who was making him feel what it was he had deep inside him—something he was already feeling about himself, prior to starting this relationship. Oh, and it turned out one of his soul lessons that he came into this life with was discipline and self-control.

Napoleon Hill, in *Think and Grow Rich*, wrote that one of the major causes of failure is the lack of self-discipline. And that discipline comes through self-control. This means one must learn how to be in control of all negative qualities and energies within their own field of consciousness.

Hill went on to say, "Before you can control conditions, you must control yourself. Self-mastery is the hardest job you will ever tackle." You see, if we don't conquer our lower self, we will be conquered by it.

At some point, though, you are going to start using this power correctly. One day, you're going to wake up, and you'll realize there's been an internal shift that has taken place within you. Before this major turnaround, however, there is going to be a process, and that process begins with the moment of awareness.

There will be a moment when you think, *Oh my gosh. I've got a power that I've been endowed with in this life, and I've been misusing it. I can see it as clear as day. Not only have I had people in my life that are very controlling; I've also been controlling. I've been controlling my mother. I've been controlling my son. I've been controlling my partner. I've been controlling my co-worker. I've been controlling my emotions—but I don't have control over my emotions, as I haven't yet achieved the place within me of true control or mastery of them.*

Remember, there's a real distinction here. When you're utilizing this power properly, you have the control that you're now choosing to utilize in the healthiest and wisest of ways.

Whenever I've worked with people who were controlling, versus having control, once they were ready to go a little deeper into their psyches, into their bodies and/or their subconscious mind, there were parts of them that would surface that could be quite pissed off at them. These parts could be so angry that it sometimes could take months to even get these parts to start to believe in them again. In other words, they didn't believe in them at all. They didn't respect them. They were pissed off at them because they often felt so repressed or pushed away, thus very controlled by them. This is one of the consequential effects of having operated this way.

If we don't conquer our lower self, we will be conquered by it.

As a person gains better control, they are able to effectively take back control of their thoughts and emotions. Recall from the section on the Power of Thought that we have around 50,000 thoughts every day. As previously mentioned, 80 percent of our thoughts are negative and 95 percent are repetitive, as reported by the Science Foundation. Too much negative thinking can cause disease. As Dr. Bruce Lipton cautions, negative thinking can kill you. Heck, I've witnessed what a continuous pattern of negativity can and will do over time, both in the form of manifesting physical diseases and/or the destroying of one's career, finances, or relationship successes as well.

So, what would it be like for you to take back control of just 5 percent of those negative thoughts? Now an important part of the overall formula is getting better at working with one's emotions or feelings. Running away from our feelings or avoiding our feelings by stuffing them down or ignoring them is not the answer here. Rather it's in learning how to consciously work towards healing them, learning from them, and releasing them, instead of acting like they don't matter. If I act like they don't matter, my feelings will end up controlling me by possibly manifesting their like with what it is I don't want to have manifest in my personal or professional world.

This is a critical point to understand, as those negative thoughts that repeat the most on the screen of our mind, and/or deep within our psyche, are rooted in suppressed negative emotional material that's buried deep within us at a subconscious level. It's these negative emotions that are controlling the thoughts of their like.

So, would you say you're currently in control of your emotions and feelings, or are they possibly in control of you? This is a great self-inquiry question to work with. Those who are truly getting better at consciously manifesting are those who have achieved a healthier degree of emotional fitness and stability.

Those who are now Manifesting Like a masterMaster... have either achieved their first degree of emotional mastery or are really close to doing so. Positive and powerful manifestations come as we fully feel higher-frequency emotions (such as joy, gratitude, love, etcetera), in our bodies on a daily basis for short yet concentrated periods of time.

You might ask, "How long do we do this for?" Well, for as long as it takes for whatever it is we most desire to have manifest.

> Speaking of our body, what would it be like if you could take full control of what actually goes into your body? Typically, for years or even decades, our bodies have been in charge of us for the most part.
>
> When in doubt, just start paying attention to what happens when you have a craving for something. Or more specifically, pay attention when that addiction comes on for whatever it is that you've been addicted to. What happens then? Does the addiction craving win over whatever it is you know might be best for your body at that time? If the addiction wins, then that implies your body is in control of you.

Or perhaps it's about gaining a better control of your spending habits, or your daily schedule, or taking better control of your emotional health. Having emotional wellness is so significant when it comes to manifesting. What we feel and how we feel (positively or negatively) greatly influences what we manifest.

Why is this all so important when it comes to manifesting? Because one of the consequences of misusing this power is that we're going to keep getting what we don't want in life. If this power is being used in a controlling way, it's going to constrict us. We're not going to have the same level of focus and fluidity in manifesting as someone who takes charge and engages in good self-control. When we're in the process of creating something that we really would like to have manifest, focus and fluidity are paramount.

The Power of Control and the Law of Consciousness

Let's go back to the Law of Consciousness... If we're going to succeed and truly expand to our very next level of consciousness, we've got to get a handle on this Inner Power by consciously practicing healthier self-control. If we're still doing the controlling thing, however, not only are we possibly resisting the active engagement for better self-control, but now we are not going to be allowed entry into this next level of consciousness—at least not just yet.

It's important to recognize that with the next level of consciousness also comes access to the next level of power to consciously and responsibly manifest with. This is why our Higher Self would never allow it. That would be dangerous. It would be like giving an eight-year-old child the keys to a Ferrari—that would be ridiculous! It's simply just too much power and responsibility for someone who hasn't earned their way yet. You wanna talk about possibly killing someone? That's a good recipe to likely kill somebody, or possibly even ourselves for that matter. All because we are accessing more power than we can handle.

Our Higher Self, thank God, will not allow us entry into the next level of consciousness because it houses that new level of power. As we expand as a Soul to that next level in our physical body, we then have access to more creative power to manifest and achieve our most important goals with.

If we're still falling asleep at the wheel in the level of consciousness that we're currently at, there's no way we're getting access to that next level. It would be an accident waiting to happen.

There's a new field of study called epigenetics, which reveals that you are controlling all of your genetic and behavioral activity. Epigenetics is a new type of science that is growing in popularity and promise in the new scientific world. It is the study of cellular and physiological traits. These traits are the external and environmental factors that turn our genes on and off and define how our cells actually read those genes. Through epigenetics, we can see the true potential of the human mind and the cells in our body.

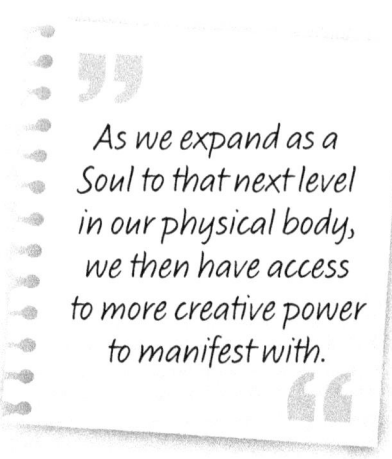

As we expand as a Soul to that next level in our physical body, we then have access to more creative power to manifest with.

This is a science that even eminent scientists are beginning to see potential in. Sir Adrian Bird defined epigenetics as the structural adaptation of chromosomal regions that register, signal, and perpetuate altered activity states. Bruce. Lipton, who is also a stem cell biologist and best-selling author of *The Biology of Belief*, writes that the idea that you cannot escape the genetics of your family is simply not true. He then goes on to say that believing we must accept and live out our family's genetics is a false and restricting belief.

When it comes to my own genetics, I took on quite a bit in this life, and little by little, I got all of these problematic genetic tendencies cleared. I love my family, and I mean no disrespect, but if you see my family and then you see me, you'll likely think, *I don't get it. What's the connection here? Are you sure this is your family?*

When I was in my early forties and my father was still alive, whenever he attended one of my events in which the seminar attendees were meeting him for the first time, they just couldn't believe it. They thought maybe I was adopted by him. Nope, he was my biological father. However, I had been clearing out the genetics that I took on from him and his father and his father's father that had been building for over a decade at that point.

My dad was very much like the character Archie Bunker from *All in the Family*—including that slouchy appearance, pot belly, and gruffness. Like Archie he was very judgmental, overly critical, could be very negative, was hard on himself and others, etcetera. His diet had a lot of unhealthy fats, carbs, and even alcohol. Uniquely enough, I found myself going down the exact same path. I began developing similar physical manifestations as well: gall bladder problems, liver problems, and heart problems. And like my father, I also needed glasses. By the time I was in my late twenties I had the same medical issues developing—and even had a pot belly!

In those earlier years, I had some of those same tendencies. I caught it fairly early on and began to shift them. As I worked through reversing many of the health challenges and the energetics I had taken on from my family lineage, my physicality, my demeanor and even the way I visually looked began changing over time. I was able to reverse my genetics and those health issues that had manifested in the rest of my family members.

I no longer had the heart issues, the gall bladder issues, or the liver problems. I was no longer negative. I had a healthier diet—and no more pot belly. *And* I didn't need glasses anymore!

Believing that we can't go beyond our family genetics—that these family genetics that we've taken on are supposedly something we have to live with until we die—is a huge limiting belief that can hold so much power over us and possibly even wreak havoc on our well-being. This is a collective conditioning on the planet. In the past, even my students had taken on this limiting belief that genetics are what you're born with, and you're stuck with them.

When I was 27 years of age, I decided to challenge that belief, as I alluded to in the comparison with my dad around taking on the family genetics. Now, I had no conscious awareness around this at the time, but I decided to challenge it. I had this sixth sense, if you will, running though my bones—I just couldn't buy into believing that this was my fate. All around me, everybody was telling me that I had to prepare for tough genetics that would come up in my life, and it was just a question of time. And I did have some experiences with these genetic tendencies—in fact, some of them almost killed me.

One heavy experience was having a heart attack at age 27. As previously mentioned, my heart issues came from my dad's side of the family genetics. These health challenges lasted until the age of 33—which was the last time one of these genetic traits almost took me out. I just refused to buy into it, even though health trouble and death were seemingly all around me until my mid-thirties.

I had a few doctor friends who were plugged into epigenetics research when it was in its infancy, and one of them said to me, "Somehow, even though you didn't know this was going on, you literally overrode your genetics. How the heck did you do that? There was no knowledge, there was no science, there was no spiritual teacher that came in and told you how to do this. There was none of that. So, how did you do it?" Well, the short and simple answer was, I did it intuitively.

This all makes more sense now because there's been more research since that time. And some doctors are now sharing this knowledge with their patients. I bring this up because the point here is, *you get to choose*. And you get to do that by utilizing this Power of Control, along with the Power of Responsibility you've been endowed with.

> *You get to choose... by utilizing this Power of Control, along with the Power of Responsibility you've been endowed with.*

And remember, if you have limiting beliefs, when you give them power, and when you attach your emotions to them, they influence the quality of your choices. They contribute to your magnetic field, manifesting more of that restrictive energy that can really limit how you are experiencing your own life.

If these beliefs have enough of your power and you were to choose to not get that power back, this choice alone (consciously or unconsciously) could have you continue on with them until your last breath—maybe even into your next lifetime or two.

To this, I suggest if you haven't already, make the decision, sooner rather than later, to stop giving these beliefs your creative power. And instead, get this power back where it properly belongs within you by dismantling those limiting beliefs. By doing so, this would be you choosing to develop and strengthen that Inner Power of Control by consciously practicing better self-control. This alone could change everything for the better if you do. This in fact is the power that has been missing, once reclaimed and regained, will truly empower you *to create the life of your dreams.*

The Power of Intention

As we deepen our understanding of what intention actually is and how to best utilize this amazing Inner Power, along with the previous two powers in this chapter, we can change our physical reality here in this 3rd dimension or frequency.

As the American Heritage® Dictionary of the English Language defines:

Intention simply signifies a course of action that one proposes to follow, as in: "It is my intention to work for a year and then go back to school." Intent more strongly implies deliberateness.

Intention is what engages another Universal Law known as the Law of Deliberate Creation. It is what we mean when we totally commit to doing something on a conscious or unconscious level. Our true intention, whatever that is and whether originating from our conscious self or some aspect of our subconscious self, will always determine the outcome. Intention is what sets things in motion. It's the inner switch that fires up the engine of manifestation.

An intention is an idea that we plan (or intend) to carry out. If we mean something... it's an intention. It's choosing or intending the way we want something in particular to go—such as an event, meeting, phone call, Zoom call, and/or even sabotaging some aspect of our life (for whatever the reason).

So, in short, it's making a clear decision of the way you want something to go.

> When you are intentional with your day, week, month and even year... you'll find that life's events fall into place more smoothly or gracefully. Both clear and unclear intentions send a message to the Universe, to the Divine, to the world, and to yourself about who it is you want to be, what it is you wish to have manifest, and what it is you want to accomplish or experience.

When we're not intentional during the course of our day, we run the risk of allowing the consciousness, thoughts, and attitudes of others (including the media) to direct the events and circumstances of our personal and professional worlds. Which can make life more difficult and/or miserable than it needs to be. This can, and often has, created pain and suffering for many in our lives. Throughout my years of teaching and coaching, I've often referred to this as the type of pain and suffering that is totally unnecessary. In my work with others, I've found there are two types of pain: one is necessary and the other is not. It's the second type where negative karma can get created and often does.

I was watching an interview with one of my favorite authors, Gary Zukav, a *New York Times* bestselling author. He was speaking on the Power of Intention that day. What he shared was profound. He said, "The world in which we live has been created unconsciously by unconscious intentions. Every intention sets energy into motion whether you are conscious of it or not. You create in each moment." It stunned me when he spoke those words... you create in each moment. For me at the time, nobody could have said something that struck me as a greater truth with a such a great level of profundity than he did that day.

Remember the Inner Power of Control—which when choosing it and utilizing it correctly, you have complete control of yourself. To that, however, you still have to say or intend the way you want it to go. This is where creation begins. You have to make a decision each day on each and every event. This is exactly what someone does when they're manifesting (or creating) like a master.

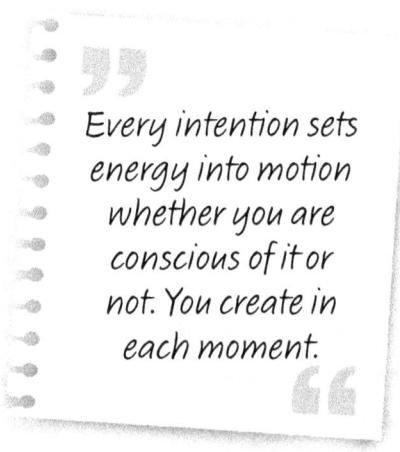

> Every intention sets energy into motion whether you are conscious of it or not. You create in each moment.

Back in the earlier days, I would experiment with my events and meetings. With some I was consciously intentional, and with others I was not. As I compared the results that would manifest with these two different approaches, I quickly realized just how life-altering the Power of Intention really was.

Later on in life, I would test this with some of my coaching clients. During this experiment, two clients would be in the process of purchasing a new vehicle or house or building. I would work with one of them on helping them to clarify their intention prior to the beginning of the process; whereas with the other, I would simply listen to them as they were sharing with me their desire to purchase something and their process of what they believed they needed to do as a way to make their purchase.

To my surprise it had the same effect that it did with me and my earlier experiences in my life. So, I decided to continue with my little experiment with other clients—and not only with their purchases but with other areas as well, such as their important meetings, phone calls, sales appointments, dating, and social events. With the ones I would practice this on, their experience with whatever it was—whether it was coming into a meeting, making a phone call, going on an appointment, planning an event, or purchasing something—was simply much smoother, more effective and productive. With the others, however, sometimes their experiences would be okay, and other times not at all. It became so obvious how much power there truly is in choosing to be intentional and ultimately living our life intentionally.

> Ask yourself: on a scale of one to ten, one being a little and ten being a lot, how often have you been living your life intentionally up until now? How often have you taken the time in advance to set forth your intention each day for how you would like your meetings, calls, or activities to go?
>
> To live with intention simply sets us up for a better, richer experience (personally, spiritually, and professionally). We could have a general overall statement of intent which we choose to live our life by, such

as: *I choose to live with intention and to be of high value to myself and to those around me.*

Those who don't live intentionally will find themselves intentionally living more from the level of their unconscious. Let's remember an intention can be conscious or it can be unconscious, subconscious, or both. In other words, there's an intention behind pretty much everything we do.

General conscious intentions might be: I intend to let go of my negative ways or negative habits. I intend to accept responsibility for my choices and decisions. I intend to be forgiving. I intend to exercise healthier self-control. I intend to close a sale today. I intend to help my son or daughter today. I intend to be more loving, kind, or compassionate today. I intend to complete this project or activity today. I intend to eat healthier today. I intend to engage in good self-care today. I intend to get to bed earlier today. I intend to get better at Manifesting Like a Master this year. The sky is the limit here.

An intention is a proclamation to the Universe or the Divine. It focuses our creative energy in a certain direction. Whether we're conscious of what we're intending or unconscious towards a shadow or light aspect of ourselves... where intention goes, our energy will flow.

Our intention behind a decision or action dictates the direction that action or decision goes. Which is why intention plays a major role regarding how something ultimately turns out.

An unconscious intention might be looking for fault in others or a reason to victimize someone or hold someone (even yourself) back. It might be looking for occasions to be offended and then lash out, or to have an outburst of anger (like a pressure cooker ready to explode) due to a lot of pent-up anger that's been building up inside. It might be sabotaging your success or happiness, or someone else's. It might be looking for someone to take care of you or looking for someone to care for who doesn't want to be cared for. And the list goes on...

Intention can move mountains. Everything is energy, and subconsciously we broadcast our intentions out into our world; and the world cannot help but to subconsciously pick up on our intentions and treat us in accordance. The solution, of course, would be to become present—to learn how to live in the *now* moment. This then would allow us the ability to become conscious of the intentions and negative programming that have been playing themselves out from our subconscious self.

> *Where intention goes, our energy will flow.*

Then the dynamic and interplay of energy becomes revealed and a whole new reality opens up to you—a reality where you become a creator or co-creator in the conscious and active creation of living your best life. Instead of the old you—as in the victim of circumstances created by your own unconscious, unresolved, unhealed intentions that simply have been living in the shadows of your own subconscious self. All of which can be totally healed and cleared.

The Power of Intention, when being utilized correctly, is also the power of a focused mind. Intention shows up in our thoughts and feelings... Intention *is* thought and feeling. Whether we're aware of it or not, we broadcast out into our own personal universe all the time with our thoughts and feelings.

If we're entertaining around 50,000 thoughts or more a day, what are the odds that at least a few hundred or possibly even a few thousand of those thoughts are being projected out into our world? Of course... how could they not be? This is another reason why it's a beneficial choice to get better at correctly utilizing this power. Now the thoughts that outwardly broadcast most are those that are fueled by corresponding emotions.

If those thoughts and feelings are more on the negative side and someone is thinking something negative about the one who is in front of them, notice what happens to them... The person who is receiving what's being broadcasted from someone who is entertaining the negative thoughts they're sending out from within their mind, might shift in their behavior and physiology. Even though we can't see what another person is thinking, it's possible to feel it.

Or our body picks up on the broadcast and responds or reacts accordingly. It doesn't matter if the one who is broadcasting is aware or not. Whether we're conscious of what we're intending or unconscious towards a shadow or light aspect of ourselves, where intention goes your energy will flow. Whatever the quality or vibrational frequency of those thoughts are in that moment... that is the intention.

These thoughts will go out as a broadcast into our personal universe whether we're aware of this or not. Even if we never act out on these thoughts, they will still broadcast outward and therefore have their corresponding effect. Whether the broadcast is coming from our conscious or subconscious self, it will influence whomever or whatever it's being sent to.

Then it eventually bounces back like a boomerang upon the sender. Whether the broadcast that's going out is positive or negative... we'll eventually get more of its like back. This is where our ego can come into the mix. If the ego has been tamed and we've been teaching it what its higher purpose really is, which is to be in service to our Soul Self, then what we've been broadcasting would now be slanted more towards the positive.

On the other hand, if we haven't been doing this type of work just yet, which would also imply that we probably haven't been exercising good self-control either, this would probably also mean that what we've been broadcasting (consciously or subconsciously) has been slanted more towards the negative. And if we've been doing that, it would be a misuse of this power. Most negative karma is a direct result of the misuse of one's ego.

> If you're interested in learning more about the nature of karma, refer back to book two in the Transformation Trilogy.

As mentioned earlier, we live in a simulation much like what was portrayed in the movie *The Matrix*. What we put out into the world around us is what we get back. At its most fundamental level, this is how karma works. The more you give into the world... the more you will receive back from the world. Now the more we try to take from the world around us... the more the world around us will take from us.

So, where does our intention come from? Well, the answer can be found in how we live. It's also found in the thoughts and feelings that show up in our minds and bodies. Ask yourself: Do you live intentionally? How often do you check your intention, or your results, which can be quite reflective of both your conscious and/or subconscious intentions that you perhaps were not even aware of? How often do you take the time to get clear on your intention prior to doing an activity? What type of thoughts have you been thinking most lately? Have your feelings been mostly positive or negative lately? Your answers to these questions give you a snapshot of where you are currently at in consciously living your life with intention.

Living Intentionally

When we're living intentionally, we recognize that intention operates on two levels. The higher level would be an energy that flows through us, whereas the other would be a lower energy that can influence us to push on something or someone that we want something from. This occurs when we are being needy—such as our needing for love, approval, attention, control, or needing to play it safe).

Five Steps to Consciously Living Our Lives with Intention
1. Connect to the Intention

Our Higher Self, when surrendered to, simply flows through us with its intention to do something or be something. Our Higher Self may appear to be doing nothing at this point, but then something happens that we notice and/or experience as miraculous. As in, something wonderful just manifested in our day-to-day life.

Whether we're parenting our children, achieving something in our career or business, or running a marathon, at some point we become aware and even emotionally moved, as it becomes obvious that what just happened in our daily life did not come from us (from our smaller self). This clearly came from a higher place that also resides within us—as in our Divine Soul Essence Self, aka our Higher Self.

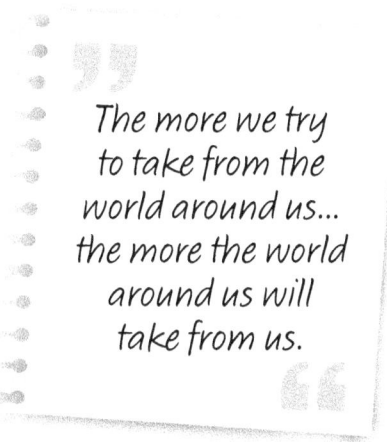

The more we try to take from the world around us... the more the world around us will take from us.

In this state of awareness, we also recognize that for this to happen, there was no pushing on something or someone; there was no trying to make something happen and no aggressing onto anything (or anyone) in order for whatever this was to have manifested in our day-to-day life. It's like breathing. For the most part, no one has to try to exhale. It just happens. These types of experiences leave us feeling amazed, inspired, or even in awe. This is us connected to something bigger, such as our Larger Soul Self, the Universe, or the Divine.

We recognize that we are not in charge—rather, there's something bigger, brighter, and greater than that of the little "I," or the small self. We often come to know this greater power through experiencing it when we least expect it. Perhaps it comes through when we're fully engaged in something else that's purer, such as being in service to someone or something beyond ourselves, or when we're fully engaged in exactly what we're to truly be doing or having a lot of fun with whatever it is we're doing. And then it happens. We're not even looking for it, as we're completely focused on what it is we're doing.

In our day-to-day life, this could happen when serving someone without any self-agenda. We could very well experience this awesome larger self or higher power as it's flowing through us when teaching or parenting a child, working with a client, having a challenging conversation with an employee, or helping a stranger in a genuine time of need. When we get over ourselves or out of the realm of our lower self, or out of our own way… this is where and when these types of experiences can simply happen.

Remember that inspiring story of the lady in Red Deer, Alberta from that hit television show *That's Incredible*. She was 80 years old when that happened. That was her larger self, aka her Divine Soul Essence Self. She was completely focused on helping the man who was laying on the ground struggling to take his next breath. She as her lower self stepped out of the way without thinking about any of this. Her only focus was to save that person in a time of great need.

> So, which level of intention have you been connected to this past week? The level of your Higher Self or your Lower Self? When was the last time you checked to see what influence you've been living under? Or choosing under? Your Soul or your ego? If it's at the Higher Level and

it doesn't happen the way you want it to happen, or when you wanted it to happen by... then know that you can choose to surrender to the experience of it all and accept it as it is. In other words, choose to see it as if it had a purpose in light of the way the experience is playing itself out.

Why? Perhaps the intention we are connected to is not the highest one at that time, and things are not going the way we want them to. When this happens, this is more than likely a time in which we are to be learning something about ourselves or the way in which we've been perceiving our life (personally or professionally). Is it possible that the way in which we have been, or have been viewing the experience, has been off?

2. Responsibility for your Intentions

Responsibility links intention to our desired outcome. This is one of the reasons why our Soul wants us to become responsible for ourselves.

Ultimately, we want to understand what our intention is that's driving or influencing the way we show up with others in our life. And to this, to also understand the intentions of others in our lives as well. For example, maybe you're dating and the other is moving in rather quickly to have sex with you. This is where you might get clear on what your intention is: are you looking for a partnership or to just have sex right away?

If you're looking for something serious, then what you need to determine is whether this person is also looking for something serious or not. If not, you're wasting your time. Or you're possibly running the risk of becoming hurt when the painful reality comes upon you that he or she had a different intention than you did.

The ego, unless taught otherwise, will attempt to have us attach to the outcome of our desires or intentions, as a way to disconnect the link of our conscious intention to the outcome. This is one of the reasons why some seem to take forever to achieve goals they've set for themselves. And this is one of the ways the ego can increase its influence over us.

On the other hand, when we accept 100 percent responsibility for ourselves and our creations, there is no more blame throwing, guilt shaming, or projecting our stuff onto others. There are only intentional experiences and happenings. This is one of the ways in which we get our power back from the ego where it properly belongs… within our true seat of center.

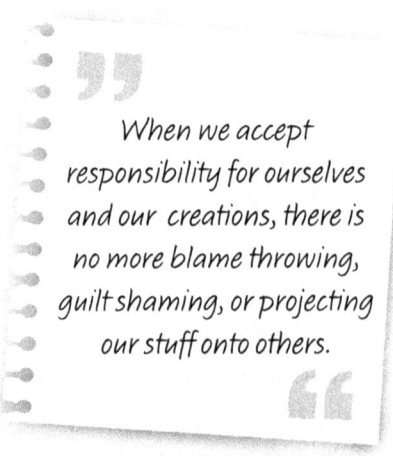

When we accept responsibility for ourselves and our creations, there is no more blame throwing, guilt shaming, or projecting our stuff onto others.

As we learned earlier with the Inner Power of Responsibility, *with great power comes great responsibility*. This is where we accept full responsibility for not only our conscious intentions but our unconscious ones as well. And if you're unsure what your unconscious intentions might be, you can look at your thoughts, then look at your choices, words, and deeds. They will always show you exactly what they are because that's where our intentions first manifest—in our choices, words, thoughts and actions. Then they can manifest in our bodies and in any aspect of our lives.

> If we find it hard to identify our intentions regarding something, we could ask ourselves, "Why?" Why am I doing this? Why am I speaking this way? Why am I acting this way? Why am I feeling this way? Why am I reacting so intensely? Where was I doing that action from? What's motivating me to do this? Why do I want this? Or do we need to be pushed into action?

3. Writing your Intentions down on paper

Putting our intentions on paper helps us to clarify them. The practice of writing them down can greatly assist us in figuring out what it is we really want. Most people don't take the time to set intentions or write them out because they haven't yet uncovered what it is they actually want.

Buddhists have this greater concept of *right intention*. Right intention is a conscious daily practice of setting an intention that can help you get where it is you want to go, or what it is you want to accomplish or experience that day.

> To practice this, simply spend a few moments focusing your thoughts and feelings on the outcome of whatever it is you want to experience or accomplish today.

> Writing our intentions down also helps us to visualize them. As we visualize our intentions, it can make the creative process more powerful in

realizing that intention. Remember, where intention goes, our energy will flow.

The act of actually writing our intentions down can also get us in touch with the feelings that naturally come as our intention actualizes. Once we know what it feels like if and when those intentions materialize that are then infused in one's electromagnetic field, it's these feelings which strengthen our inner clarity to post-visualize the end result of the intention.

4. *Voice your intentions*

> What's even more powerful is when we voice our intentions into creation. Recall the Inner Power of the Spoken Word... everything that exists is created through vibrations. This speaks directly to the Law of Vibration that we covered earlier in the book.

Our voice amplifies our ability to manifest through intention because it is using sound, which is vibration. This is the way in which the Universe responds to us... through vibration. If my intentions that I speak out loud, whether through my actions, thoughts, feelings, decisions, or words are more on the negative side of the vibrational scale, then I'll get more negative. If, on the other hand, my intentions are more on the positive side of the vibrational scale, then I'll get more positive.

It's our words, however, that carry the strongest vibration. It all plays out in how we choose to use our Inner Power of the Spoken Word. We ultimately want our words to be the best representation of the reality we intend to have manifest in our day-to-day life experience.

5. Become Intentional in your thinking

As previously mentioned, this is where ALL your intentions first show themselves—in your thoughts. Reflect on yesterday: what were your thoughts mostly focused on? Your answer to this question will tell you exactly what your intention was. So, are these the type of thoughts that you want to have manifest in your day-to-day life? If yes, simply keep your focus on those thoughts. Now if you don't like the answer, *you can change it*. That's the beauty here.

You can release and clear out those thoughts or thought patterns. Here's a little golden nugget for you: when the thoughts appear like they don't want to go, it's because of the repressed past emotional material they've taken root in. As we release the old, buried emotions or feelings, the thoughts corresponding with those emotions release as well.

The truth is: When you change your thoughts, you change the way you think... and when thinking changes, your intentions also change. Once you change your intentions... *your reality changes.* It's the correct use of one's power to intend for something to happen. If the subconscious can utilize this Inner Power and intend something to happen, so can you! This is you stepping into your own mastery in doing so.

The more we can come from our true seat of center... the more creative power we access to live the life of our happiest and most fulfilling dreams. Now this greater power does require great self-control and personal responsibility in living our lives intentionally. This also means building and gaining inner focus. To become master of our own thoughts and feelings and become really good at manifesting whatever it is we really desire to manifest, is the strongest reason for gaining a steady inner focus. This focus will not only empower us to manifest but to remain steady on the path of accomplishing those things we know we need to have accomplished as well. Our focus itself... is a superpower.

> To become intentional in your thinking, practice conscious intention setting. Intention setting is the process of clarifying on paper specifically what it would take to make your life (personally, professionally or entrepreneurially) exactly the way you would like it to be. To do so, start and maintain a daily focus on what your heartfelt desires, activity objectives, and most meaningful goals would be.
>
> Then break it down to a daily task where you purposefully think of what it is you wish to accomplish TODAY. And then set an intention for whatever that is by writing it down. Then, with feeling and conviction, SPEAK IT OUT LOUD. Not only does intention serve as an ignition switch; it's also like the fuel that powers up your desires for your intentions to be realized as well.

A clear intention helps to set a clear path before us that guides us to a specific action. Therefore, IT IS THE ACTION, or act of intending, that guides us to right action. I learned long ago that the right action, aka aligned action, is what empowers not only our intention but our spoken word as well. The action taken is where the transformational magic happens. Which is always found in our determination to follow through.

When you become masterful at following through with impeccability, with what you say you will do or you're intending to do... this is where your reality can and will change. And sometimes in the biggest, in the best, and in the brightest of ways!

As we get into the habit of intending daily—both at the start of our day, and prior to each event or activity we're about to engage in, we will notice a momentum building from within our own field of consciousness. At that point, a clear, concentrated thought that we intend to see manifest will turn out exactly as we imagine it to be.

When we're conscious of what we're intending, the Universe simply responds; whereas when we're unconscious of what we're intending, we run the risk of our subconscious possibly still carrying any unhealed past programming or negative karma that could manifest it's like in our day-to-day reality. This is why it's a wise and powerful choice to maintain the ongoing intention to become conscious of the transformative energies in the healing of our subconscious self.

The life-altering experiences that will happen in our life, as we choose to correctly utilize these inner superpowers, can literally change our reality and place us on an upward path of trajectory where we can do, be, or have anything we want.

CHAPTER 12

YOU CAN MANIFEST ANYTHING

What if I was to tell you that you could manifest anything you want? Well, what just came up for you as you read those words? Do you believe me? Now be honest... It's important that you are honest if you want to get to the truth. I know this is a higher truth; that I can manifest anything I want to manifest. It doesn't matter whether you believe me or not. What matters is what you believe.

I'm only suggesting that you possibly question what it is you believe, as it might not even be a greater truth. It's perhaps something you've chosen to simply believe as true. And if that's what you've done, then whatever it is you've been believing in... must come true. It's a Law of the Universe: whatever we wholeheartedly believe in must come true.

Again, we are an energetic creator, co-creating with the Universe and/or the Divine, to which we've been endowed with an inborn natural ability to manifest. No one can turn this off. We could, however, fall asleep to this higher truth and manifest more from our unconscious, or subconscious, reality. Additionally, this ability is only limited to what we choose to impose upon it. As in, if I choose to believe this natural ability doesn't exist, then it won't exist. If on the other hand, I truly believe it exists then it will exist.

We can manifest anything. To quote the lyrics in the 1982 song by the rock group America, "You Can Do Magic... you can have anything that you desire." In this, our final chapter, we'll learn the five guidelines and five steps to mastery for creating or co-creating with the Divine anything we truly desire. Ready to dive in? Here we go…

> When you read this greater truth, that you CAN have anything that you truly want... does this bring anything up for you? If so, what is it? Positive or negative? Either way, it doesn't matter. What matters is where you're at with your current level of understanding of this truth. So check and see how this truth makes you feel. Whatever that is, you're now aware of it. Now, if you need to, give yourself some time to be with whatever it is you're feeling around this greater truth.
>
> In fact, this might be a good time to bring out your journal and start writing down your thoughts and how you find yourself feeling. Let your journaling take you to where your Higher Self wants you to go to discover something of value or spiritual significance about you.

Let's remember here that within whatever truth we're in the process of uncovering is an energetic code for freedom, as in that beautiful ancient sage teaching, *the truth shall set you free*. In other words, once we come to truly know this at a deeper cellular level, nothing is impossible. To reiterate a part of Audrey Hepburn's revealing quote on this, "… the word itself says, I'M POSSIBLE."

With the exception of the following five simple guidelines, there are no limitations, except, of course, those you impose on yourself.

The 5 Guidelines

1. We know what it is we want.

> There are your larger goals and your smaller goals. With your larger goals you're going to need a higher level of creative power. The creative power from your Higher Self or Soul is released into the manifestation process as you come into the clear and true knowing of what it is you most genuinely desire from Soul level.
>
> In other words, what are your three most important goals? Another way of asking the same question is; what are your *Soul goals?* Not sure? Go back and revisit the action exercise at the end of the Power of Goals section in Chapter 7.

Now as we get better at connecting with our Higher Self, we at some point come into full conscious contact with what it is our Divine Soul Self truly wants us to have. This is where the goal-setting process becomes most powerful, as we now have the full support of our Highest Self guiding us, strengthening us, revealing to us exactly what to do next along our journeys in the realization and/or achieving of our goals.

2. We never create anything that will harm another person.

If we harm someone, we create negative karma. If this act of harming someone creates karma or a negative consequence, then this throws a monkey wrench into the creative process of manifesting what it is we most desire.

Here's another little hint: if you do create this type of karma... go with it. Embrace the consequence. From this side of the coin it now presents an opportunity to heal or transform some part of us. In this healing of embracing our karma or consequence, we learn something about ourselves and more than likely a lesson that we're to be learning.

3. We never create anything that would take away from another person.

To receive is one thing; to take is another. Taking from life is not the best strategy; rather, the greater life strategy is to become better at receiving that which we've been given. When we take from the world, the world then takes from us. It's cause and effect. Again, taking is not receiving. It's choice, which then causes an effect or consequence. Every choice has a positive or negative consequence. This is another reason why choosing to live our life intentionally is a great choice, as it leads to the creation of a dream life.

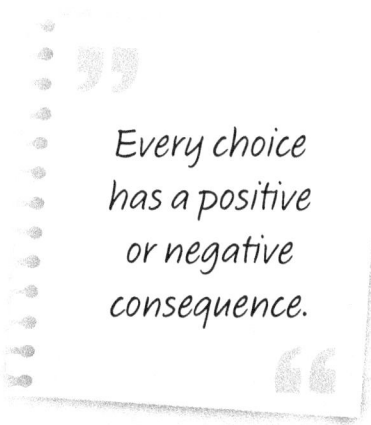

Every choice has a positive or negative consequence.

I'll say it one more time... taking is not receiving. Recall the Three Pillars for Manifesting from Chapter 9. One of the pillars is receiving. On a scale of one to ten, one being a little, ten being a lot, how receptive are you? How easy or natural is it for you to simply receive? For many, this in itself appears to be a Soul lesson–learning how to receive.

4. The goal, dream life, or intention is in complete alignment with our Divine Soul Essence Self, or Higher Self.

This is what will give an extra magic to the overall process of creating whatever it is we would like to have manifest in our day-to-day world.

> One practical way in telling whether the goal, dream, or intention has been inspired by our Higher Self is by the amount of desire that is burning within for the goal, dream, or intention. On a scale of one to ten, one being a little, ten being a lot, how strong is your desire to achieve this? How much do you want this?

Like a clear intention, a strong desire is the ignition switch to the engine of manifestation. To quote Napolean Hill, *"When your desires are strong enough, you will appear to possess superhuman powers to achieve."*

As we covered earlier, whatever it is you desire... your soul or Highest Self has already created for you to now receive. If you really want it, you are destined to have it. To receive it however, you are required to go through a true and complete transformation.

If we feel like we are blocked or held back in the manifesting of our desire, it's because we haven't evolved or expanded our consciousness, in our physical form, to the point where we are now matched at the correct frequency level to that of our greatest desire. This brings us back to being required to first go through a true transformation.

> *Whatever it is you have a heart-felt desire for... you can have..*

As I've often said, whatever it is you have a heart-felt desire for... you can have. To fully experience the achievement of your goals, intentions, and dream life, you must follow your heart's desire. This desire will show up in your gut. In other words, you will feel the strength of this desire. This is your Highest Self speaking to you, prompting you, guiding you to move in the direction of your desire.

In addition, when you follow your desire, it will always lead you to more personal and spiritual growth as well as to the expansion of your consciousness.

> And to open this up even more, check again to see where you're currently at with what your Soul is wanting you to have. It might be something even bigger or better for you than you currently think. Perhaps

your Soul wants you to have a different version of what you're thinking or feeling your exact desire is. Again, how open are you to receiving what your Soul wants for you and knows is best for you?

This is where you might revisit the Principle of Non-Attachment found in Chapter 8. If we become too attached to our desired outcome, we run the risk of temporarily cutting ourselves off from our Magnanimous Soul or Higher Self. So, a transformative affirmation here might be *"I am now open and ready to receive far beyond that of my current dreams, goals, and intentions."*

5. We're in harmony with the Universal Laws.

There is a real magic that occurs as we live our lives in alignment with Universal Law. This is why there are laws in each of the books within the Transformation Trilogy. The laws found under each title are specific to the teachings in each of the three books. As the great Atlantean God Thoth wrote about in the Emerald Tablets, *"Magic is not about illusion or tricks but rather understanding Universal Laws and working in harmony with them."*

To the degree in which we are living our life in alignment with these Universal Laws is the exact degree in which we access the power to create and manifest with. The Universe follows set principles. Living in alignment with these laws and principles brings balance into our personal, professional and spiritual lives.

> When we integrate these *five guidelines* into the choices we make in our lives when it comes to our manifesting, we can have anything that we truly want.

As the late and great world-renowned hypnotherapist Dolores Cannon in one of her public appearances said, the most important lesson we can learn when we come to earth is how to manipulate energy. Her definition of manipulating the energy meant *to create*. We have to learn how to create. We don't realize the power we have. Physical things are the easiest to create.

She would go on to say, it's the Universe's job to give us anything we truly want. We just don't believe it; therefore, some don't realize the creative power they have.

> Now you still have to ask the Universe for what it is you want. It's also super important to recognize that the Universe does not know what you want until you ask. Ask and ye shall be given. Now the more specific and clear you are in what you're asking for, the more powerful the process of being given it becomes.

5 Steps to Mastery

In addition to the Principles of Manifestation, the Inner Powers, and the Universal Laws contained within the covers of this book, we're going to hone in on five steps to mastery for creating or co-creating with the Divine and the Universe.

1. Believe it…

The truth is and *has been*, as we learned with the Principle of Becoming in Chapter 10, we *can become anything we want to become*. I can, you can, become anything we want to become. This also implies that we can manifest anything we want, as long as it's in alignment with those five baseline guidelines mentioned earlier.

What's worthy to note is that your Soul is already wise to this. It knows that in order for you to have whatever it is you have a heartfelt desire for, you are first to become it. You start this conscious process by keeping your focus on the question: Who do you want to become? Or who do you need to become in order to have what it is you really want?

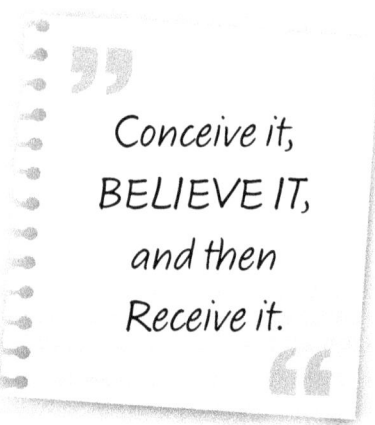

Conceive it, BELIEVE IT, and then Receive it.

Then comes the next question: Do you believe that you are what you have declared out loud that you need or want to become. When you completely believe in it, you'll have it. Now you've got to believe it all the way through until you become it.

This was another one of the core messages in *The Matrix*. Neo had to completely believe it before he could actually become it. Morpheus believed with all of his being that Neo was the one and yet even with this strong belief in Neo that Morpheus carried in his consciousness, it still wasn't enough. It was a very important part of Neo's journey to have Morpheus enter into his life. Come the end of the day, though, it was Neo who had to believe within all of his being at a cellular level that HE was the ONE.

This Principle of Becoming is so powerful, and at the same time, it's quite amazing how many don't yet truly understand how it all really works. Recall again the three pillars for manifesting that we learned about earlier in this book: Conceive it, BELIEVE IT, and then Receive it. And in that order. There is a direct inner connection between these first two. Once we conceive who it is we need to become, to have what it is we really want, the very next part of this journey will be to believe in it to where your subconscious completely believes it as well.

Now to fully believe it, check yourself to see how easy it is for you to practice faith in yourself and the Universe, for there is a direct connection between believing in something and having faith in that something.

Which brings us to the 11th Inner Power of our journey together through this book...

The Power of Faith

We've all heard these types of sayings umpteen times before: "You just need to have more faith," or "Have faith in yourself," or "Take a leap of faith," or "Have faith in the Universe," or "Have faith in God," etcetera. Faith is considered a belief and trust in God, the Universe, or one's Higher Self based on evidence but without total proof.

Among all definitions, faith holds a common theme... TRUST. Whether we're putting faith in a person, duty, or belief, trust is a necessity.

Without the conscious act of trusting, there is little access to our Inner Power of Faith.

When faith, supported by the conscious act of trusting, is practiced correctly and consistently, it becomes a powerful force field. Remember in the original *Star Wars* movies during the seventies, the phrase in what is likely the most quoted *Star Wars* line of all time. This iconic phrase has ascended beyond th *Star Wars* franchise itself. "May the Force Be with You."

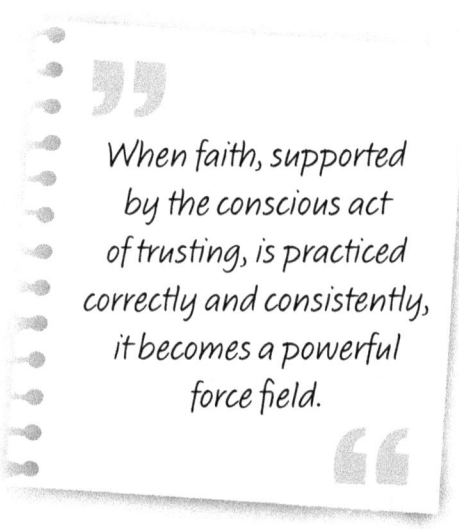

The Force itself, of course, is invisible. You might recall Obi-Wan Kenobi teaching Luke that the Force exists within all living things, emphasizing the importance of togetherness in the eyes of the Force. Just as the Force itself is invisible, so is the higher and greater process of manifestation or achievement.

It's the higher act of trusting and living in the faith that what we can't see does exist, whether it's a positive and welcomed change in our life or an exciting and real opportunity that alters our path of trajectory in the best and brightest of ways.

> The question here would be, will we continue to trust in this higher and greater manifestation process and ultimately keep the faith? This in and of itself becomes a testing ground for us to see where we're really at with our ability to actually apply our Inner Power of faith that will be required to achieve whatever it is we're in process of achieving.
>
> On a scale of one to ten, how much faith have you given to your convictions? If those positive opportunities were to fall away or be taken away, what would you do then? Would you give up or continue on? When this type of thing shows up in our lives, it's often been designed to test our faith in ourselves and/or our truest desires. Will we pack it in, or will we keep moving progressively forward?

To quote Einstein once again, "Life is like riding a bicycle. To keep your balance, you must keep moving."

> Will we continue to keep the faith, even if those opportunities or good things aren't coming our way like they did before This is another place along our journey's where we're possibly being tested yet again. Will we continue to believe in whatever it is that we know is true? Will we survive through the testing phase regardless of how long it might last? These are the experiences in our life that will test our faith. Another way of saying this: *Luck changes for people who never give up.*

If we were to give up on these things that were coming our way... then the Universe or the Divine would say to us, "Okay, we were taking these things for granted, and there'll be no more, at least for a while."

It would be beneficial if we were able to see this, as a result of our experiencing what it was like to have that kind of flow, grace, or success in our lives (prior to what is happening now along our current journeys). Now if during that time, we got to see what it was we could do with something that is positive, wonderful, and more graceful when it showed up in our lives this would empower our ability to manifest even further.

This past experience gave us a great heightened awareness of where we could go in our lives if we stayed true to following the path during the time or those times we were traversing through the testing phase. Then, if we graduated from the kind of testing, which would be totally unique to each of us, it would then become clearer what we could do with this level of success.

> If and when this beautiful gift of Divine grace, and this higher energy of greater flow were to materialize again, how would you show up?
>
> Now if you feel anxious, stressed, or weighed down, remind yourself that both fear and faith require you to *believe* in something unseen, implying the choice is in your hands to either worship the fear or honor your heart's desire by choosing to activate your Inner Power of Faith and turn the act of faith into a *way of being*.

For some this might mean releasing the need to control someone, or something—as in the outcome. Or perhaps for some of us it's the need to know... to always need to have the answers in order to move forward.

What we need is to strengthen our Inner Power of Faith. To have more faith we can't always expect to know or have the answer, or to know how things will turn out for us in advance of just stepping forward. To do this, however, we need to become comfortable with uncertainty. We need to apply or practice more faith in the unseen world of creative manifestation, faith in the unknown, or faith in a higher power or our Greater Self.

In book one of the *Transformation Trilogy*, I invite the reader to make peace with the world of the uncomfortable. "Why?" you might ask. This is often where we make the greatest strides in moving our lives forward. It's also where we often have the most powerful life-changing experiences.

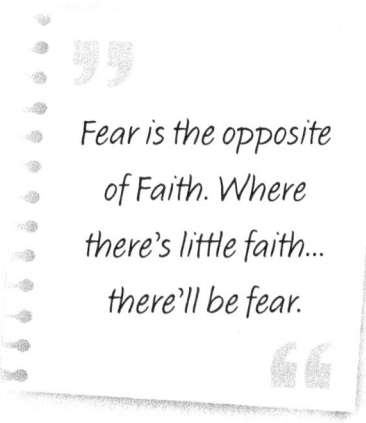

Fear is the opposite of Faith. Where there's little faith... there'll be fear.

When we choose faith, we then let go of the struggle—the influence that fear has had on us. Fear is the opposite of Faith. Where there's little faith... there'll be fear. When we let go, we begin to operate in the field of the Divine or the quantum field. It's this consistent practice of faith in ourselves and the Universe that places us on this path where we begin to do things and experience things we never thought possible. We develop in ways that totally surprise us in the most magical of ways. This is where we're not only creating the life we love… we're now living our best life.

When you are in the experiential process of BELIEVING IT and you're consciously utilizing this Inner Power of Faith, it unlocks a direct connection to your Higher Self, the Universe, or the Divine—which will support you in manifesting whatever it is your heart genuinely desires. I love what Saint Augustine once said, "Faith is to believe what you do not see; the reward of this faith is to see what you believe."

> Do you believe that there is a Higher Self, as in your Highest Self (even though you perhaps can't see it, feel it, or truly know it at a deeper cellular level yet)? Do you believe in the loving Divine, or in a generous Universe? Do you believe that your most genuine desires are in their own unique process of materializing *(even though you can't fully see them on a physical level just yet)*? If so, on a scale of 1 to 10, 1 being a little and 10 being a lot, how strong is your belief right now?

If our belief is on the weaker side, it's likely we've been living in fear of something. The greater goal or intention here would be to transmute the fear and ultimately become the master of that fear. If you haven't done so just yet, then a real good starting point would be to choose and learn how to release your fear. Even if you were to choose not to master fear, it would still be beneficial for you to transmute it by releasing it.

A suppressed fear might reveal itself when it is activated by some experience you're having in your day-to-day life. Maybe you just found out your partner wanted to leave you, or you took a major financial loss, or you simply felt afraid of something you were in resistance around doing—something you knew would be in your best interest to go out and do.

An Exercise for Working with Fear

> When you find yourself confronting one of your fears, you can begin by acknowledging the fear. Observe the fear as you give yourself permission to consciously feel into the fear (instead of resisting or running away from the fear). Running away from my fear is equivalent to giving the fear my power. This is what makes the fear stronger and me weaker.

This is a very important part of one's transformational process when clearing or releasing the fear... which is to not give our creative power away to the fear, or whatever it is we're afraid of. The reason for this is that if we give our power to fear we run the risk of it disconnecting us from the source that fosters our well-being.

> At this point, grab your notebook and do some journaling around this fear. This is where you simply write everything down on what the thoughts and feelings are that come up for you with the intention to put to paper what it is you're afraid of.

Transformational journaling, (which I often refer to as Transjournaling: Trans taken from the word, transformation), can really help jar the energy of the fear lose and get it moving—which is exactly what we want here. (The other option would be to give it more of our personal power by resisting it or avoiding it, and then possibly run the risk of it gaining even more influence over us and our choices.)

> The next step would be to purposely and courageously engage in an act of faith by doing the very thing you've been afraid to do. This would be us now consciously choosing to replace fear with faith. As we step into this thing that we've been afraid of doing or experiencing, we simply stay in the observing of the fear—the acknowledging of the fear—and intentionally use our breath to help us process it. This is done by remembering to breathe.
>
> When I choose to replace fear with faith and determined action, it also means I'm now committing myself to that act of stepping through the fear. This is when providence or my greater power moves in to support me in this courageous endeavor.

Let's recall the parable of the mustard seed, which is considered to be one of the greatest light-body teachings of Jesus: *"If you have faith as small as a mustard seed, you can say to this mountain, 'Move from here to there', and it will move. Nothing will be impossible."*

The mustard seed serves as a metaphor for a tiny thing that was encoded with massive potential—a small seed that grew into a mighty plant. We too, just as that tiny seed, have been encoded with phenomenal potential, which with faith, can be recognized and then realized. So, if we were to conquer our fears, just as that tiny mustard seed did, what could we now consciously manifest?

Think of the process or journey Neo had to go through to ultimately arrive at that place of truly believing. Here's the deal, if we don't believe within the 50 trillion-plus cells that our physical form is currently comprised of, we won't have it or receive it—at least not just yet. It's our subconscious that must totally believe in this. If it doesn't believe in it, then we won't have it.

> For us to accomplish anything of significance, we have to become it. To completely become it, we'll have to believe it. To believe it, we'll need to practice having *faith* not only in ourselves but in the Universe as well. For when we do, our believing eventually reaches the point where our subconscious completely believes it too. This is where whatever it is we've been in the process of accomplishing magically materializes in our physical reality.

2. Keep walking towards it...

For as you walk, the way appears.

> Are you currently walking towards what it is you really want? If not, what have you been moving towards? Has it been towards more complaining, excuse making, cheating, staying stuck, waiting for something to change, waiting for everything to be perfect, getting too comfortable, partying too much? Or having too much dreamy time, too much alone time, too much impulsive spending, too many processed foods, or perhaps too much laziness? Laziness breeds inaction.

I recall what Dale Carnegie said decades ago, "Inaction breeds doubt and fear. Action breeds confidence and courage. If you want to conquer fear, do not sit home and think about it. Go out and get busy."

> If you want to conquer fear, do not sit home and think about it. Go out and get busy." To do this we want to master the dynamics in becoming engaged in determined action in our lives. Let's remember nothing comes without a form of consistent action, and everything gets easier with practice. An attitude of determined action is what brings us to the place of experiencing something. Without the actual experiencing of something, the whole thing is pointless. Whereas the experiencing of something itself is priceless, as it gives us valuable feedback as to where we are to be adjusting our approach and/or refining or even *redefining* our dreams, goals, or intentions.

This is also what brings us closer to our Inner Power of Aligned Action. This is where we are right on the money, so to speak. In other words, this is where our action bears great fruit. Again, action could be the highest active form of prayer. Another form of prayer is intention. As in, a prayer of intent. And I say *active* because if we were to choose in advance to have our actions for today become a clear reflection of our intentions for the day, we really could have anything we truly desire.

> By committing to aligned, intentional action we can achieve all that we truly want, especially when we're living our personal, professional, and spiritual lives intentionally.

Action is the fuel that powers the Law of Attraction. It's in plain sight; it's in the word itself... ACTION. It's also the intentional energies, whether our intentions are coming from our conscious or subconscious self, that will express themselves through our actions.

Another key to conscious manifestation is to specifically take determined action in conjunction with powerfully using our imagination to create our desires with.

If we were to continue to only engage our imaginations and intentions with whatever it is we truly desire, but our actions speak to the contrary of this desire, we will have only have kept ourselves in a holding pattern for achieving our most important goals. In this scenario our subconscious will get the message loud and clear that we don't want to manifest the imagined desire.

As a direct result, the subconscious will then steer us away from our dreams, goals, and even intentions. So, we want to become more conscious and even more careful when it comes to our actions. Are they in alignment with what we say we want? And are we determined enough to carry them out?

> This is also where taking action can really assist us in becoming even more specific and clear on what we want and what it is we need to do. To have this be a powerful process for us, we could ask ourselves: What is it I need to be doing that will challenge me the most? To be clear, the action that is most right for us to be engaged in *is the action* that will catapult our creative process forward... toward the achieving of our goal or intention.

Now if your intention for this day is to become more productive, you could adopt an even more progressive approach to action by implementing Brian Tracy's metaphor of eating a frog at the start of your working day. Brian referred to this unique type of activity or action of doing something as a frog in one of his best-selling books, *Eat That Frog*. He came across this powerful idea from a summary written by Mark Twain in which he said, "If the first thing you do in the morning is to get up and eat a live frog, you'll have the satisfaction of knowing that's probably the worst thing that's going to happen to you all day long."

Now what you choose to do shortly upon awakening when your energy has been restored and replenished from the night of rest that you're waking up from is totally up to you. Shortly thereafter is the time of the day where you might consider eating a frog. The frog, of course, is to be taken symbolically. As it represents something specific and unique to you. The frog represents the very thing we usually don't want to do, and yet, it's the very thing that when done that moves us faster and more specifically propels us towards our greatest desire—quicker than anything else we could do at the start of our working day.

Most people resist the very thing they're truly to be doing or BEING. Now in all fairness most are not even aware that they're doing this. This is also highlighted in the first book of our trilogy, where I coined the phrase *unconscious resistance*. I often refer to this as the silent killer to that of living our greatest life... our best life... our dream life.

In this context, this is where someone always goes for what comes easiest to do or most comfortable to do. Unconscious resistance is a lower shadow dynamic of one's untamed ego that is designed to protect us from the world of the uncomfortable. This is all done as a way to make sure we stay safe by keeping things as they are, rather than the way they need to BE in moving our life onward and upward.

This unconscious resistance can have a heavy and even devastating effect on our psyche and overall life. When we're in that shadow lower energy pattern of unconscious resistance as a way to keep ourselves safe from something, the resistance is rooted in fear. It's something we're afraid of.

Perhaps we're afraid that we'll get hurt, or be made wrong, or make a mistake, or they'll reject us… the list goes on. It's clearly the strongest reason why we resist the action that we're really to be taking. Yet if we're to embrace the action, we'd be on our way to transmuting the fear. As Emerson said long ago, "He who is not every day conquering some fear has not learned the secret of life."

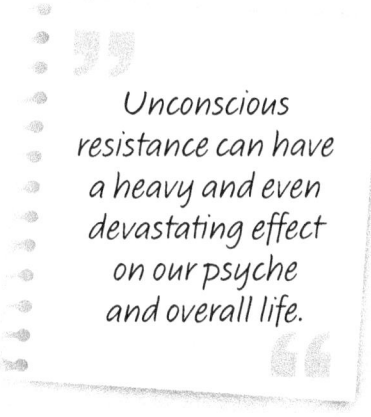

Unconscious resistance can have a heavy and even devastating effect on our psyche and overall life.

What we often don't realize is that resistance is a pushing away or pushing down type energy. This is clearly an unconscious strategy that drives the need to play it safe in life, whether it's in our personal or professional world. Until, of course, the individual becomes conscious and realizes what it is they've been doing. At this point, they also realize that these lower-energy patterns have been holding them back from creating the life of their dreams.

Most who are under the influence of this shadow lower energy patterning haven't yet realized that when they are acting out on this pushing energy, they're not only pushing away what it is they are possibly afraid of, they are also pushing away their heartfelt desires, most meaningful goals, and greater dreams. In other words, we can't have it both ways here. We cannot continue to resist the negative and somehow embrace the positive—it simply doesn't work that way.

> So, what is it? What's your frog? What have you been in resistance of doing? Or what is it you've been afraid to do? Go ahead, grab a sheet of paper, and write down up to three doable action steps that you've been avoiding doing recently...

An example of this might be: As a manager, is there a tough conversation you're to be having with someone in your sales organization or department that you've been avoiding? Or perhaps there's an important personal project that needs to get done that you find yourself resisting even getting started on? As a parent, are you to be getting your child out of bed earlier in the day, rather than letting them sleep through the day? Or maybe you've been resisting helping them with their homework. If you've been in resistance of taking action, you might ask yourself, "Do I need to be pushed into action?" And if by chance you do, just know, somehow, some way the Universe or your outer world will find a way to push you into action.

To continue on with a few more examples: As a career professional, have you been resisting some activity at work? Perhaps it's an important task to complete or a new one to start. Or maybe it's setting up phone appointments, Zoom meetings, a webinar, or making actual sales calls or perhaps even customer service calls? Is this your frog—the act of making calls earlier in the day?

Or perhaps you've been in resistance towards the act of prospecting for your sales business? Or how about a project at home? Have you been resisting completing the new build out, the garage, or the new patio deck that you started many months ago—where you know it would be in your best interest to get on with the project?

Becoming too comfortable is another dynamic that can easily fuel resistance. Once we become too comfortable with anything, we, without even trying, start the process all over again with our unconscious resistance to that of which is uncomfortable.

Whether it's an uncomfortable conversation we're to be having, getting started on our to-do list for the day, re-entering the dating scene, starting a new relationship again, or getting back up on the stage to sing or speak again... the antidote, of course, is intentional, determined action.

You might recall from Chapter 7: The Inner Manifesting Powers, that the 6 percenters, just like the 94 percenters, had a lot of things to accomplish too. The big difference, however, was they would save the things that were lesser than a 9 or 10 for another day or delegate those things to someone else. These were the activities that would lead them to the success of their goals and greater happiness. Whereas the 94 percent never even got to their nines or tens, as they were too busy with the zeros, ones, twos, and threes on their lists of priorities.

The 6 percent, rather, got very clear on what their tens were for the day and did them first. They knew it wasn't just the act of doing, doing, doing or running around that got them to their goal—like what was happening for the 94 percent. It was the act of doing their tens that got them there.

Determined action gets us moving towards living our dream life, as it can cause us to believe more in ourselves and our most important goals. It'll increase how you feel about yourself. You'll start to feel more worthy of having your goal or heartfelt desire materialize.

Whatever it is, the master key here is to first identify it. Why is this so important? Because we first need to recognize what it is that's up for us to be changing. The very thing we're truly to be doing... could be the very thing we've been avoiding. It's a fear that's been trapped within our subconscious that we perhaps didn't even know was there. Until, of course, we begin to recognize our shadow pattern of avoiding.

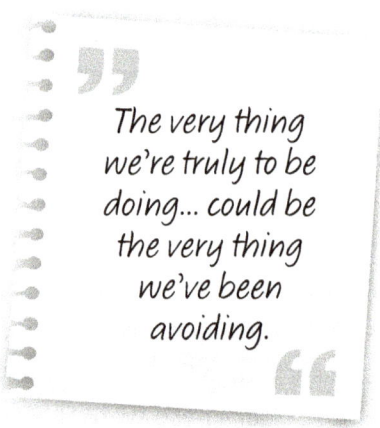

The very thing we're truly to be doing... could be the very thing we've been avoiding.

However, the moment we step into this thing is the exact moment when the changing process begins. Why? Because of what it brings up for us. It's the *transforming* of some part of us. It's this powerful act of changing something, or anything for that matter, which always begins with us being able to see what it is we're to be transforming within ourselves and our own lives. And if there was a spiritual reason for embracing determined action... this would be it.

Know that whatever it is we truly need to be doing will more than likely challenge us the most. As I've taught over the years, what challenges us the most has already been designed to change us the most. This comes directly from the wisdom of your own *Magnanimous Soul*. The action or act of doing what is right for us to be fully engaged in... is the exact action that moves the creative process forward. Alan Watts illuminated this even further when he said, "This is the real secret... to be completely engaged with what you are doing in the here and now. And instead of calling it work, realize it is play."

> Deciding to overcome the fear that's been stopping us from simply embracing the action that we know in our bones will be life-changing is a very empowering choice to make.

Then, should we choose to go the distance and become the master of fear while continuing on in mastering the art of right or divine-aligned action, this is where we successfully set ourselves up to live our best life... our happy dream life.

3. Step out of your comfort zone...

> Getting too comfortable can easily hold us back from stepping into action, thus also hijacking the manifestation process from accomplishing what it is we really want. So, check your comfort zone. How have you been using it? Have you become too comfortable? Do you *intentionally* use this zone for pure enjoyment? Or do you use comfort as some form of device to go non-present?
>
> Does this comfort zone slow you down from moving towards your dreams, goals, or intentions? Are you willing to step out of the comfort zone? When was the last time you consciously stepped out of your

comfort zone? What happened then? Stepping out of our comfort zone is where transformational magic can happen. It's also where we can experience the most growth.

It's when we step out and do the thing we've been afraid to do… that ultimately stretches us. Which causes us to heal, expand and grow. There's a powerful quote by John A. Shedd that speaks to this, *"A ship in harbor is safe, but that is not what ships are built for."*

In my experience, it's been all about becoming, expanding, healing, and growing. As we embrace the action of doing the thing we know we are to be doing, we become one with the action. When we become one with the action, it creates a fresh, new neuropathway in our brain. The two most common ways of creating a positive or negative pathway are through immersion or hardship.

Immersion: Choosing to engage in determined action.

Choosing to embrace the more shadow-oriented, lower-energy feelings or emotions such as anger, shame, sadness, guilt, or fear. This requires determined intentional action, as it's not easy or pleasant to do this type of inner transformational work. Now if we were to choose not to embrace this, we would then likely never rise to experience the higher octaves, frequencies, or dimensions.

In other words, we're left in a 3D world of separation where we find ourselves experiencing more stress, strife, and struggle. We must transform and transmute the energies from within us that have driven a lower expression of those parts of us that have been living in the lower rungs of existence. This will lead us to becoming one with a higher expression of life that is divine,

Furthermore, to deny that these lower dynamics need to be consciously embraced and transmuted, you might think again. We see this throughout the spiritual communities around the world where some of these people have often done what's known as the bypass.

> *It's when we step out and do the thing we've been afraid to do... that ultimately stretches us.*

This is where they've been attempting to get to that state of nirvana. And yet, it just seems to allude them. They might be very spiritual within their mental construct. Yet their lives reveal something else, as in their health or finances might not be that good. Their day-to-day lives also don't seem to work all that well.

A great question here to ask is, "If I'm so spiritual, then how much of my Higher Self have I actually embodied?" And what proof of this do I have in my day-to-day life or physical body? Or "How well have I been doing in the embodiment process of actualizing my own sovereign divinity?" Or we might even ask, "As of now, how much have I embodied my Divine Soul Essence Self? Not sure? Then ask yourself, "How connected am I to the Divine, to God, to the Creator?"

In this new era, collectively speaking, we are now on a spiritual transformational journey for the greater purpose of embodying the wholeness of our true sovereign divinity. This is done through the transmuting of ALL of our lower energy patterns, limiting beliefs, and the pain of our past—so that we can shine the divine light of our *Magnanimous Soul* into our personal and professional lives. As we successfully transform the wounds of our past into the power of our Soul, our future becomes brighter, more beautiful, and even limitless. It's where we can truly co-create with the Creator, along with our higher-level guides and the Ascended Masters, a heavenly dream life in the here and now.

The greater truth is: the way to the highest state of nirvana is through accepting and consciously working through the real challenges that confront the initiate within the inward journey of transforming every unhealed or wounded lower part of themselves. It's through clearing the way. It's the willingness to do the inner work. This is the road less traveled that Scott Peck back in the eighties wrote about in his bestselling book. I've often said, the way to the Soul is through the ego. The way to our higher path of destiny is through our lower path of destiny.

Hardship: even though hardships can often be tough to get through, they can be taken as an amazing opportunity for transformation, healing, and growth. As Freud wrote, "One day, in retrospect, the years of struggle will strike you as the most beautiful."

Everything changes once you know that your Soul or Higher Self is behind everything that happens in your life. You see, whatever it is that's currently challenging you has already been designed by the power of your Soul to change you (as a way to support you in the creating those new neuropathways in your brain and nervous system, thus transforming of you).

For those of us who are truly dedicated and committed to our own sacred path of healing, growing, maturing, evolving, and expanding, we will want to become comfortable with the world of the uncomfortable. As we do, we'll notice that the hardships of life become less. Doing the inner work of transforming is not a comfortable process. Change is not comfortable. More specifically, it's the process in which we go through that's uncomfortable—and sometimes downright inconvenient.

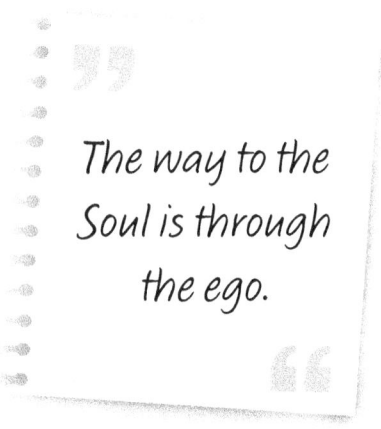

The way to the Soul is through the ego.

So, when we become more comfortable with what it is that's uncomfortable in our personal, professional, and spiritual lives… we also become comfortable with uncertainty—and the fear of the unknown as well. This changes everything for the best when it comes to the transformation of ourselves. Why? Because we're no longer in the fight around resisting the changes our Soul has been prompting us to make. Rather, now we recognize when it's truly time to change something within or without and we step into inner or outer action and fully embrace it. This is what aids us the most when it comes to transforming ourselves when we show up this way.

In moving forward, remind yourself on a regular basis that movement is good… it's beneficial, and it feels good, as it keeps all energies moving. This is what energy in and of itself has wanted to do all along. This would be you living your life in alignment with the Law of Energy that we learned about in Chapter 2.

As a powerful conscious daily practice, simply continue to walk towards whatever it is that's truly important to you… for as you do, the way will always appear.

4. Focus on it…

There's another law that says, "Whatever we focus on expands." If I'm focused on who and what it is that is positive, I'll get more positive. If I'm focused on who or what it is that's negative, I'll get more negative. If I'm focused on getting more done, I'll get more done. If I'm focused on being lazy or easily distracted, I'll get more of that.

If I'm focused on becoming strong, vibrant, and healthy, I'll get more of that. If I'm focused on eating junk food, staying depressed, and lethargic, I'll get more of that. If I'm focused on becoming kinder, more honoring, and more loving, I'll get more of that. If I'm focused on becoming more self-centered, controlling, bitchy, or grumpy. I'll get more of that. If I'm focused on becoming an addict, I'll get more of that. If I'm focused on becoming the best version of me, I'll get more of that. And so on…

> The master question for those who genuinely want to manifest their deepest truest desires, is: Am I focused on becoming who it is I need to become to truly have what it is my heart desires? Whether it's my

relationships, my finances, my family, my health or my career? Again, the truth is... we CAN manifest whatever it is we truly want. This is the larger purpose as to why we were born with the natural ability to manifest.

Let's remember that our most vibrant point of attraction is when we become what it is we desire. To understand this from another perspective, when we become who it is we need to become in order for us to have what it is we want, it'll then materialize in our physical reality. In other words, to manifest what you want... stay focused on who it is you truly want to become or need to become.

Recall from earlier in this book one of Jim Rohn's most powerful teachings: *"Success is not something to pursue; rather, it's something we attract by the person we become."* It's all about BECOMING.

You can become anything you truly intend to become. This also implies that you can manifest anything you genuinely desire. You will not be rich, happy, or successful *(at least in a way that is sustainable)* in whatever you choose to do until you become it. When you become it, your actions show it, as they're all in alignment with who it is you've now become. In other words you're no longer struggling with the engagement of the action that you know in your bones you're to just be doing.

If we, on the other hand, choose to focus on trying to get something, we'll more than likely continue looping around the energy of trying. When we're focused on trying to get, we're operating at our lowest point of attraction. Alternatively, if we choose to focus on what it is we wish to become, we're now operating at a higher point of attraction. Ultimately, what counts the most is our state of *Being*. When we're focused on becoming something, it raises our state of being. As our state of being lifts, so does our point of attraction.

Trying to get something is not very empowering at all; rather, what is empowering is when you're becoming something. Instead of trying to get married... become a well-balanced, integrous, mature partner first.

So, ask yourself, "What do I really want, and who do I want to be or need to be?"

There's another principle on alignment. It's focuses in on correctly aligning the "having" part of you with the "being" part of you correctly. In my next book we'll take a much deeper dive into this powerful principle for going quantum with our manifesting.

A great exercise here in the meantime would be:

Identify what you wish to have in your personal, professional and spiritual life. Then fill in the blank that follows the "I HAVE" and "I AM" statements below:

I HAVE _____
(*write down a specific want or desire you have*)

Some examples of this might be: I HAVE a strong, healthy, vibrant body. I HAVE a prosperous and profoundly meaningful career. I HAVE the courage, the power, and discipline to achieve the life I love. I HAVE a thriving relationship with a great partner, who is my best match. I HAVE a 4.0 GPA. I HAVE $100,000 in my savings account or a safe interest-bearing account. I HAVE the best boss or employer. I HAVE the best employees or team. I HAVE a great and trustworthy dear friend.

I HAVE a well-balanced abundant life. I HAVE a fulfilling family life. I HAVE a rich, dynamic spiritual life.

I AM _____

(*follow your I am with who or what it is you want to become*)

Some examples of this might be: I AM healthy and vibrant. I AM a great mother or father. I AM a highly skilled manager or leader. I AM a happy wife or husband. I AM an independent, creative, mature, loving woman. I AM a powerful, disciplined, responsible, well-balanced man. I AM an excellent A+ student. I AM happy, heathy, and rich. I AM a masterful copy writer. I AM a true professional. I AM loving, joyful, fearless, and alive. I AM a spiritual being having a human experience. I AM enough just as I am.

> Recall the Power of Control from the previous chapter. Here is another great application for utilizing this power correctly. The master key here is in consciously taking control of the re-direction of our creative energy toward what we it is we want to become. And that means we now have actively removed the element of "trying" and have moved into the action and ownership that we are now in a state of "doing". Remember that most people use their control to TRY to get something. Utilizing this master key means we are no longer in that trying energy but have risen above that into an action of doing. A strong, steady, positive focus will and does promote an overall state of wellbeing.

In my next book, we'll also take a deep dive into another way in which we can utilize our Inner Power of Focus. That said, I'll touch on it here in this last book that completes the trilogy. I call this a Focused, Relaxed, Knowing–which I'll refer to here forward as FRK...

The FOCUS part of this powerful equation is when we're operating from the place of a real clear knowing of exactly what it is we want to create that translates into a laser-like-focus

RELAXED is the conscious act of dropping deeper into the KNOWING what it is we want, and who it is we truly are as a manifestor. This could be one of the biggest roadblocks in really getting better at conscious, intentional manifesting. When we can keep this type of focus in a way that's relaxed into the knowing of who we already are as a manifestor, we can achieve anything that we intend to or we set our mind to.

This, in my experience, is an ultra-clear state of focus one could rise to. I stumbled across this higher-vibe state within myself some time ago. In this state of FRK, we're acutely aware of our focus in what it is we now know about ourselves and what it is we want. To this, we're able to hold and maintain this crystalized knowing in our own body-mind consciousness.

In other words, this is where it becomes more natural for one to do this. With this type of Focused Relaxed Knowing, the emphasis is to be placed on the relaxed part. The more relaxed we become in our mind and physical vessel, the better we get at this. Another way of saying this is there's no trying and no aggressive energy. No trying to be someone or something, nor trying to stay focused on our goal or intention–or on anything for that matter. This relaxed state of concentrated focus is completely free of "trying," aka the unconscious resistance we learned about in step two of this chapter.

Bruce Lee, the great martial artist and famous movie star, would teach his students to become like water. This is what he meant. His focus was beyond what most on their best of days have ever experienced. It was so intensely laser foccused—and yet so relaxed. His level of focus was piercing, as there was zero resistance both consciously and subconsciously. His body was not filled with tension when he fought or performed. Rather, it was like water running through his vessel. He knew where he was going next, for he was already there in this relaxed higher state of focus (before he even got physical with whatever move or action he was going to engage in or act out on his opponent).

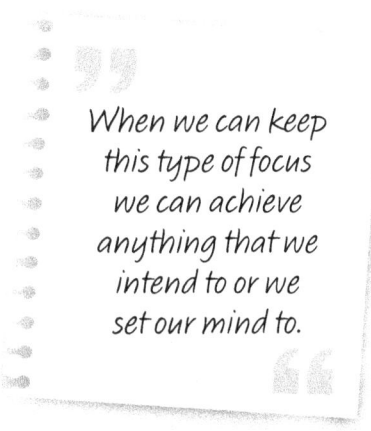

When we can keep this type of focus we can achieve anything that we intend to or we set our mind to.

As a master martial artist, his fluidity and flexibility were like nothing we had ever seen with a fighter or athlete during his time. It's still talked about to this day. He was operating in a purely non-resistant, focused, and knowing state, in which he was totally relaxed and yet intensely focused. All at the same time.

He had become what, at the time he was teaching others to become. He would often emphasize with great passion the key was to become like water. And he became like water. There was no trying or aggressing upon himself or another. Rather, he achieved a state of being where there was zero resistance both on a conscious and subconscious level. His mind-body consciousness was totally at one.

This embodied consciousness that he was a walking example of is equivalent to the FRK State of Being. And in this state, we can manifest anything.

This Focused Relaxed Knowing State can help us to successfully manifest our goals, dreams, and intentions. It is worthy of mentioning here, as this is also an aspect of Self-Mastery. This means we don't have to become a martial artist to rise to this state. Rather, we would become a master of this Focused Relaxed Knowing State within ourselves, to which our mind and body consciousness become one to manifest with.

Our focus is also very much like a superpower, as our creative energy automatically goes to whatever it is we're mostly focused on. Consider the beliefs you have on the world. Whatever it is we believe about the world is what's going to create the world around us. As Wayne Dyer said long ago, "It's why 2 percent manifest and 98 percent don't." And he was referring to consciously manifesting.

You see, if I'm focused on the world I would like to see… as in everybody living the life of their happiest dreams, I'm more likely to be living the life of my happiest dreams. If I'm focused on the world growing into a better healthier happier version of themselves, then guess what? I'll more than likely get the same. I'll sometimes say to my audiences, that if we're still the same person we were just two to three short years ago, we simply have not yet received the memo from our own Higher Self. This is so powerful when we get it, which is also why it's one of the steps to mastery.

5. Commit to it...

Just as our energy always simply flows to whatever we're mostly focused on, so does our commitment. This brings us to our last power, which is the 12th power of the inner powersInner Powers highlighted in this book...: The Power of Commitment.

The Power of Commitment

As soon as we commit to whomever or whatever, we create the power source. Which then releases itself and is directed into whatever it is we get committed to.

Commitment is also about our word being completely congruent with our action. Now this alignment will require a greater degree of self-discipline, as it is the driving force which can propel one towards their own success or their own demise. If it propels us to our demise, this is where we often sabotage something we truly value–including life itself. If it propels us forward to the manifestation of our dreams, goals, and intentions, it then is a transformational catalyst for manifesting our truest desires into reality.

In other words, our commitment is very much like a directional device for where it is our creative power is to move towards. It doesn't matter whether we're aware of this or not. It simply happens the moment we become committed. The commitments we make can happen on both a conscious and unconscious level, implying that we could be unconscious of a commitment that has been taken on by our subconscious self.

This all depends on how conscious we become of our Inner Power of Commitment and how we are using it or directing it. If I'm directing it under the influence of my Highest Self or Soul, it can also be a dynamic catalyst for effectively transmuting lower energies into their higher octave or frequency. Or a powerful catalytic dynamic for creating the life I love, living my most authentic life, living a spiritually rich life, or becoming the greatest version of myself.

Yes, this power that's inside of you is that powerful. It's all up to you, however, how you choose to use it.

Commitment is also about our word being completely congruent with our action.

Another way to look at commitment is that it's a state of being where we become dedicated to something that matters to us. It's a sacred promise we make to ourselves and others, which then plays a pivotal role in the shaping of our personal, professional, and spiritual growth. This can also have its own unique effect on the level of success we experience in our lives and whether this success will be sustainable, fulfilling, and enjoyable.

In my own life, I learned some time ago that my deepest, most authentic commitment reveals itself in the answer that follows the following question: *Am I willing to do whatever it takes, for however long it takes, to achieve the life I deeply love, respectfully value, and humbly appreciate?*

Shortly after I first started teaching, one of my students shared a poem with me that I have since shared in my classes hundreds of times over. The poem is titled "Commitment" and was written by William Hutchinson Murray, from his 1951 book entitled *The Scottish Himalayan Expedition*.

> *Until one is committed*
> *there is hesitancy, the chance to draw back,*
> *always ineffectiveness.*
> *Concerning all acts of initiative (and creation),*
> *there is one elementary truth,*
> *the ignorance of which kills countless ideas*
> *and splendid plans:*
> *that the moment one definitely commits oneself,*
> *then Providence moves too.*
>
> *All sorts of things occur to help one*
> *that would never otherwise have occurred*
> *A whole stream of events issues from decision*
> *raising in one's favor all manner*
> *of unforeseen incidents, meetings*
> *and material assistance,*
> *which no man could have dreamt*
> *would have come his way.*
>
> *Whatever you can do, or dream, you can begin it.*
> *Boldness has genius, power, and magic in it.*

Once again, our power is in whomever or whatever it is we're committed to. I'm either committed to becoming a more negative, judgmental, critical, intimidating person or a more positive, caring, compassionate, and likeable person—and whichever I'm committed to, I will become more of. My creative power is in who or what it is that I'm becoming.

My power is in what I'm committed to. It could be a project that I'm completing. It could be to the sabotaging of some part of my personal, professional, or even spiritual existence (whether I'm aware of this or not). The commitment I have towards either end will bring the project or that sabotage all the way through to completion. In fact, this is where my resolve to do whatever, to become whomever, for however long it takes will reveal itself.

As the opening paragraph from the poem "Commitment" reads: *"Until one is committed there is hesitancy, the chance to draw back, always ineffectiveness. Concerning all acts of initiative (and creation), there is one elementary truth, the ignorance of which kills countless ideas and splendid plans: that the moment one definitely commits oneself, then providence moves too."*

What happens with this Inner Power is that whatever we're committed to, be it positive or negative *(conscious or unconscious)*, is where the creative energy of our Inner Power goes. To quote the legendary Carl Jung, "Until you make the unconscious conscious, it will direct your life, and you will call it fate."

Recall the story from earlier in the book of the couple wanting a baby. Until they made what was unconscious to them... conscious–nothing changed. All that was happening for them was the "trying harder" to become pregnant. Until we make the unconscious, CONSCIOUS... it will drive our lives and then we will call it fate. Just like the couple was getting ready to do...questioning that maybe it wasn't meant to be. But it turned out it was meant to be. All they needed to do was become conscious of what was really happening, (that at the time they were unconscious of), and what it was they could actually do that would open everything up where they could have a baby.

Our conscious and unconscious commitments will show themselves in the stories we tell, the conversations we have with ourselves and others. They can also show themselves in whatever it is that we've been focused on. Maybe it's lying, cheating, being a know-it-all, being dishonest, acting like we can do it all by ourselves, getting stuck, remaining unproductive, or being lazy. Or maybe they will show themselves in truth-telling, being kind, responsible, fair, honest, forward moving, being productive, calling upon help when they genuinely need it, or becoming well-disciplined.

> To examine this further, it could be very beneficial to go over the conversations you've had with yourself and others over the last seven days. If there was an overall theme in these conversations, as in more towards the positive or more towards the negative, what was it?
>
> Look at the stories you've been telling. Are you telling the same story over and over again? How many times have you told that story over the last 30 to 90 days? Where has your focus been? Has it been more on what it is you really want to create or have manifest in your life? Or has it been on the drama of the day? Have you been too focused on the things that have been going wrong for you in the last 30 to 90 days? Or have you been focused on the things that have been going right for you?
>
> As you go through the day, do you find yourself more focused on the victories or positive accomplishments of that day? Or possibly on the things you did wrong that day? And then, if you did something wrong, what was your focus then? Beating yourself up, making yourself even more wrong? Or were you focused on what you were to be learning from what you felt you did wrong?

Have you been more focused on embracing the change that you're really to be making in your own life—whether that's with your health, your finances, or the way you've been in your relationships? Or have you been resisting the change that would be beneficial for you to be making?

Whatever our answer is to these questions, they simply show us what we've been directing our Inner Power towards, or how we've been utilizing this Inner Power. You see, here's how it goes... we simply get more of whatever it is we've been mostly committed to. If I'm really more committed to acting out my addictive behavior, then my addiction to whatever it is I'm addicted to simply becomes stronger. And more than likely it causes more pain. On the other hand, if I'm more committed to having more positive conversations with others, then I'll have more positive conversations.

If I'm more committed to truly changing something about myself or some aspect of my life expression (personally or, professionally or spiritually), then those changes will manifest in kind. Why? The answer is found in my resolute commitment—as it will release my creative power to manifest those changes. So, if I now want to bring this power into my goals, I will then look at what I'm more committed to. Maybe it's the materialization of my goals, or possibly it's complaining about why my goals haven't manifested yet. This is what that last line in the paragraph of the *Commitment* poem means, that the moment one definitely commits oneself, then providence moves too. My creative power will support whatever it is I'm most committed to.

Live Long and Prosper

If you made it this far, dear reader, I suggest that you revisit the content of this book—many times. Perhaps you start back at the beginning, or you just pick it up and bring your attention to whatever section you divinely happen to fall upon. Whatever the case, trust that the message or teaching found on the page or pages you land on is for you, and more than likely is coming at just the right time.

Take something from the page or section and purposely work with it for a while. Let it integrate into your life and beingness. Then come back and grab something else and work with that. Remember, as mentioned at the beginning of starting this journey together, this is not only intended to serve as a book but as a textbook and guide, to further assist you in getting better at consciously manifesting whatever it is you have a genuine desire or need for.

Should you choose to really work with the teachings and exercises contained within this book… whether that's weeks from now, months from now, a year or two from now… you'll be so glad you did.

We can all make this a wonderful journey by simply getting crystal clear about what it is we really want, by successfully releasing the energetic blocks that have been standing in our way, by believing that we can become anything we want to become, and by choosing to step out of our comfort zones. I can still hear those thought-provoking words from Bob Proctor during my early days when I was an ambitious young man, "you can be, do or have anything you really want." He would sometimes pause, and then with his powerful voice, he would follow it with… "ANYTHING!!"! And at the time I completely believed him, and I continued to believe him until I eventually believed it within myself.

You could purposefully use these teachings for creative and conscious manifesting as another way to authentically empower yourself. An example of this would be... select one or two Inner Powers, and/or principles that speak to you or ring true for you in current time. Would it be the Power of Feeling, the Power of the Spoken Word, or possibly the Power of Aligned Action? Is it the Principle of Detachment, or is it the Principle of Aliveness?

Here are a couple of examples of how to apply this teaching...

Think of a time when someone in your life gave you a reality check on how you were acting. Perhaps a friend or business associate pulled you aside and said, hey, have you noticed lately that your actions haven't been congruent with what you say you're going to do? Or with what you want others to do, but you haven't been willing to do?

Or perhaps you've been speaking poorly about yourself, your kids or some aspect of your life? If so, with any of these examples start working with the Power of The Spoken Word and the Power of Aligned Action.

Maybe you haven't been feeling alive in your body for the last couple of months. If that's been the case, you could work with the Principle of Aliveness along with the Power of Feeling. Whatever it is, if this has been affecting your natural ability to manifest that of what you truly want, odds are that your answer to correcting this mis-alignment is somewhere within this book.

By continuing to walk towards what we want through turning intentional, determined action into a conscious practice, placing our focus on what it is we want to see more of in our lives, and keeping our commitment on what it is we most desire and value, we will ultimately live our best life as if it's a heavenly dream.

Well, there you have it... all the teachings you need to *Manifest Like a Master*. What you choose to do with it, however, is now up to you. Will you take the time to learn how to embody the teachings that are most aligned with you at Soul Level? This is also up to you. Whether you choose to use this book or textbook as a tool to assist you in learning the teachings of manifestation, or not, is in your hands. Whether you choose to also use this book as a framework or roadmap for changing your reality for the better, imagining your best life into BEING, or achieving one of your most important goals... is up to you.

The speed at which you travel in the manifesting of your goals and dreams is partly up to you as well—which we'll leave for another time... perhaps in my next book, should it be divinely meant to be for us to travel together yet again, as we explore the next frontier of your Soul's amazing journey in becoming one with the quantum field.

I lovingly and respectfully leave you with the iconic words of the original Spock played so masterfully by the late Leonard Nimoy, "Live Long and Prosper!!!"

This is Dale Halaway, wishing you much Godspeed along your journey... *in creating the life of YOUR GREATEST DREAMS!*

Acknowledgments

I wish to express my appreciation to all the beautiful souls, beings, and people who have contributed to this book so generously. Thank you to both those who gave knowingly and willingly... and to those who may not have been aware of the gifts they shared as well.

A very special thank you to the many dedicated transformational seminar students and avatar clients who have allowed me whether in the classroom or in sessions over more than four decades to assist and witness in the awakening of their natural, inborn ability to consciously manifest the life of their dreams.

I would also like to give extra recognition to my amazing, incredibly supportive publishing team who have brought this book *(the final one within the trilogy)* to life with me. I am endlessly grateful for the love, encouragement and belief you've poured into me and my work. From the depths of my being, THANK YOU.

Jesse Krieger, my visionary publisher and a true champion of my work for almost 10 years. From that special moment of recognition we shared over the phone in the spring of 2016, I knew... as did he, that we were divinely meant to step into this project together. Since then, Jesse has never wavered in his unconditional and loving support for my work, my vision, and my spirit... not only for *Manifest Like a Master*, but for the entire Transformation Trilogy. I honor the greater vision he so consistently holds, along with his pure enthusiasm for the trilogy and the countless lives he believes, with all his heart, will be touched. What began as a publisher-author relationship has blossomed into a soul-family bond. I have a very thankful heart when it comes to Jesse. His support as gone far beyond publishing, having touched my life in ways I will always cherish.

ACKNOWLEDGMENTS

Mycki Manning, my soul mate editor and creative director for our company. I could not have asked for a more gifted person for guiding me in refining my grammar and helping me express myself in English with greater clarity and precision, especially within my books. I'm convinced she must have been a highly skilled English teacher in a previous life. Since leaving high school in the 10th grade to pursue entrepreneurship, I always trusted that, when the time was right, I would be aligned with the right person or schooling to help refine my English. That person was Mycki. Through our work together, my grammar has continuously improved and yes, if you're thinking I consciously manifested a loving, thoughtful and caring grammar teacher, you're right. This book would not be what it is without her kind guidance, artistic creative energy, and exceptional organizational skills. I am very thankful for you Mycki.

Zora Knauf, a truly professional editor with an eagle eye for detail. I so appreciate her expertise and dedication. I remember the first book she edited for us. The sheer number of edits made it feel like it would take forever. This ignited in us a new passion in which elevated my ability as a writer and catapulted us as a team in our editing process overall as well. And it paid off. As with this book, it was completely different: her edits were few, clear, and encouraging. Zora clearly got us moving in the right direction, and I am so happy she did.

Irena Kalcheva, our talented interior layout designer for the trilogy. She has worked with great skill and care behind the scenes, creating layouts that are sequential, organized, and reader-friendly. Her design work has made it easier for readers to step into a truly empowering experience with each book. Many thanks to your wonderful work with us Irena.

Lastly, to all of you, and to everyone who has contributed to this journey in ways both seen and unseen, my heart overflows with gratitude.

Congratulations on completing Manifest Like a Master!

WONDERING WHAT'S NEXT?

Become a part of Soul Speed, our manifestation community...

Right now, you're probably really feeling it... like anything's possible... like you're destined for more.

Here's what we've learned after guiding thousands through this work...

The moment you put this book down, life starts pulling you back. Your kids need dinner. Your boss sends that email. Your old patterns jump back in the driver's seat of your life. And suddenly you're trying to manifest alone in your living room, wondering why it felt so clear when you were reading about it, but now it feels so... hard. We've seen it happen too many times.

That's why Dale created Soul Speed...

Where he personally guides our intimate group deeper into the work. You bring your specific situation, whether it be a relationship you're calling in, a dream that keeps you up at night, or a block you can't seem to shift (on your own)... together with Dale you'll explore what's really happening in your vibrational field.

The people in Soul Speed get it. When you're surrounded by others walking the same path as you, when you have Dale there to guide you through your specific challenges, you're never alone in this. The journey becomes so much clearer.

> *"Dale has this amazing ability to take these grand concepts that could be very confusing and break them down into bite-sized pieces. I can gain a deep level of knowledge and understanding and just grasp it so easily. I have a lot of "aha" moments when he's teaching where all of a sudden these pieces of things that I have felt or experienced in my life all of a sudden make sense. The community of people that I've met is genuine and it's strong and it's pure and it's powerful. To be connected to that sort of group of souls is a beautiful blessing within itself. And I'm just happy and grateful that I took the time investment, I took the money investment, and I realize I'm worth being better."*
>
> —Sara Mathis

If that resonates with you, go to ManifestWithSoulSpeed.com to get immediate access.

Inside, you'll get instant access to our past group calls that you can start absorbing right away.

Plus, you'll have access to our very next live call with Dale.

Your soul tribe is waiting for you...

Go to **ManifestWithSoulSpeed.com** to join today!

Essential tools for your daily practice...

Vibrational Alignment Meditation Pack

We'll bet you've had those powerful moments of clarity when you feel completely aligned and anything seems possible. But then tomorrow comes, and that feeling fades...

What if you could tap back into that alignment more frequently? What if you could start or end your day feeling more centered?

Most of us carry hidden resistance we can't even see. Old programming running in the background. Protective patterns that once served us but now hold us back.

You can read all the books, understand all the principles, but if those deep patterns are still running? It's like trying to drive with the parking brake on.

That's exactly why Dale created these guided meditations...

They're your daily maintenance tools for better vibrational alignment.

Just like you wouldn't go weeks without brushing your teeth, you shouldn't go days without clearing your energy field and realigning with your desires.

Each morning (or evening), just press play. Let Dale guide you through releasing yesterday's static, clearing today's resistance, and opening to tomorrow's possibilities. Twenty minutes of maintenance now saves you from months of feeling stuck later.

This collection contains meditations for morning alignment, evening release, quick mid-day resets, and deeper exploration. They're designed to fit into your real life because daily practice only works if you actually do it daily.

> *"I feel enriched and grateful for Dale's guidance on the path of transformation, even when I'm challenged up and down–it is SO worth it. Dale's meditations are always amazing, and they get better each time. I use the Answer Within meditation every week when my heart wants to connect with my Higher Self. My 5-year-old and I call it the Higher Self Meditation! She loves to listen to all of Dale's meditations before bed and falls asleep to them almost every night."*
>
> —Charlyn F

Your vision needs daily attention, just like everything else that matters to you.

Get your Vibrational Alignment Meditation Pack for just $47

Go to: **DaleHalaway.com/vamp**

Bring Transformation to Your Organization

What if your next company event could spark a shift that ripples through your entire organization for years to come?

For over 40 years, Dale has had the privilege of guiding leaders at FedEx, AT&T, Johnson & Johnson, Century 21 and many more through transformational experiences that unite teams from the CEO down.

As a Success Coach, Master Strategist and Evolutionary Teacher, Dale blends practical business insights with deeper principles of human potential.

Whether your team needs to break through self-limiting beliefs, chart new paths to success, master the art of selling beyond price, become champions of change, or tap into their fullest potential, Dale has programs designed for exactly where you are.

His sessions deliver something different…

Not just another motivational talk that fades by Monday, but practical wisdom that shifts how your people see possibilities in their work, their relationships, and their results. They leave inspired, aligned, and equipped with tools they'll use immediately.

Dale's programs range from focused 3-hour sessions to immersive full-day or multi-day experiences. Each one is crafted to meet your organization where it is and take it where it needs to go.

The results speak for themselves. Here are some reported improvements:

- 165% increase over sales quota
- 65% revenue increases
- Record-breaking performances
- And most importantly, teams that are unified, purposeful, and unstoppable

> "Dale, your speaking content was thoroughly informative and motivating. There was never a dull moment… the multiple standing ovations you received were proof of your effectiveness in motivating my people."
>
> —FEDEX

If you're ready to bring this level of transformation to your next event, let's explore which program is right for your organization.

Discover how to bring Dale Halaway to your next event.

Go to: **BookDaleHalaway.com**

Experience Deep Personalized Growth with Private Intensives

If something in this book got to you, you know there's more work to do...

Dale works with high-level leaders, celebrities, and people with serious influence who need something most consultants can't offer: complete privacy and sessions built around your actual challenges and problems.

This isn't a one-size-fits-all experience. It's a deeply tailored, private immersion designed for people who carry influence and responsibility–those ready to move through long-standing challenges, big life shifts, or the next phase of personal and professional growth.

Private Intensives with Dale - Real Transformation, On Your Terms

For leaders, celebrities, and change-makers who need more than surface-level support, a Private Intensive with Dale offers an experience unlike traditional therapy or coaching. This is a deep, soul-level recalibration focused on your most urgent personal, professional, or spiritual challenges.

Wherever feels safest–your home, office, or a retreat of your choosing, Dale comes to you. He brings decades of experience, intuition, and a presence built to meet you exactly where you are.

This Is For You If:

- You're someone who leads, influences, or serves at a high level and you're ready for your own next breakthrough
- You're at a major turning point in life, work, or relationships
- You want support that's private, powerful, and deeply aligned with who you really are
- You value real depth, substance, and results over quick fixes or hype

"Before we began the private intensives, things felt stuck. Communication had broken down, progress was stalled, and it seemed impossible to get everyone aligned. But from the first session, everything shifted. What stood out most was the unity it created - the sessions became a catalyst for real, honest communication and healing. As each of our sessions came to an end, Dale designed practical transformational strategies for us to use that have been leading to deep changes improving each of our lives. We didn't just rebuild what was broken–we evolved to a new and healthier place. If you're ready to create change that lasts, not just in your relationships but in every aspect of your life this is where it begins."

—Theresa T

Curious to See What This Could Look Like for You?

Each year, Dale offers a small number of private consultations for people exploring this kind of work. This 60-minute conversation is focused and confidential. It's a chance to see if an intensive is the right next step for you.

To request your private consultation, visit:
www.DaleHalaway.com/intensive

Stay Connected on Your Manifestation Journey

We'd love to continue supporting you beyond these pages…

On social media, Dale shares daily insights, manifestation tips, and practical wisdom to keep you aligned in between our deeper work together. Plus, you'll be the first to know about new offers, free resources, and special opportunities for our community.

Our online family is filled with like-minded souls walking this path alongside you. It's a beautiful space for inspiration, encouragement, and reminders of what's possible.

Come be part of our fast-growing community. Your journey doesn't end with this book—it's just beginning.

> *"Thank you so much, Dale! I can't tell you how much I appreciate your work. I listen to you every day, and it's become an essential part of my routine, especially during my drives. Your insights and energy resonate deeply with me, and your delivery brings the content to life in such an impactful way. It's inspiring, uplifting, and truly transformative. You've made a lasting impression on my personal journey, and I can honestly say your work is helping me shape a brighter, more purposeful future. Thank you for sharing your wisdom with the world!"*
>
> —Maria Fregoso Delgado

Join Dale on your favorite platforms:

- **Facebook:** facebook.com/dalehalaway
- **IG:** @dalehalaway
- **YouTube:** https://www.youtube.com/@dale.halaway
- **X:** @dalehalaway
- **TikTok:** @dalehalaway
- **LinkedIn:** linkedin.com/in/dalehalaway
- **Website:** DaleHalaway.com

www.ingramcontent.com/pod-product-compliance
Lightning Source LLC
Chambersburg PA
CBHW050847160426
43194CB00011B/2064